Violence Within the Family

Violence Within the Family
Social Psychological Perspectives

Sharon D. Herzberger
Trinity College

WestviewPress
A Division of HarperCollinsPublishers

Social Psychology Series
John Harvey, Series Editor

Empathy: A Social Psychological Approach, Mark H. Davis

Violence Within the Family: Social Psychological Perspectives,
Sharon D. Herzberger

Social Dilemmas, Samuel S. Komorita and Craig D. Parks

*Self-Presentation: Impression Management
and Interpersonal Behavior*, Mark R. Leary

*Experimental and Nonexperimental Designs in Social
Psychology*, Abraham S. Ross and Malcolm Grant

Intergroup Relations, Walter G. Stephan and Cookie White Stephan

Copyright © 1996 by Westview Press, Inc., A Division of HarperCollins Publishers, Inc.

Published in 1996 in the United States of America by Westview Press, Inc., 5500 Central Avenue, Boulder, Colorado 80301-2877, and in the United Kingdom by Westview Press, 12 Hid's Copse Road, Cumnor Hill, Oxford OX2 9JJ

Herzberger, Sharon D.
    Violence within the family : social psychological perspectives /
Sharon D. Herzberger.
        p.   cm.
    Includes bibliographical references and index.
    ISBN 0-8133-3002-5 (pbk.)
    1. Family violence. 2. Family violence—Psychological aspects.
I. Title.
HV6626.H43   1996
362.82'92—dc20

96-1278
CIP

The paper used in this publication meets the requirements of the American National Standard for Permanence of Paper for Printed Library Materials Z39.48-1984.

10   9   8   7   6   5   4   3   2

For My Parents

CONTENTS

Preface   xiii

1   The Incidence of Family Violence   1

What Do We Mean by ''Family Violence''?   2
Rates of Family Violence   5
   The Validity of Information about Violence   5
   Child Abuse   8
   Spouse Abuse   10
   Sibling Violence   12
   Elderly Abuse   13
   Multiple Forms of Violence in the Family   15
Violence in the Home versus outside the Home   17
Universality of Violence against Family Members   21
   Cross-Cultural Variations   21
   Temporal Variations   23
Concluding Remarks   25

2   Attitudes about Violence in Families   27

Evidence of Tolerance for Aggression against Family
Members   28
Explanations for Tolerance of Aggression   30
   Lack of Empathy for Victims   30
   Belief in a Just World   31
   Illusions about Ability to Prevent Violence   32
   Tolerance of Victimization of Family Members   33
Variation in Levels of Tolerance of Violence   34
   Variation Due to Context   34
   Variation Due to Gender Roles   39

Variation Due to Education and Socioeconomic Status   40
Variation Due to Ethnic, Racial, or Other Cultural
Differences   40
Variation Due to Professional Orientation   41
Variation Due to Characteristics of the Victim and
Perpetrator   43
The Relationship between Attitudes and Behavior   44
Concluding Remarks   46

3   Victims' Reactions to Violence   47

Victims' Beliefs about Themselves and Their
Victimization   48
Causal Thinking   48
Learned Helplessness   53
Problem-Solving Abilities   54
Perceptions That Their Treatment Is Unusual   55
Are Victims Masochistic?   56
Decreased Sensitivity to Aggression   57
Why Do Abuse Victims Stay?   60
Fear and Dependence upon the Abuser   60
Lack of Support from Police and Social Services   61
Affection for the Perpetrator   61
Other Victim Reactions   62
Help-Seeking   62
Retaliation   63
Perpetrator Desistance: Which Strategies Work?   63
Concluding Remarks   65

4   The Dynamics of Family Life   67

The Social System of the Family   68
Parent-Child Relations   69
Parent Factors   69
Child Factors   72
The Interaction between Parent Factors and Child
Factors   72
Relationship to Other Family Subsystems   74
Spousal or Partner Relations   75
Perpetrator Characteristics   75
Victim Characteristics   76
Couple Characteristics   78
Inequality   78
Relationship to Other Family Subsystems   83

Sibling Relations   83
Adult Child-Elderly Parent Relations   85
Family System and Social Environment Influences   86
   Economic and Social Stressors   86
   Lack of Social Support   88
   Societal Norms   90
Concluding Remarks   90

5   Theories of Aggression   93

Thinking about the Causes of Violence   93
An Illustration from the Cyclical Hypothesis Literature   94
Concluding Remarks   101

6   Learning to Be Aggressive   103

How Is Behavior Learned?   104
Is Family Violence Learned?   107
What Are the Mechanisms through Which Family Violence
May Be Learned?   108
   A "Direct" Path to Aggression   108
   The Role of Alternative Disciplinary Methods   110
   Assertiveness and Problem-Solving Skills   112
   Social Cognitive Information Processing   113
   Cognitive Appraisal of Violence   114
   Emotional Support   115
Who Is Susceptible to Learned Aggression and Who Is
Immune?   116
   Victimization versus Observation   116
   Gender of Parent and Child   118
   Age of Onset of Abusive Treatment   119
Concluding Remarks   120

**7   Biological Contributions to Family
Violence   121**

The Evolution of Family Violence   122
   The Relationship between Natural Selection and Wife
   Beating   125
   The Relationship between Natural Selection and Child
   Abuse   127
   Final Thoughts on Evolutionary Explanations   130
Genetics and Family Violence   131
Hormonal Contributions to Aggression   136

Temperament and Physiological Reactivity   139
Other Biological Relationships   140
Concluding Remarks   141

8   Nature and Nurture on Display   143

Empathy   144
   Relationship to Violence   144
   Biological Determinants of Empathy   144
   Social Determinants of Empathy   145
   Interaction between Biological and Social
   Determinants   146
Alcohol and Drug Use   147
   Relationship to Violence   147
   Biochemical Determinants   148
   Social Determinants   149
   Alcohol or Drug Use by the Victim   151
Concluding Remarks   153

9   Legal and Social Service Interventions in Cases of Family Violence   155

Moving from Tolerance to Intolerance of Family
Violence   156
   The Growth of Mandatory Arrest Policies   158
   Theory and Evidence about the Effect of Arrest   159
   Victim Involvement with the Arrest   163
Prosecution of Family Violence Cases   163
   Victim and Witness Accuracy   164
   Variations in Interview Techniques   168
   Confidence in the Testimony of Witnesses and
   Victims   171
   Expert Testimony   174
Professionals' Failure to Report   178
   Ambiguity of the Evidence   178
   Victim Denial   179
   Biased Processing of Evidence   180
   Belief That Reporting is Wrong   181
   Benefits of Reporting   183
Compassion versus Punishment   184
Concluding Remarks   185

10 The Prevention and Treatment of Family Violence   187

Prevention   188
   Education and Support to Potential Perpetrators   188
   Education and Empowerment of Potential Victims   193
   Changes in the Law   194
   Changes in the Media Portrayal of Violence   195
   Multifaceted Prevention Efforts   198
Treatment Programs   198
   Determinants of Behavior Change   199
   Therapeutic Interventions with Offenders   202
   Self-Help Groups   204
   Intervention with Victims of Partner Abuse   207
   Intervention with Victims of Child Abuse   209
   Intervention with Victims of Elderly Abuse   210
   Intervention in Cases of Sibling Violence   211
   Individual Reactions to Intervention   211
Concluding Remarks   213

References   217

Index   243

PREFACE

Pick up any newspaper and you can probably find a story about a case of family violence. One prominently featured case involved two brothers who killed their parents to escape from abuse (as the defense claimed) or to inherit their parents' estate (as the prosecution contended). Another story featured a wife who mutilated her husband allegedly after being raped. Less sensational stories, receiving only fleeting and local concern, can be found almost daily. Although we like to think of our home as a place of refuge and support, the stories remind us that the home can be dangerous and depressing for all too many people.

Perhaps one-fifth of all marriages are tainted by violence, and an equal number of parents may harm their children. Violence against elderly relatives is not well understood, but we are beginning to recognize it as a major social problem. And the most common form of family violence, receiving little attention and less sympathy, occurs between siblings. We do not even understand its impact.

Over the years there have been many books written on family violence. This book is different because it places the topic of family violence within the disciplinary perspectives of social psychology. Family violence is an ideal subject for the application of social psychological theory and research. It draws upon the familiar topics of aggression, attitude formation and change, self-perception, social cognition, gender roles, and group processes. In this book you will learn about the biological and social causes of aggression within families and its consequences. You also will study ways to prevent violence, as well as to treat it, and examine characteristics of families that facilitate or inhibit the use of aggression to solve conflicts.

Finally, the book investigates how society reacts to aggression against family members and how the reaction has changed over time and varies across groups.

The book provides an overview of research on child abuse, partner abuse, abuse against elderly relatives, and sibling violence, but it does not cover all types of violence. Its focus is on physical violence; sexual and emotional maltreatment are discussed occasionally, but only when relevant to the primary topic of physical abuse. This book addresses such questions of current interest as: Does a child who is abused grow up to become an abuser? Can anyone become an abuser, given the right circumstances? Why do victims of partner abuse stay with the perpetrator? Should we arrest perpetrators of family violence? What are the impediments to successful prosecution of crimes against family members? And, Why do people demean victims of family violence?

The book is intended for advanced undergraduate students in special topics classes or as an accompaniment to a text in an introductory social psychology course. But it is also designed to be read by intelligent laypeople who want to understand this difficult and widespread social problem.

I want to thank several people for their diligent help with this volume. First, I thank Trinity students, Kirsten Olson and Kristin Maki, who helped me to find interesting material to include in the book and who commented upon early drafts of each chapter. My secretary, Tracy Knight, provided invaluable editorial and organizational help. Reviewers, Robert Burgess of Pennsylvania State University, Irene Frieze of the University of Pittsburgh, and John Harvey of the University of Iowa made insightful suggestions on the first draft of the manuscript. I am most grateful, however, to my husband, David, for encouraging me throughout this process and to my parents, Marion and Robert Dickman, whose love and support during my childhood provided an environment so contrary to those featured in this book.

1

The Incidence of Family Violence

CHAPTER OBJECTIVES

What Do We Mean by "Family
Violence"?
Rates of Family Violence
  The Validity of Information
    about Violence
  Child Abuse
  Spouse Abuse
  Sibling Violence
  Elderly Abuse
  Multiple Forms of Violence in
    the Family

Violence in the Home versus
  outside the Home
Universality of Violence against
  Family Members
    Cross-Cultural Variations
    Temporal Variations
Concluding Remarks

We are supposed to feel safe at home. Home should be where we are loved, protected, and restored after a day at work or school. For many people, however, the home is not a safe haven from the stresses of life. Instead, it is a dangerous place where mental, physical, or sexual suffering occurs, often on a regular basis.

This book explores physical violence within families from the perspectives offered by social psychology. Social psychologists are interested in the forces that affect our behavior in the social world. They study the influence individuals or groups have on other people and how, in turn, the individual influences the surrounding environment. Social psychologists recognize that reality is in the eyes of the perceiver and that to understand a person's behavior or thoughts, we must understand how the individual interprets and evaluates the behaviors of others. Gordon Allport (1985) said this well: Social psychologists "attempt to understand and explain how the thought, feeling, and behavior of individuals are influenced by the actual, imagined, or implied presence of others" (p. 3).

While scholars from other areas of psychology and from anthropology, sociology, and biology also study human interaction, social psychologists focus on the individual in relation to his or her various social groups. The groups examined by social psychologists range from small groups, such as dating partners or married couples, to large groups, such as religious organizations. Groups that can influence and be influenced by the individual may be formally connected, such as a family, or may be formed by haphazard circumstances, such as when people are together in an elevator that stops functioning.

In exploring family violence you will study the themes that have fascinated social psychologists for decades: attitudes, self- and other-perception, and how behavior develops and changes. You will investigate such questions as: What are the prevailing attitudes about violence in the home and how might these attitudes influence patterns of violence? How do victims perceive their own victimization, and do differences in self-perception relate to the consequences experienced by victims? What are the biological and learned origins of aggressive behavior and to what extent can these origins be overcome? How can we prevent violence in the family, and once it occurs how should society respond? Throughout this book you will study whether violence in the family can be explained by the same factors as violence outside the home. You will also address the special characteristics of families and family life that distinguish violence within the home from violence in other social groupings.

What Do We Mean by "Family Violence"?

Let us start our exploration of family violence with a definition of *violence*. A good definition helps us to distinguish violent from nonviolent acts, or at least to describe points on a continuum from total nonviolence to extreme violence.

Violence can take many forms, from physical and sexual assault to emotional degradation. This book concentrates upon physical violence, with discussion of emotional and sexual abuse only in recognition of the fact that they often accompany physical harm.

Information that researchers have gleaned from studies of other forms of abuse are often relevant to understanding the causes and consequences of physical violence in families. Both emotional and sexual abuse, however, are well developed, independent research areas (Finkelhor, 1984; Garbarino, Guttmann, & Seeley, 1987), and their inclusion would necessitate a discussion that is beyond the scope of this small volume. It is not the intent of this book to review the literature on all of the harmful activities of family members. Instead, it will combine a study of the well-investigated social psychological literature on aggression with the study of physical violence in the context of family relationships.

We also need to define *family* (Weis, 1989). This book concentrates upon violence among people who share kinship (i.e., they are related through birth or marriage) and who share a home. It does not address violence among dating partners or close friends, or even among distant relatives. By narrowing our topic, you will learn about the special dynamics of family interactions and how living together and sharing a relationship contribute to violent behavior.

Beyond this, deriving a suitable and generally accepted listing of specific acts that constitute *family violence* is difficult. One common definition concentrates on the parent's action and suggests that child abuse refers to an intentional use of force aimed at injuring or damaging the child. This definition seems reasonable, but we might also consider the consequences of the act and the circumstances surrounding the victimization (Weis, 1989). For example, knowing that a parent hit a child with a stick and did so intentionally may not be sufficiently informative to warrant a label of abuse. If the parent hit a child on clothed buttocks, some may not regard this as abuse. However, knowing that the stick left welts would be more likely to prompt the abuse label. Of course, the perpetrator's aim, whether the victim ducks, or how the victim falls affects the degree of injury (Gelles & Cornell, 1985). Thus, consequences by themselves cannot be used to define abuse.

The defining characteristics of abuse within families also depend upon one's perspective. Since spanking is an intentional use of force, it may be seen as abuse according to some definitions; in this case most parents could be labeled abusers (cf. Garbarino, 1989b). Some injurious behaviors stem from beneficial intent. Consider the Vietnamese-American parents who bruise their child's body by rubbing it with coins to cure minor illnesses (Gray & Cosgrove, 1985). The parents intend no injury; in fact, they want to aid the child. Although the procedure leaves no permanent physical damage and causes no emotional trauma, some might call this violence. And how should we react to parents who have their infant boys circumcised or who pierce their infant daughter's ears (cf. Garbarino, 1989b)?

The definition of child abuse that will guide discussions in this book is one proposed by Garbarino (1989b), who recognizes that child abuse is a socially defined phenomenon:

> Child maltreatment can be defined as acts of omission or commission by a parent or guardian that are judged by a mixture of community values and professional expertise to be inappropriate and damaging. (p. 220)

Garbarino encourages us to consider the analogy between a fever and child abuse. An elevated body temperature indicates infection that must be treated, just as child abuse signifies an underlying problem within the family. And, just as the fever by itself may not be dangerous and is rarely the real problem, physical violence toward a child may indicate an impaired family relationship that ultimately may produce lasting emotional damage. Acts of violence against children may be seen as a sign of an ill-functioning family; accordingly, attention to more than just the violence is needed for us to understand the derivation of the violence and the means of correction.

Similar reasoning applies to efforts to define violence against other family members. "Intent to harm" is part of most definitions of spouse abuse, but intentions are notoriously difficult to assess. For this reason many people concentrate on the actual behavior involved, such as kicking, hitting, pushing, or threatening to harm (Straus, 1979b). Consistent with the community standards criterion that is useful in defining child abuse, notions about "acceptable" behavior between partners are used in definitions of spouse assault. However, whereas community standards often exclude minor acts of violence against children (e.g., spanking, slapping) from the category of "child abuse," community standards promote the inclusion of such acts under the definition of "spouse abuse." Even relatively mild physical violence between adult partners is usually regarded as nonnormative and unacceptable (cf. Hotaling & Straus, 1989), not only because of the pain involved, but because the use of violence may alter the balance of power between partners and create a sense of inequality in the victim (Frieze & Browne, 1989). In our society we are generally unconcerned about children's feelings of inequality in relation to their parents; therefore, parental behaviors that promote inequality are not in and of themselves seen as abusive.

Even though the act itself may be the primary defining characteristic of spouse abuse, some suggest that it is helpful to know the force used to carry out the act, how frequently the act occurred, and how many different acts are "clustered together" in one event (Frieze & Browne, 1989). These characteristics help to determine the severity of the abuse. "Both the repetition of violent acts and a clustering of types of acts within a single incident increase the potential for injury, as victims are overwhelmed by the rapidity of events and are unable to recover in time to protect themselves from the next blow" (Browne, 1987, p. 69).

Arguments over definitions do not have trivial consequences. Estimates of the incidence of family violence vary widely depending upon the definition chosen, leading us either to see violence as a major or relatively minor public health concern. Weis (1989) notes, for example, that varying definitions have led to estimates ranging from 1 percent to 30 percent of all children in the United States suffering from physical abuse. Let us take a look at the various estimates of family violence and how they are derived.

Rates of Family Violence

Although it is impossible to define precisely what is meant by family violence, we can estimate its occurrence using various indices. However, we also need to discuss the problems that arise when we try to measure the incidence of violence.

The Validity of Information about Violence

The statistics on family violence only estimate the rate of this phenomenon and, as later chapters will attest, they dramatically underestimate the true incidence of maltreatment. Figures based upon official statistics gathered from the police or social service agencies are faulty because some unknown number of cases of abuse are not reported to authorities (see Webb, Campbell, Schwartz, & Sechrest, 1966, for a discussion of the problems associated with the use of archival data). Physicians, psychologists, teachers, and to a lesser extent ministers and school nurses decline to report confirmed cases of abuse, preferring to work with the family themselves (Garbarino, 1988). Also, even when a case secures the attention of authorities, the evidence may not be sufficient to substantiate the allegations (e.g., some states substantiate only 5 percent of the allegations through the perpetrator's admission or through a conviction; Garbarino, 1988). Furthermore, suspicions against white, middle-class individuals and against mothers are often dismissed (cf. Herzberger, 1988; Garbarino,

1988), signifying that not only will official statistics underestimate the rate of family violence, but will do so disproportionately among some groups.

Written surveys or interviews conducted with a sample of the population also have drawbacks. Characteristics of the interviewer, such as warmth or ability to establish rapport, strongly influence the amount and type of information disclosed by the respondent (Groth-Marnat, 1990). Some people who are contacted may not agree to participate in the project, and we cannot know precisely whether those who do participate are similar to those who do not participate in their experience with maltreatment. People who choose to participate also may deny the truth about their involvement in violent relationships, or, while not actually lying, may interpret questions in a manner that allows them to put their ''best foot forward'' and to underplay their negative characteristics (Crowne & Marlowe, 1964). Arias and Beach (1987), for example, found that husbands' and wives' willingness to admit to violence against their spouse was related to their tendency to place themselves in a socially desirable light. People who had such a tendency were more likely to deny being aggressive. Once they admitted to being violent, however, the tendency to respond in socially desirable ways did not affect disclosures about how seriously or how frequently they abused a spouse.

Although men may underreport their own victimization by a spouse (Szinovacz, 1983), in general we may feel more confident about reports of violence by victims than by perpetrators (Arias & Beach, 1987). For example, Riggs, Murphy, and O'Leary (1989) asked college students to rate how likely it is that they would report their own or their partner's positive and negative activities. While no differences were found in expected reports about positive behaviors, Figure 1.1 shows substantial differences in expected reports about the use of physical violence. As measured by items on the Conflict Tactics Scale (Straus, 1979b), students expected that they would be less likely to report their own violent behavior than their partner's, especially as the behavior becomes more serious.

Another problem with surveys or interviews is that they cannot be used with all people. The involvement of young children as victims or perpetrators is usually measured by speaking to parents, not by questioning the children themselves. Parents, of course, may not be privy to all instances of violence involving children or may not want to disclose their knowledge of these events.

Another way of trying to gather information about family violence includes the use of uninvolved informants (cf. Weis, 1989).

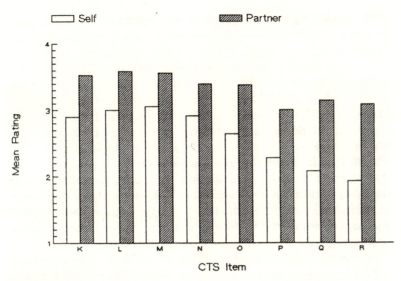

FIGURE 1.1

Mean likelihood to report CTS physical aggression items: self versus partner reports

Note: K = threw something; L = pushed, grabbed, or shoved; M = slapped; N = kicked, bit, or hit with a fist; O = hit or tried to hit with something; P = beat up; Q = threatened with a knife or gun; R = used a knife or gun.

Source: Riggs, D. S., Murphy, C. M., & O'Leary, K. D. (1989). Intentional falsification in reports of interpartner aggression. *Journal of Interpersonal Violence, 4,* p. 226. Copyright 1989, Sage Publications, Inc., Newbury Park, CA. Reprinted by permission.

Gil (1970), for example, found that few people admit to injuring their own child, but many report on injuries inflicted on neighboring children by their parents. Furthermore, when children are questioned about fights between their mother and father, estimates of the rate of spouse abuse exceed rates estimated from official statistics (Weis, 1989).

Research on family violence also depends extensively on retrospective designs, in which people are asked to recall their involvement in abusive situations and to identify key information about the abuse. Adults, for example, may be asked to recall their childhood experience with or witnessing of violence by a parent. Such designs are fraught with the potential for error (Sudman & Bradburn, 1982). People dramatically err in estimating the frequency of past events and have difficulty gauging the timeframe in which events occurred. Unless demarcated by a salient occurrence (e.g., the year in which a relative died or a child was born), we often mistake when behaviors, such as abuse, began and when they ended. Furthermore, the meaning of events changes over time and people may not recall accurately their feelings and perceptions as they experience the abuse.

Child Abuse

Now that we have some appreciation for the limitations of research in this area, let us examine statistics from some of the most valid research. One survey (Burgdorf, 1980) collected data from schools, hospitals, social service agencies, as well as from the police and court system, in a randomly selected sample of twenty-six counties in ten states. Analysis of these *known* cases of violence suggests that at least one out of one hundred children is maltreated each year through physical, sexual, or emotional abuse or through neglect of their physical, educational, or emotional well-being. About one-third of these children suffer from physical abuse. Table 1.1 shows the judged severity of the forms of maltreatment, along with the ages and percentage of children experiencing each form.

Another survey (American Humane Association, 1987), again using cases that were verified by social service agencies, shows that official maltreatment rates may reach as high as three per one hundred children. While not all cases of child maltreatment involve parents or other relatives as perpetrators, the American Humane Association (cf. Garbarino, 1989b) estimates that 83 percent of the cases of physical injury involve parents; only 12 percent of physical injury cases involve people not related to the child.

As noted above, another way to estimate the incidence of child abuse is to randomly survey the general public. When we do so, we find much higher rates of child abuse. Straus and Gelles (1986) conducted one such national survey through the use of phone interviews with a randomly selected sample of adults in two-parent households. The interviewers questioned the parents about their involvement with various forms of violence using the Conflict Tactics Survey (Straus, 1979b). The parent was recorded as having engaged in "child assault" if the child about whom they were questioned was kicked, bit, hit with a fist, hit with an object, beaten up, threatened with use of a knife or gun, or actually shot or stabbed. Of the 2,688 parents interviewed, fully 18 percent admitted to assaulting a child during the past year.

These figures are undoubtedly underestimates, given that some parents falsely deny their involvement in assault. Also, many families have more than one child, and the relationship between the parent

TABLE 1.1 Severity of Maltreatment-Related Injury or Impairment by Form of Maltreatment and Age of Child: Estimated Percentage Distributions by Severity Category

Form of Maltreatment and Age of Child	Severity of Injury or Impairment		
	Fatal	*Serious*	*Moderate*
Form of maltreatment:			
Physical assault	72	14	40
Sexual exploitation	1	5	3
Emotional abuse	0	16	22
Physical neglect	28	36	9
Educational neglect	0	19	34
Emotional neglect	0	34	1
Age of child:			
0–2	49	16	5
3–5	25	7	9
6–8	2	17	18
9–11	0	19	18
12–14	1	14	23
15–17	23	27	27

Note: Percentages may sum to more than 100 since a child may have experienced more than one form of maltreatment at a given level of severity.

Source: Burgdorf, K. (1980). *Recognition and reporting of child maltreatment: Findings from the National Study of the Incidence and Severity of Child Abuse and Neglect* (p. 50). Washington, D.C.: National Center on Child Abuse and Neglect.

and only one child was examined. Finally, children who might be at greatest risk of abuse, those in single-parent homes and those under 3 years of age, were not included in the survey. For these reasons, even more children may be exposed to parental violence than are indicated through survey or interview methods such as these.

Both sons and daughters are victims of family violence. While girls are three to four times as likely to be the target of sexual abuse than boys, most evidence suggests that boys tend to be physically maltreated more often (cf. Finkelhor, 1984; Garbarino, 1989b; Gelles, 1979; Hartman & Burgess, 1989). Gelles (1979), however, suggests that the most serious forms of violence are directed equally to sons and daughters, and Burgdorf's (1980) results show that daughters are more likely to be the victims of physical assault during adolescence.

Reliable figures are unavailable on whether mothers or fathers are more likely to physically assault the children under their care (cf. Pagelow, 1984; Weis, 1989). Some reports (Burgdorf, 1980; Gelles, 1979) suggest that mothers, who often spend more time with their children, are more likely to assault them. This conclusion contrasts with the figures showing that men are overwhelmingly the perpetrators of sexual abuse of children (Finkelhor, 1984) and points to the importance of studying the problems inherent in parenting to understand physical child abuse.

Spouse Abuse

Straus and Gelles (1986) also interviewed family members about their involvement in spousal assault. Because, unlike with children, spouses do not have the legal right to hit each other, the authors counted as "assault" both minor forms of violence (e.g., hitting, slapping, throwing things at the spouse) and the more serious forms that had also been counted as child assault (e.g., kicking, punching). Eighteen percent of those surveyed reported that they had employed assaultive conflict tactics toward a spouse within the last year. An earlier study (Straus, Gelles, & Steinmetz, 1980) revealed that 28 percent of a nationwide sample of adults had experienced at least one incident of spouse abuse during their current relationship. (See Box 1.1 for a severe example of spouse and child abuse.)

Which partner is most likely to be aggressive? Contrary to popular opinion, some reports suggest that women and men are about equally likely to aggress against a partner. In the Straus et al. (1980) nationwide survey, 49 percent of the people who admitted to being involved in a violent relationship reported mutual physical violence between partners, 27 percent reported male violence, and 24 percent reported female violence.

However, estimates of gender differences in spouse abuse vary according to the source of the information (cf. Frieze & Browne, 1989). Battered men are less likely to seek help from social service agencies or the police, except following severe injury (cf. McNeely & Mann, 1990). Thus, surveys of individuals rather than social service agency records result in a more even picture of abuse by men and women.

More importantly, perhaps, estimates vary with the definition of abuse. Repeated and severe violence is more likely to be perpetrated by men, with four times as many husbands killing wives as wives killing husbands (cf. Bograd, 1990; Sigler, 1989). The inclusion of

BOX 1.1

A few years ago in New York City a severe example of spouse and child abuse rose to national attention. Hedda Nussbaum and Joel Steinberg were arrested for the murder of their adopted daughter, Lisa. Charges were dropped against Hedda Nussbaum when her systematic and brutal victimization by Joel Steinberg became known. *Newsweek* (Hackett, McKillop, & Wang, 1988) presented a detailed account of the trial testimony, which is summarized here.

On the day that Lisa was killed, Steinberg became angry at Nussbaum and their daughter for not drinking enough water, and he made them eat hot pepper. Steinberg, who often took Lisa to business appointments at restaurants, started to get ready for a meeting. Lisa questioned her mother about whether her father would let her go along. Nussbaum suggested that she ask him. A few minutes later Steinberg brought Lisa to Nussbaum, holding her limp body. Nussbaum testified:

> "And I said, 'What happened?' He said, 'What's the difference what happened? This is your child. Hasn't this gone far enough?' " Nussbaum later explained that Steinberg said he was angry at Lisa for staring at him. "He said, 'I knocked her down and she didn't want to get up again. This staring business had gotten to be too much'." Steinberg put Lisa on the bathroom floor and got ready to go out. (pp. 57–58)

Nussbaum tried to arouse her daughter, but Steinberg told her to "relax, go with her." Then he left for his appointment. Nussbaum was asked why she did not call for help and she said that Steinberg had:

> "healing powers." . . . "I looked at the phone and I started thinking, 'Should I call 911 or . . . a pediatrician?' And I said, 'No, Joel said he would take care of her . . .' And I didn't want to show disloyalty or distrust for him. So I didn't call." Lisa died three days later. (p. 58)

Steinberg, a criminal lawyer, and Nussbaum, a children's book editor, lived together for two years before Steinberg began to assault Nussbaum seriously. According to the *Newsweek* account, it was in 1978 when Nussbaum first went to the hospital.

(continued on next page)

While she initially told the truth about the beating, she later asked the doctor not to record who hit her. As happens frequently in cases of spouse abuse (Walker, 1984), Steinberg was affectionate when she returned home. Then, three years later, he ruptured her spleen.

> Over the next six years, Nussbaum says Steinberg broke her knee, broke her ribs, choked her hard enough to damage her vocal cords, burned her body with a propane torch, hit her hands, feet and sexual organs with a broomstick, urinated on her, forced her to sleep while handcuffed to a chinning bar. . . . (pp. 60–61)

Throughout this time neighbors suspected the abuse and once even called in the police. A teacher reported suspected child abuse to school officials. Doctors also wondered about the injuries. Somehow, though, no one intervened to stop the abuse or to conduct an investigation.

''threats'' and other mild forms of violence in the definition produces more equal estimates of the rates of violence by women and men. Also, violent acts by women more often than similar acts by men are in retaliation for the violence of a partner (cf. Frieze & Browne, 1989; Sigler, 1989). Studies that do not separate provocative from retaliatory violence confuse the picture. For example, Browne and Williams (1989) found that the decline between 1976 and 1984 in the number of husbands murdered by women correlated with the development of social support and legal services available to women who needed to leave abusive partners. With such services, women may not resort to such dire actions.

Sibling Violence

You may be surprised to see a heading for sibling violence in this listing. If so, you are similar to the vast majority of professionals and parents who pay little attention to aggression between siblings. Most people regard sibling violence as so common that it is a ''normal'' part of growing up in a family (Gelles & Cornell, 1985; Pagelow,

Tooley (1980) describes a case of serious sibling aggression of a middle child named Allen:

> Allen reacted with obvious terror to the presence of his eight-year-old brother and to the threat of his three-year-old sister to "hit him with a sock." Allen was referred to Children's Psychiatric Hospital for inpatient treatment. The mother, Mrs. J, recounted without much evident concern that over a period of a year the older boy had: tried to drown Allen in the bathtub; pushed him down the stairs; cut his head to the degree that he required a dozen stitches to close the wound; and had set fire to the family home. In the last instance, which was never fully clarified by the parents, Allen had been trapped in his bedroom and had to be rescued by firemen "with hoses and axes." (p. 28)

1989). But just because it is common does not mean it should be ignored. Tooley (1980), in Box 1.2, describes a particularly troubling case of sibling violence.

Straus et al. (1980) reported that sibling violence *is* the most common form of violence in families. Fully 82 percent of parents surveyed reported aggression among their offspring; two-thirds of parents reported that their teenage children hit a brother or sister on average nineteen times a year. Families with boys report more violence than families of boys and girls or just girls. Another study (Roscoe, Goodwin, & Kennedy, 1987), which gathered information directly from seventh graders, found even higher rates of violence; 88 percent of the boys and 94 percent of the girls reported being victims of sibling violence during the last year, and 85 percent of the boys and 96 percent of the girls reported being perpetrators. Although more similarities than differences emerged in the types of violence experienced by boys and girls, boys both suffered from and perpetrated more serious forms of violence (see Table 1.2).

Elderly Abuse

Violence against parents by young children or by adolescents is rarer than other forms of family violence, and when present in a family is usually a response by the child to a consistent pattern of violent parenting (cf. Hotaling & Straus, 1989). However, when the parents are

TABLE 1.2 Percentage of Violent Behaviors Involving Siblings as Victims and Perpetrators

	Victim		Perpetrator	
	Sisters N = 123	Brothers N = 121	Sisters N = 123	Brothers N = 121
Pushing/shoving/pulling	70	62	73	62
Kicking	58	55	47	32
Throwing an object	44	50	35	40
Hitting with an object	41	52	27	36
Hitting with a fist	41	50	45	56
Scratching	44	34	50	12
Pinching	41	36	37	20
Pulling hair	44	35	28	14
Slapping	41	34	48	21
Biting	17	21	16	7
Smothering/holding pillow over sibling's head	15	13	15	11
Locking in a room or closet	14	13	11	16
Holding against one's will	11	13	10	18
Choking	10	13	7	9
Beating up	5	7	14	14
Threatening with a knife or gun	0.8	7	0	0.8
Being bodily thrown	0.8	6	2	8
Shooting, stabbing or cutting with knife or gun	0.8	0	0	0.8
Other	5	2	4	3
None of the above	6	12	4	15

Source: Roscoe, B., Goodwin, M. P., & Kennedy, D. (1987). Sibling violence and agonistic interactions experienced by early adolescents. *Journal of Family Violence, 2,* 131. Copyright 1987, Plenum Publishing Corp., New York. Reprinted by permission.

elderly, parent abuse is not uncommon, nor is abuse by grandchildren or other members of the family. Estimates of the number of abused elderly each year range from one-half million to over two million cases annually, with at least 70 percent of the perpetrators being family members (cf. Pagelow, 1984, 1989). Approximately two out of each one hundred people aged 65 or older experience physical violence and most of the studies show that the majority of the abused elderly are women, as might be expected given their greater longevity (cf. Wolf & Pillemer, 1989). Abused elderly people are likely to reside with the abuser and, more often than the nonabused elderly, to suffer from a physical or mental impairment (Wolf & Pillemer, 1989). Box 1.3 illustrates cases of elderly abuse that were brought to the attention of the House Select Committee on Aging (Elder Abuse: An Examination of a Hidden Problem, 1981).

Information about abuse of the elderly has only recently begun to surface (Gelles & Cornell, 1985). Because the elderly tend to be more isolated and have fewer social networks than younger people, their victimization is less likely to be noticed by others. In addition, the elderly may be hesitant to report abuse because of their fear of alternative living arrangements, should they have to leave the abusive home.

Multiple Forms of Violence in the Family

When a family member suffers from one type of abuse, often other types of abuse exist in the household as well. Many women who have suffered physical assaults by their husbands also have experienced marital rape (Frieze & Browne, 1989). Surveys of students and the general populace conducted from 1972 through 1985 (cf. Hotaling & Straus, 1989) find that approximately 20 percent of violent families are like those of Joel Steinberg (see Box 1.1); they experience both child and spousal assault. As Table 1.3 shows, the 1985 national survey data revealed an increased likelihood of child abuse in families where one parent assaults the other; if both spouses are assaultive, the likelihood of a child becoming the victim of assault increases substantially.

The respondents in this survey were also asked about sibling violence. Parents were asked whether they considered fights between siblings to be a ''problem.'' The wording of this question dramatically underestimates the amount of violence, since, as we discussed above, parents regularly ignore sibling violence or consider it normal (cf. Pagelow, 1984). However, Table 1.4 shows results that are consistent with other relationships in the family. Sibling fights were seen as more problematic in families which had experienced spouse abuse or child abuse and were especially problematic in families which had experienced both. When the statistics were examined separately for boys and girls, the same relations among the forms of family violence emerged.

BOX 1.3

Consider the following excerpts from cases of elderly abuse presented to the U.S. House of Representatives Select Committee on Aging (Elder Abuse: An Examination of a Hidden Problem, 1981). As the examples illustrate, perpetrators vary in relationship with the victim and both men and women are subject to abuse, although most often the victims are women.

. . . (A)n elderly woman with a heart condition was being routinely abused by her 15-year-old grandson. On one occasion, he threw a suitcase at her, hitting her head. She also had bruises on her arms from beating. He hit her only in places where it would do no damage according to the grandmother. The grandson did not really know why he hit his grandmother except that she made him angry. (p. 4)

An elderly man, aged 87, was being abused by his daughter. He, in turn, took out his anger on his senile and incontinent wife. In periodic rages over her inability to care for herself, and for wetting the bed and dirtying herself, he would physically attack her. (p. 7)

Here is direct testimony from one of the victims, who was abused by her well-educated daughter who was a social worker:

My husband died 10 years ago. The house where we lived became mine . . . My younger daughter, who had two unfortunate marriages, was welcomed by us and helped in every way we could with her and her children. This began over 18 years ago. The past 3 years, things have gotten steadily worse. My daughter locked me in the garage and left me there for more than an hour. She always parked her car behind mine in the garage so I could not get my car out except by her permission. She insisted upon a weekly time schedule of when I wanted my car in or out of the garage. . . .

. . . Several times she locked me out of the house. One of those times it was very cold and snowing with ice on the ground. I had to get to a pay station to call a friend to come and get me. My daughter's treatment of me kept getting worse. Always hurting me physically and mentally; kicking me, pushing me, grappling with me, telling me to get out, at one time throwing a drawer down the stairs at me. . . . She told me I was senile and paranoid and my brain was all shriveled up. (pp. 114–115)

TABLE 1.3 Percentage Likelihood of Child Assault by Mothers and Fathers for Each Spouse Assault Type (1985 National Resurvey Data)

	No Spouse Assault (N)	Wife Only Is Assaultive (N)	Husband Only Is Assaultive (N)	Both Husband and Wife Are Assaultive (N)
By mothers	15.5 (1,213)	28.6 (63)	28.9 (76)	36.1 (138)
By fathers	14.7 (992)	19.2 (62)	15.7 (41)	41.1 (103)

Source: Hotaling, G. T., & Straus, M. A. (1989). Intrafamily violence, and crime and violence outside the family. In L. Ohlin & M. Tonry (Eds.), *Family Violence* (p. 337). Chicago: University of Chicago. Copyright © 1989 by the University of Chicago. Reprinted by permission.

TABLE 1.4 Rate of Sibling Violence by Parent-to-Child Assault and Spouse Assault (1985 National Resurvey)

	Child Assault		
Spouse Assault	Absent (N)	Present (N)	Total (N)
Absent	3.6 (1,289)	8.5 (141)	6.0 (1,430)
Present	6.0 (168)	11.5 (84)	8.8 (252)
Total	4.8 (1,457)	10.0 (225)	7.4 (1,682)

Note: Rates are per 100 and are therefore equal to percentages.

Source: Hotaling, G. T., & Straus, M. A. (1989). Intrafamily violence, and crime and violence outside the family. In L. Ohlin & M. Tonry (Eds.), *Family Violence* (p. 338). Chicago: University of Chicago. Copyright © 1989 by the University of Chicago. Reprinted by permission.

Violence in the Home versus outside the Home

The statistics cited above present a startling picture of home life. But we have said nothing about our chances of involvement in violence outside the home. America is a relatively dangerous place to live. In

1990, 23 thousand people were killed and about 6 million people were victimized by violent crime (Reiss & Roth, 1993). Residents of the United States are more violent than the populations of any other industrialized country. If our chances of being harmed at home are insignificant compared to our chances of being harmed outside the home, then we perhaps should refocus this volume to concentrate on the peace-inducing qualities of the family.

Unfortunately, informative comparisons of rates of violence in and out of the home are rare. While it would be helpful to compare rates of violence gathered through police statistics to known cases of domestic violence, we cannot do this. Family violence is usually a private matter; consequently, substantially more underreporting of violence against family members occurs than against nonfamily members. So, direct comparisons for most forms of family violence are not feasible.

However, we can obtain evidence about extreme violence, such as murder, since these cases are quite likely to be discovered and investigated. The statistics show that family members are involved in a substantial number of murder cases and just how dangerous the home is depends upon one's gender (Browne & Williams, 1993). A study by Browne and Flewelling (1986), for example, showed that approximately one-quarter of the homicides committed during 1980 to 1984 involved family members. Women seem to be especially vulnerable to be murdered by a male partner; they are more likely to be killed by partners (52 percent of the time) than by all other categories of people combined (e.g., children, strangers). Only 12 percent of male victims are killed by their partners. Looking at the statistics another way yields the same conclusion. Most murdered men are killed by acquaintances or strangers (73 percent), but among men killed by women the murderer is most likely to be a partner (55 percent of the time). These statistics suggest that, at least with respect to the most serious forms of violence, women are much more likely to be involved in violence in the home, while men are victims and perpetrators more often outside the home.

Logic tells us that child abuse is more often perpetrated by family members than by outsiders. There are little or no published comparisons of rates of parent-to-child physical violence versus rates of acquaintance- or stranger-to-child physical violence, but one might presume that outsiders who prey on a child would get reported quickly.

Are the same people engaging in violence at home and on the street? Again, to the extent that there exists substantial overlap in the people who are violent in each place, we may not need to search for special characteristics of *family* violence. However, if people who are violent toward family members would rarely or never think of lifting a hand to their neighbor, then it is important to elucidate characteristics of home life that evoke aggression.

A survey of college students reveals a connection between sibling violence and violence toward peers. Male college students who admitted being violent to a brother or a sister were more likely to be violent toward people outside the family (Mangold & Koski, 1990). College women who were violent toward a brother were also more likely to aggress outside the home, but those violent just toward a sister were not. These findings are interesting because they reiterate earlier conclusions (e.g., Browne & Flewelling, 1986) that, while girls are aggressive in the home, boys are more generally aggressive. Also, the presence of a brother may provide an aggressive training ground for girls.

Children who fight in more than one setting are more maladjusted than children who fight only in the home or at school (Loeber & Dishion, 1984). Loeber and Dishion's study of fourth, seventh, and tenth grade boys revealed that boys who fought across settings were not only more likely to lead delinquent lifestyles and to be disobedient to parents, but were more likely to be in contact with the police than were adolescents who only fought with peers or in the home. Furthermore, the parents of ''cross-setting'' fighters monitored their children's behavior more poorly, more frequently displayed inconsistency in their discipline efforts, were more likely to reject their children, and had poorer marital relations than parents of nonfighters or ''single-setting'' fighters. The study also found that boys who fought only at home were more likely to suffer from some of the same behavior problems and home deficits as those who fought across situations, whereas boys who fought only at school were more likely to resemble nonfighters in these characteristics.

Hotaling and Straus (1989), in a summary of the 1985 national survey, report that people who assault family members are more likely to assault nonfamily members as well. In fact, as Table 1.5 shows, husbands who assault their wives are four times more likely to have hit a nonfamily member than nonassaultive husbands. The highest rates of assault of nonfamily members are found among people who had abused both a spouse and a child.

Cross-cultural studies also demonstrate the overlap between family and nonfamily violence. A study of ninety small-scale societies around the world revealed support for the notion that some cultures promote widespread forms of violence (Levinson, 1989). While Levinson found no connection between family violence and warfare

TABLE 1.5 Rates of Nonfamily Verbal and Physical Assault by Family Assault Type and Gender of Adult Offender (1985 National Resurvey)

Indicator of Nonfamily Aggression	Nonviolent (N)	Child Assault, No Assault by Husband (N)	Assault by Husband, No Child Assault (N)	Both Child Assault and Husband Assault (N)
A. For husbands who assault wives:				
Husband got angry at nonfamily person and yelled at him/her	49.8 (1,931)	59.3 (158)	69.2 (234)	77.3 (120)
Husband got angry at nonfamily person and smashed something	6.1 (1,960)	11.8 (363)	19.4 (235)	25.7 (118)
Husband got into fight with nonfamily member and hit him/her	2.3 (1,960)	3.7 (364)	9.0 (236)	11.4 (120)
Husband got into fight with nonfamily member and injured him/her	.8 (1,964)	.2 (364)	.9 (236)	6.6 (120)
Husband got arrested in last twelve months	1.4 (896)	.6 (158)	3.2 (95)	5.1 (49)
B. For wives who assault husbands:				
Wife got angry at nonfamily person and yelled at him/her	41.9 (1,937)	46.4 (358)	55.5 (242)	73.7 (120)
Wife got angry at nonfamily person and smashed something	3.8 (1,948)	5.1 (356)	10.7 (240)	20.0 (121)
Wife got in fight with nonfamily person and hit him/her	.6 (1,954)	.9 (362)	2.4 (242)	4.1 (122)
Wife got in fight with nonfamily person and injured him/her	.2 (1,960)	.0 (362)	.7 (242)	.0 (127)
Wife got arrested in last twelve months	.3 (1,077)	1.3 (210)	3.0 (132)	.5 (68)

Note: Rates are per 100 and are therefore equal to percentages.

Source: Hotaling, G. T., & Straus, M. A. (1989). Intrafamily violence, and crime and violence outside the family. In L. Ohlin & M. Tonry (Eds.), *Family Violence* (pp. 360–361). Chicago: University of Chicago. Copyright © 1989 by the University of Chicago. Reprinted by permission.

against other groups, he demonstrated that violence within the community (e.g., men's brawls, women fighting other women) was more common in societies in which wife beating was prevalent. Again, the use of physical punishment against children generally failed to correspond with the presence or absence of other patterns of violence.

These studies suggest that many people who assault family members aggress against nonfamily members as well. However, as the tabled figures show, substantial independence remains between the two types of violence. Also, research such as that conducted by Shields, McCall, and Hanneke (1988) suggests that individuals who aggress only against family members differ from more generally violent people in the nature of their violent acts, in their attitudes toward violence, and in other characteristics. For example, men whose only assaultive behavior is toward a wife are more violent than more generally assaultive men, are more remorseful about the use of violence, and tend to hold more prestigious jobs. Thus, we need to examine the conditions that foster and inhibit violent family life and the socialization patterns that produce different types of violent people (Fagan, 1989).

Universality of Violence against Family Members

With all the media attention to family violence today, we might wonder whether this social ill is a sign of something gone awry with our current way of life. Perhaps the financial pressures or complicated social roles pervasive in modern-day families have fostered an environment particularly ripe for violent interchanges. One way to place today's violence in perspective is to compare our current record to the record of violence throughout history, as well as to evidence of violence in other nations and cultures around the world.

Cross-Cultural Variations

People often wonder whether family violence is a phenomenon that is restricted to the United States and a few other societies in which aggressive resolution of conflict is common. The answer to this question appears to be *no*. Family violence is nonexistent or rare among some peoples, but many studies reveal at least occasional physical violence against children and women in a majority of cultures (e.g., Levinson, 1983). Levinson (1989) used information on ninety small-scale or peasant societies around the world (e.g., the Arapaho, Pawnee, and Copper Eskimo societies of North America and the

TABLE 1.6 Regional Variation in Family Violence

	North America	South America	Oceania	Africa	Asia	Middle East	Europe & Soviet Union
Wife beating	2.5	2.3	2.4	1.9	2.3	2.5	3.0
Child punishment	1.8	2.0	2.3	2.7	2.2	2.5	2.3
Sibling fighting	1.5	1.3	1.9	2.0	1.6	2.7	1.5
Husband beating	1.5	1.5	1.4	1.3	1.1	1.3	1.1
Wife beating severity	3.6	2.0	2.9	2.9	2.1	3.0	3.5

Note: Wife beating and child punishment are coded on a 1–4 point scale, with 4 meaning that it occurs in all or nearly all households; sibling fighting and husband beating on a 1–3 point scale, with 3 meaning that it occurs in a majority of households. Wife beating severity is coded from 1, absent in the society, to 4, mutilation or death is present.

Source: Levinson, D. (1989) *Family violence in cross-cultural perspective,* (p. 113). Newbury Park, CA: Sage. Copyright, 1989. Reprinted by permission.

Malays, Thai, and Okinawa societies of Asia) that had been well described by information available in the Human Relations Area Files. He compared the societies, grouped by area of the world, on the frequency of wife beating, husband beating, child physical punishment, and sibling aggression, and on the severity of wife beating. Table 1.6 shows regional variations in each form of violence. Wife beating is rare among the studied societies in Africa, while it is relatively common and tends to be severe in North America, the Middle East, Europe, and the former Soviet Union. Physical child punishment is most common in Africa and the Middle East. The data are least reliable about the incidence of sibling aggression, since few reports examine this behavior explicitly, but recorded sibling violence appears to be highest in the Middle East. Across cultures husband beating is reported less frequently than other forms of family violence.

Ethnographic data of this kind suffer from a number of deficiencies. Different ethnographers produce different estimates of the frequency of family violence, and the estimates vary with, for example, the gender and language skill of the ethnographer (Levinson, 1989). Furthermore, some behaviors, such as sibling aggression, may not be recorded consistently by the ethnographer; yet they may exist within the society. Also, consistent with our definition of violence as a socially constructed concept, it may be unwise to compare specific practices across cultures without a thorough grounding in the cultural rationale for the practice and its consequences.

For these reasons the comparisons presented in Table 1.6 should not be regarded as accurate representations of the rate of abuse in each society. Nevertheless, the statistics suffice to demonstrate that family violence is not confined to the United States and, in fact, exists around the world.

Temporal Variations

Has violence towards family members increased over the decades or centuries? We certainly have heard a lot about it recently. Is this an indication of just more attention given to the phenomenon, or of a real increase in violent behavior?

One way of looking at this question is to examine historical records for signs of family violence. When we do so, we see that abuse of family members has been a prominent feature of family life throughout history (Zigler & Hall, 1989). In ancient Rome, for example, families were forbidden to rear children with defects or deformities, and fathers, who were the rightful owners of children, were granted the right to sell their children and to mutilate or kill them. Through the 1700s in Sweden and the mid-1800s in Norway and Denmark, fathers who chose not to lift their newborn infants into their arms condemned the infants to be killed or left to the elements through ''exposure.''

Even the Bible provides evidence about child maltreatment. Although the Bible refers to children as gifts from God that bring happiness, importance, and wealth to parents, biblical references to infanticide and child beatings abound (Hastings, 1963; Zigler & Hall, 1989). Proverbs 23:13–14, for example, extols: ''Withhold not correction from the child, for if thou beatest him with the rod, he shall not die. Thou shall beat him with the rod and deliver his soul from Hell.'' To this day parents whose religion urges literal translation of the Bible are more likely to believe in corporal punishment of children (Wiehe, 1990).

Although there have been times and cultures in which at least some women seemed to have escaped domination and violence by male partners, this also is rare throughout recorded times (cf. Pagelow, 1984). In ancient Rome, marriage laws dictated that husbands should rule over wives and gave husbands the right to physically punish or kill their wives for infractions. Some historians (e.g., Pleck,

1989) claim that an eighteenth-century English judge gave us the expression, the "rule of thumb," when he proposed that husbands could hit wives with a stick (and parents could do the same with children), as long as the stick was no larger than the adult's thumb.

Some maltreatment has been recorded in early American times as well. Women generally were treated with respect among Native American populations, although some groups, like the Chipewyan tribe in the Arctic region, treated women poorly (Garbarino, 1976b). The Chipewyan fed women last and, in times of famine, withheld food from them. Native American tribes are often depicted as treating children in a loving fashion and rarely using physical punishment, but in some tribes twins and deformed children were killed because they were believed to bring bad luck (Garbarino, 1976b).

The Puritans regarded family violence as a sin and neighbors were supposed to report signs of violence to ministers or constables (Pleck, 1989). However, they occasionally permitted the use of physical force by parents against disobedient children and by husbands against wives.

One of the interesting policy issues that will be discussed in this book is whether family violence is best regarded as a private matter or as a matter of public concern. Until the end of the nineteenth century in the United States there existed a pervasive belief that family matters were private and not a threat to social and religious order (cf. Pleck, 1989). While courts might punish serious cases of spouse abuse, state statutes that banned abuse generally were not enacted until the late 1800s. Children received even less protection from the court and the law until a case in 1874 led to the birth of the Society for the Prevention of Cruelty to Children (cf. Sigler, 1989). However, concern about maltreatment of children and efforts to apply legal remedies waxed and waned for the next hundred years (Pleck, 1989).

Because of the absence of good records and the secrecy about family matters during many periods of history, we cannot determine whether any particular form of violence is more pervasive at this moment than a century or more ago. However, this brief account illustrates both the consistency of family violence throughout recorded history and its sanctioning by governmental and other authorities.

What about the recent past? Is family violence on an upswing or a downturn now? The evidence is mixed (cf. Gelles, 1990). When estimates are derived from official statistics, gathered through social service and other agency records, child abuse, for example, appears to increase. The American Humane Association data suggest that the years between 1976 and 1986 brought a 212 percent increase in the rate of child maltreatment. But when estimates of child abuse are derived from surveys of a random sample of the population, rates of violence appear to wane, at least among white Americans (Gelles & Straus, 1988; Hampton & Gelles, 1989). The same surveys also reveal a 27 percent decline in the incidence of wife abuse among white Americans and a 43 percent decline among African-Americans (Hampton & Gelles, 1989).

Conflicting figures may be interpreted in several ways. The increases in *reported cases* may be attributable to an increased rate of violence in present-day homes (Knudsen, 1988). At the same time, the decreased voluntary disclosure of violence to survey researchers may reflect a burgeoning awareness of societal disapproval of violence. Fictionalized and nonfictionalized media accounts of spouse or child abuse may inform people that family violence is wrong and that help is available, thus increasing the likelihood that abuse will be reported. But it is also possible that the media portrayal of violence may make some people less talkative about the violence they inflict.

The increase in reports may also be attributable to enhanced funding to social service agencies that investigate reports and to broader definitions of abuse among police officers and social service professionals (Gelles, 1990). In this case, reports of abuse may increase, even though the actual rate of violence may decline.

Concluding Remarks

We began this chapter with a discussion of the various defining characteristics of family violence. You may be uncertain about which behaviors are included in this definition, but, as was noted, there is no reliable, universally valid definition. The cases presented in this chapter are not ambiguous; they would be regarded by almost everyone as instances of abuse. But most cases are less serious than those depicted and, therefore, are likely to be judged differently across cultures and even within a given culture. Estimates of each type of abuse vary depending upon the definition used by the investigator, but the most common form of abuse probably occurs between siblings. And family violence exists in many societies and has been present throughout recorded history.

Researchers have found that often a pattern of violence exists within a family. If one form of abuse is present, another form is likely to occur as well. Similarly, there is some correspondence between people who abuse others in the home and outside, but considerable independence in family and nonfamily violence has been found as well.

Throughout this book you will find that the issues raised in this chapter will reemerge. For example, several chapters will address the *social construction of violence;* that is, the ways in which our definition of violence depends upon our background experiences and who we are. Also, as you read the studies presented in subsequent chapters, you will be reminded often of the difficulties of measuring family violence and eliciting information about it.

In the next chapter we will talk about attitudes toward violence and explore why we tolerate aggression in families. We will see how attitudes vary according to gender, education, and professional or socioeconomic status. We will also study how our beliefs about violence are influenced by the characteristics of the perpetrator and victim. Finally, you will examine whether knowing someone's attitudes tells you anything about the likelihood that the person will engage in violence.

2

Attitudes about Violence in Families

CHAPTER OBJECTIVES

Evidence of Tolerance for Aggression against Family Members
Explanations for Tolerance of Aggression
  Lack of Empathy for Victims
  Belief in a Just World
  Illusions about Ability to Prevent Violence
  Tolerance of Victimization of Family Members
Variation in Levels of Tolerance of Violence
  Variation Due to Context
  Variation Due to Gender Roles

Variation Due to Education and Socioeconomic Status
Variation Due to Ethnic, Racial, or Other Cultural Differences
Variation Due to Professional Orientation
Variation Due to Characteristics of the Victim and Perpetrator
The Relationship between Attitudes and Behavior
Concluding Remarks

Violence has pervaded the history of the United States, and some of this violence is justified as being for the good of society. Death and destruction during war, such as during the Revolutionary and Civil Wars, are regarded as necessary and inevitable byproducts of positive

social change (Sigler, 1989). Violence by police against student pro-
testors or urban rioters is deemed by many Americans an important
means of social control (Blumenthal, Chadiha, Cole, & Jayaratne,
1975). Movies, news reports, and even video games bombard us with
violence for our entertainment and relaxation. There is no question
that the vast majority of us tolerate a great deal of violence without
doing much to counter it, and some of us confidently believe that a
little violence, at least in some circumstances, for the most part is a
good thing.

It should not surprise us then that many of us also approve of, or
at least tolerate, aggression against family members. In this chapter
we will see evidence for acceptance of violence in the family and
study why people tolerate aggression, especially in family settings
(see Box 2.1). We will study how gender roles, education, the context
in which the aggression transpires, and other personal and situational
factors influence our attitudes. We will also examine the connection
between attitudes and behavior: Are people who approve of violence
more likely to behave aggressively, and does disapproval typically
signal a nonaggressive style of interpersonal behavior?

Evidence of Tolerance for Aggression
against Family Members

One of the early studies of attitudes toward violence was a survey of
200 Baltimore residents conducted by Rossi, Waite, Bose, and Berk
(1974; see also the study depicted in Box 2.2). The authors' goal was
to construct an index of the seriousness of crimes as judged by a cross-
section of people and then to see what characteristics make some
crimes seem more serious than others. The survey results permit us
to compare crimes against property with crimes against people, and
to look for variations in judgments depending upon the type of victim
involved. Fortunately, their design allows us to compare reactions to
the murder, beating, or assault of nonrelatives with the same acts
committed against family members.

Baltimore residents did not greatly distinguish among murder
victims, except for the higher rating earned by the killing of a po-
liceman (8.21 on a 9-point scale). The impulsive murder of a spouse
(7.84) and a stranger (7.82) were seen as gravely and equally serious.
Lesser acts of violence, however, were judged less severely when
committed against a family member than against a stranger. Rape,
beating, and assault with a gun toward a spouse generally were seen

Consider this anecdote from an article about parenting (McIntire, 1973):

> A mother and daughter enter a supermarket. An accident occurs when the daughter pulls the wrong orange from the pile and 37 oranges are given their freedom. The mother grabs that daughter, shakes her vigorously, and slaps her. What is your reaction? Do you ignore the incident? Do you consider it a family squabble and none of your business? Or do you go over and advise the mother not to hit her child? If the mother rejects your advice, do you physically restrain her? If she persists, do you call the police? Think about your answers for a moment.
>
> Now let me change one detail. *The girl was not that mother's daughter.* (McIntire, 1973, p. 36)

Now consider some other questions: Would your handling of the situation vary depending upon the age of the child or the harm done, or whether the family was like yours or different (in race/ethnicity, socioeconomic status, for example)? Would your handling differ if you knew that the child deliberately spilled 37 oranges? Does the child's provocation matter in judging parental actions?

Change the locale: Imagine you are listening to physical blows delivered to a child (or a spouse) in a nearby apartment. Does location affect your willingness to act?

If you were the mother (or daughter), how would you interpret a bystander's intervention or nonintervention? And what type of intervention would be most/least beneficial?

---

as less serious offenses than the same act committed against a stranger or acquaintance. Consider the average ratings of the following crimes (Rossi et al., 1974):

Beating up:	stranger	6.60
	spouse	5.80
	acquaintance	5.03
Assault with a gun on:	stranger	7.66
	acquaintance	7.51
	spouse	7.32

BOX 2.2

Rossi et al. (1974) are not the only ones to show that family violence is regarded less seriously than other forms of violence. One of the most vivid examples of acceptance of spouse abuse comes from a study by Shotland and Straw (1976). Participants in the experiment overheard a man and a woman arguing in a nearby room. The man then was heard to violently shake the woman, who screamed and shouted, "Get away from me!" At this point one-half of the participants heard the woman shout, "I don't know you," while the remainder heard, "I don't know why I ever married you." As you undoubtedly will guess, at least twice as many people were likely to aid the victim of the stranger (from 40 to 80 percent, depending upon the acting team) than the victim of a spouse (from 17 to 20 percent).

Crimes against family members also generally elicited more variation in judgments across people than did other crimes, revealing substantial disagreement among the populace about the seriousness of these crimes. Later in this chapter we will explore factors that lead people to view aggression against family members more or less seriously. And we will explore the types of victims and perpetrators that elicit the harshest judgments.

Explanations for Tolerance of Aggression

In an ideal world families are supposed to be a source of comfort and support. Why then do we tolerate aggression within the home setting? Efforts to answer this question suggest that many of the reasons for tolerating aggression within the home correspond to reasons for tolerating it outside of the home. Most of these explanations revolve around ways of thinking that lead us to derogate victims.

Lack of Empathy for Victims

One component of our tolerance of violence is that people are not particularly empathic toward victims. Perry, Williard, and Perry (1990) found that children expected to gain more benefits and to suffer fewer negative repercussions from aggression against classmates who were most likely to be picked on than against less victimized classmates. Children expected victimized classmates to show more suffering following aggression than would other classmates, but the children cared little about the victims' reactions.

Similarly, Coates, Wortman, and Abbey (1979) asked Chicago area students and residents to read materials about rape and then to listen to a taped interview with an alleged rape victim. Depending upon the tape heard, participants listened to the victim's disclosures either that she had managed to go on with her life and look forward to the future or that she was still focused on the rape, was no longer a happy person, and had lost interest in her studies and hobbies. Unfortunately, the more suffering the victim displayed, the less well liked she was by listeners.

In some circumstances our ability to withhold empathy from victims may protect us from feeling guilty about failing to do something to help out. A study by Cialdini, Kenrick, and Hoerig (1976), for example, found that when people are assured that they are not at all responsible for victim suffering, they do not derogate the victim.

Belief in a Just World

Another reason why people may tolerate violence is that many of us tend to believe that the world is ''just'' and that people get basically what they deserve (Lerner, 1980). Given that the world is fair, we surmise, bad things will only happen to bad people. When a bad thing does happen to someone, then, we seek explanations for why this person suffered the victimization. When we hear about a child being abused by a parent, we ask what the child did to provoke the incident (Herzberger & Tennen, 1982). When a woman is abused by her husband, we point to her nagging as provocation, and thus justification, for the violence (Dobash & Dobash, 1979; Lavoie, Jacob, Hardy, & Martin, 1989; Schur, 1983). And we are not particularly scrupulous about assessing the legitimacy of the justification. As Dobash and Dobash (1979) have observed:

> The types of behavior that have been defined as provocative either
> by researchers or by husbands are diverse and contradictory,
> ranging from aggression and nagging, to submission, through
> dominance . . . , or emasculation (i.e., failure to be submissive), and
> on to insinuating language or gestures. Being too talkative or too

quiet, too sexual or not sexual enough, too frugal or too extravagant, too often pregnant or not frequently enough all seem to be provocations. (p. 135)

Schur (1983) aptly summarizes that the "provocation can mean virtually anything of which the husband disapproves" (p. 159); it is merely a "retrospective rationalization" that allows us to derogate the victim and, hence, better understand the violence.

This kind of thinking has led victims to feel that they have to show evidence of brutal maiming for police officers, court officials, or others to believe that they did not "encourage" or provoke the perpetrator (cf. Gelles, 1976). The perpetrator's action must be so egregious that others see it as without justification.

Illusions about Ability to Prevent Violence

Another way to derogate victims and, thus, to tolerate the violence around us, is to assume that victims can prevent violent episodes and should know better than to place themselves in dangerous situations. An interesting example of this kind of thinking was demonstrated by Janoff-Bulman, Timko, and Carli (1985). Students read an account of a date between a man and a woman and, while half of the accounts ended with the man taking the woman home, the other half ended with the man raping the woman. In all other ways the accounts were identical. The readers were then asked to disregard the ending and from the clues in the account to predict the likelihood of various types of endings, including being taken home or being raped. Those who read the rape scenario were more likely to predict that the date would end in a rape and were more likely to blame the rape on the woman's behavior (e.g., letting the man kiss her). But remember that the events leading up to the rape or to being taken home were identical; so, they were blaming the woman for not foreseeing circumstances that readers of the non-rape scenario also did not anticipate. Similarly, we can find in the literature on spouse abuse writers who question how abused women can be so "insensitive" as to the effect their "irritating" behavior would have on their husbands (see Dobash & Dobash, 1979, for examples).

When we blame victims for their failure to forestall violence, we feel more secure (Frieze, 1987). To the extent that crime or violence can happen to anyone, the idea that it could happen to us threatens our sense of safety. By assuming that the victim is somewhat responsible for his or her fate, we are able to shield ourselves and continue to think that we will be unscathed.

Tolerance of Victimization of Family Members

The explanations offered here explain why we tolerate aggression toward victims in general. What is it about *family* violence that makes it especially vulnerable to approval? Why should we feel more comfortable about violence in the home than outside of it?

For one thing, we all know that family life is intense. The close and constant contacts build pressure upon family members and result in frequent conflicts. If once in a while this conflict results in minor aggression, we learn that the negative consequences are slight. Furthermore, it may be that the negative consequences of aggression are outweighed by the possibility of garnering positive consequences—such as gaining power over another and getting one's way. When behavior is rewarded in such a manner and rarely punished, it is likely to be repeated (Bandura, 1986). Therefore, minor acts of aggression may become more frequent.

Let us take sibling conflict as an example. Although children know that parents disapprove of aggression against siblings and that siblings are likely to retaliate (Herzberger & Hall, 1993a, 1993b), they also learn that parents rarely punish them for their aggressive disputes (Pagelow, 1984). Parents may not notice most of the aggressive acts, or they may believe that it is best not to interfere. In fact, siblings who start conflicts may derive more satisfaction than punishment from their aggressive activity (Patterson, 1984). In this way, we may come to regard minor forms of aggression in the family as "basically harmless."

Research on aggression also shows that over time children and adults (with the possible exception of adult women) habituate to scenes of aggression and experience less of a physiological reaction (Thomas, Horton, Lippincott, & Drabman, 1977). Thus, our own experience with repeated, minor forms of violence in families, coupled with our awareness of the difficulties of family life, may make us especially tolerant of those who are aggressive toward their family members.

Some theorists have suggested that the most significant explanation for tolerance of family violence stems from the continuing hierarchical and largely patriarchal nature of society that is exacerbated in the family situation (Dobash & Dobash, 1979). Women and children are often still regarded as property, and husbands and parents accordingly are charged with the responsibility to keep less powerful family members in line. Violence is a means of asserting one's control over others, and to the extent that we continue to accept patriarchal control, we will continue to find people who believe that they have the right to violate family members. An example of this is the battering husband who informed a *New York Times* reporter that he cut telephone cords in the house because, "Why should she talk on something I paid for?" (Hoffman, 1992, p. 64).

Another factor that creates a fertile climate for tolerance of family violence is the presumption that family matters are "private" (cf. Goolkasian, 1986). We often hear such statements as, "How can some outsider tell me how to rear my child?" or "What my spouse and I do in the privacy of our own home is our business!" A legitimized hierarchical family structure coupled with an unwillingness to "invade the privacy of families" by proscribing violent acts creates a situation that promotes tolerance for displays of power and aggression. A Justice Department task force, recognizing the danger of this situation, recently stated that family violence is not solely a family matter and that, "The legal response to family violence must be guided primarily by the nature of the abusive act, not the relationship between the victim and the abuser" (Attorney General's Task Force on Family Violence Final Report, 1984, p. 4). We will discuss this issue in more detail in Chapter 9.

Variation in Levels of Tolerance of Violence

You will recall that Rossi et al. (1974) found substantial variation in the way people viewed acts of violence against family members. It is quite likely that any given act, such as the beating of a spouse, will be regarded differently depending upon the characteristics of the victim, the perpetrator, the person rendering the judgment, and the context in which the violence occurred. In this section we will discuss factors that are known to influence judgments of family violence.

Variation Due to Context

Tolerance for violence against family members depends upon the circumstances in which the violence transpires. Stark and McEvoy (1970), for example, asked a nationwide sample of adults whether "under some circumstances" it is appropriate for one spouse to slap the other. About 20 percent of the respondents agreed. More recently, Greenblat (1985) decided to investigate the circumstances that foster acceptance of violence. Contrary to Rossi et al.'s (1974) results, Greenblat found widespread disapproval of violence toward family members when she surveyed college students. Her sample rated a man beating up his wife as extremely wrong (an average rating of 9.7 on a 10-point scale) and more wrong than the man beating a stranger (8.5). A man slapping his wife earned a rating of 8.4, while a woman slapping her husband earned 7.9. Furthermore, more than 70 percent of the sample agreed that husbands who beat their wives should be put in jail.

Greenblat (1985) noted that her findings might have been heartening for those who hoped that violence in the family was becoming less tolerated. The problem was that, while people rejected the use of violence against family members in the abstract, they accepted its use when placed in the context of marital or family disputes. Listed in Table 2.1 are twenty contexts in which to imagine a husband slapping or beating his wife. Greenblat (1985) first asked survey respondents whether they approved or disapproved of the husband's action in the situation and then to note how wrong they believed the husband's action to be. As you can see, substantial numbers of respondents approved of slapping more than beating and they approved of violence in self-defense or in protection of a child, in retaliation, and in response to marital infidelity. Only 12 percent of the respondents uniformly rejected slapping under all featured circumstances and only 56 percent uniformly rejected beating.

Reactions to physical discipline of children vary with circumstances too. Almost all parents at least occasionally use corporal punishment with children (Gelles & Straus, 1988; Stark & McEvoy, 1970), and when presented with a hypothetical disciplinary situation people readily admit that spanking or slapping children is an option they consider. For example, Blumenthal and her colleagues (1975) described a situation in which a 5- or 6-year-old boy declines to do something a parent has requested that he do right away. The child is busy watching television and says that he will do it in about an hour. Residents of Detroit and four southern cities were asked to imagine themselves as the parent in this situation and to report on their likely response. Sixty-seven percent of the respondents said that they would "usually" or "sometimes" spank or hit the child in this situation. Only eight percent said that they would never hit him. In fact, 48 percent noted that they would at least "sometimes" hit the child with a belt or paddle and 13 percent would at least sometimes spank the child so hard that "he can't sit down."

But how do people *feel* about harsh treatment of children? Do we recognize that it is bad, even though we simultaneously recognize that we sometimes engage in this behavior? Sigler (1989) surveyed adult residents of Tuscaloosa, Alabama about the kinds of acts that they would label as "child abuse." Residents labeled the parent's

TABLE 2.1 Approval of a Husband Slapping or Beating a Wife under Various Circumstances

Circumstance	% Approving Husband Slapping Wife (N = 124)	% Approving Husband Beating Wife (N = 124)
She is threatening him with a knife.	78	34
She is physically abusing their child.	47	13
He catches her in bed with another man.	37	16
She is screaming hysterically.	28	8
He learns she has been having an affair with another man.	24	10
In an argument, she hits him first.	23	5
She is sobbing hysterically.	19	4
She comes home drunk.	7	2
He suspects she has been having an affair with another man.	4	1
She insults him in public.	3	3
She insults him when they are at home alone.	3	2
She insults him in front of the children.	2	3
He comes home drunk.	2	2
He has great problems at work and is very frustrated.	2	2
She won't do what he tells her to do.	2	1
She won't listen to reason.	2	1
She hasn't cleaned the house all month.	2	1
She doesn't have dinner ready when he comes home from work, though she's been home all day.	1	1
He's furious at her and wants to show how angry he is.	1	1
He wants to force her to attend to an issue.	0	0

Note: The circumstances were listed in order of those eliciting the most to least approval of violence.

Source: Adapted from Greenblat, C. S. (1985). "Don't hit your wife . . . unless . . . ": Preliminary findings on normative support for the use of physical force by husbands. *Victimology, 10,* p. 232. Reprinted by permission from Victimology: An International Journal, Vol. 10. © 1985 Victimology Inc. All rights reserved.

behavior as abusive when the action presumably would cause substantial harm (e.g., 91 percent of respondents said "hitting occasionally with a fist" was "always child abuse"). Frequent physical
punishments were more likely to garner child abuse labels than occasional physical punishment. And, if the parent's behavior resem-
bled typical discipline, it was less likely to be regarded as abusive.
For example, "hitting occasionally with a belt or stick" earned the
label "always child abuse" from 43 percent of the respondents. "Hitting occasionally with an open hand" was regarded by fewer people
as "always child abuse" than was "cursing" the child (18 percent
versus 63 percent).

Another example of this phenomenon comes from Giovannoni
and Becerra (1979), who asked a representative sample of adults in
the Los Angeles area to rate the seriousness of certain acts on a scale
from 1 to 9, with 9 indicating the most serious acts. On average,
people believed that spanking by using the hand was moderately serious (4.35) and that spanking by using a strap was more serious
(6.42). The acts that elicited the most severe ratings, however, were
unusual forms of discipline such as burning a child with a cigarette
(8.63) or immersing a child in a tub of hot water (8.32). Banging a
child against a wall (7.65) and punching a child in the face (7.77)
might do as much damage as burning with a cigarette, but perhaps
because they more resemble normative modes of discipline, they received less severe ratings.

This survey illustrates what social service professionals and researchers have known for a long time: that "normative" or
"common" violence is more acceptable to us than atypical violence.
Just as each night we can, without much emotion, read about or listen
to news about another gang slaying or a fire that killed several people,
we get used to certain acts of violence in the family. Since we live in
a culture and in a time period in which spanking children is common,
we tolerate it and tolerate acts that resemble it as well. Also, as noted
before, when the violence appears to take place during the context of
a disciplinary interaction or a spousal dispute, the victim is believed
to provoke the perpetrator's retribution. The Menendez trial, featured
in Box 2.3, shows that even jurors are willing to exonerate retaliatory
aggression.

Some researchers (e.g., Gil, 1970; Giovannoni & Becerra, 1979)
suggest that acceptance of any act of violence may set the stage for
more widespread acceptance of harsher violence. Consider an analogy
derived from research on helping. We have long known that people
who comply with a small request often will comply subsequently with

BOX 2.3

A well-publicized court case appears to demonstrate that we excuse violence that is retaliatory (i.e., that responds to aggression by someone else). The trials of Lyle and Eric Menendez, brothers who killed their parents as they watched television in the family den, ended with deadlocked juries. The brothers planned the attack on their parents and purchased shotguns surreptitiously, leading the prosecution to claim that they killed their parents to have control over a $14 million inheritance (Mydans, 1993; Quindlen, 1993). The defense claimed that the men grew up with a physically and sexually abusive father and an unstable mother. Faced with information about their murderous behavior and their past, the brothers' separate juries apparently could not decide upon a guilty verdict.

Even young children believe that retaliatory violence is different from unprovoked violence (Ferguson & Rule, 1988; Perry, Perry, & Weiss, 1989). They expect to feel less guilt about committing retaliation and expect less parental and peer disapproval (Perry et al., 1989). The Menendez trial results suggest that children need not expect anything different when they get older.

larger requests. Salespeople (and social psychologists) call this the *foot-in-the-door* phenomenon. Underlying this behavior is the notion that, once labeled as a person who helps others, the individual tries to behave consistently in similar situations. This phenomenon is believed to underlie the escalation of undesirable behaviors as well, such as the willingness of participants in psychology experiments to administer larger and larger doses of electric shock to another person (Milgram, 1974).

According to this perspective, parents and others who approve of hitting children who misbehave have already accepted the notion that under some circumstances physical violence is beneficial or at least tolerable. Those who approve of slapping a spouse under some circumstances do not adhere fully to nonviolence as a philosophy for social interaction and problem-solving. It may be hard for people who condone violence under some circumstances to draw the line between the conditions under which violence is tolerable and those under which it is not, and between levels of violence that are tolerable versus those that are not. In fact, according to this argument, drawing the line to include any forms of violence only encourages the subsequent inclusion of more serious forms of violence.

Some perusal of the research literature, however, will suggest that escalation does not always follow minor acts of violence. After all, almost all parents spank their children (Garbarino, 1989b); yet only a minority of parents abuses them. Nevertheless, the idea of an escalating tolerance for violence may help us to understand some cases of abuse within the family.

Variation Due to Gender Roles

You can see from the statistics presented earlier that, while some people approve of or at least tolerate violence in the family, others do not, and you might wonder who is likely to hold more positive attitudes. Women generally approve less of violence than men both in non-intimate (Macrae & Shepherd, 1989) and in intimate relationships (Greenblat, 1985; Koski & Mangold, 1988; but see Arias & Johnson, 1989, for counterevidence). Women are also more likely than men to assign blame for the origin of the violence to the perpetrator, as opposed to the victim (Sugarman & Cohn, 1986), and women tend to pay less attention to the circumstances of the violent act when they judge the violence. For example, college students at the University of Aberdeen in Scotland were given a fictionalized account of the rape of a young woman (Macrae & Shepherd, 1989). Women blamed the perpetrator more than men did and assigned more punishment for the crime. The characteristics of the victim, whether she was a virgin or whether she was sexually promiscuous, generally did not affect the women's judgments. Men, however, believed that the perpetrator deserved more blame and more punishment when the victim was a virgin.

Perhaps women reject violence more than men because women are portrayed so often as the victim and people empathize more strongly with similar others (Barnett, Feierstein, Jaet, Saunders, Quackenbush, & Sinisi, 1992; Barnett, Tetreault, & Masbad, 1987; Thorton, 1984). Along the same lines, women, being generally less aggressive than men across all cultures (Maccoby & Jacklin, 1985), may not empathize with violent perpetrators.

Men and women who reject patriarchical values and subscribe to feminist principles are more intolerant of violence against women (e.g., Burt, 1980; Coller & Resick, 1987; Greenblat, 1985). For example, people who subscribe to such statements as "Men should share the work around the house with women . . ." and "A woman can live a full and happy life without marrying" are more likely to reject a husband's violence against a wife (Greenblat, 1985).

The same phenomenon can be found with attitudes towards children (Baumrind, 1971). Parents who practice *authoritative* child rearing methods include children more in the family decision-making and thereby eliminate some of the status and power differences between parents and offspring. These parents also tend not to use harsh corporal punishment. In contrast, *authoritarian* parents dictate policy to children, establish rigid rules to guide children's behavior, and employ harsh physical punishment as a means of discipline. Thus, parents who see themselves as "in charge" are more likely to adopt violent methods of displaying their power, while parents who deliberately deflate the family hierarchical structure reject these methods.

Variation Due to Education and Socioeconomic Status

Surveys generally reveal that better educated people and wealthier ones judge violence against family members less seriously than others do (Giovannoni & Becerra, 1979; Stark & McEvoy, 1970). Wealthier or more educated people may become more tolerant of deviation from moral norms (Giovannoni & Becerra, 1979), or perhaps they become inured to the traumas experienced by victims in society. Because they have the resources to rise above the traumas they have experienced, they may underestimate the seriousness of the traumas experienced by the less fortunate.

Findings contrary to this, however, are reported by Rich and Sampson (1990) in a survey about marital rape completed by Chicago residents. Better educated people urged prosecution of such cases more than the less well educated (55 percent to 42 percent). Why this difference occurs and whether it is reliable are unknown, but it is possible that with recent widespread media coverage, well educated people are more aware of legal and social sanctions against at least some forms of family violence.

Variation Due to Ethnic, Racial, or Other Cultural Differences

Giovannoni and Becerra (1979) found substantial ethnic or racial differences in judgments of the seriousness of violent acts. Controlling for the respondent's income and education level, they found that whites inevitably rated violence against children as less serious than did African-Americans or Latinos. Latino respondents were given the choice of answering interviewers' questions in English or Spanish. Those who answered in English rated the acts more like the non-Latino white respondents than did those who answered in Spanish. This suggests that assimilation to the majority culture in the United States, at least as shown by language preference, may bring greater tolerance for harsh treatment of children.

Other examples of variations in attitudes include the case of Vietnamese-Americans in Hawaii, who bruise their child by rubbing his or her body with coins to cure illnesses, but whose treatment is accepted by the adults, the children, and caseworkers (Gray & Cosgrove, 1985). What about circumcision, so widely performed in the United States? While some might argue that this practice is an unnecessary medical procedure, done for religious and social—but not medical—reasons (Wallerstein, 1980), those who perform circumcisions in this and many other countries have no fear that they are going to be charged with child abuse.

Of course, Korbin (1987) argues that we cannot blindly accept practices out of concern for cultural sensitivities. We might want to discourage the Ecuadorian practice of breast-feeding boys longer than girls, which leads to higher infant mortality among girls, or the painful and dangerous procedure of removing the girl's clitoris practiced in many African societies, even while we understand the cultural mores that promote these behaviors.

It is important to remember that norms for proper treatment of family members evolve over time. In the last chapter we saw examples from history of normative practices that would not be tolerated today. A modern example of a norm in transition in this country is the debate over a pregnant woman's right to take chances with the health of her unborn child by smoking, drinking, or taking illicit drugs. A few years ago no one labeled these acts as abuse or became intolerant of them. Today, however, women are being charged with "risk of injury to a minor" and other criminal offenses when caught engaging in these acts (Myers, 1990; see Box 2.4).

Variation Due to Professional Orientation

One of the most interesting questions is whether professionals who deal with violence against children on a daily basis feel differently about such cases than laypeople. We might predict that a special empathy draws certain people into social service careers where they can help unfortunate victims, or that, through training or experience on

BOX 2.4

Two waiters in Seattle were fired for being rude to a pregnant customer when they protested against serving her the strawberry daiquiri that she ordered. The story has drawn mixed reactions from around the country. *Newsweek* (Kantrowitz, Quade, Fisher, Hill, & Beachy, 1991) reports, for example:

> One newspaper columnist praised the two for caring, "which is more than 90 percent of us ever do." But in New York, feminists recently battled a new state law requiring liquor sellers to post alcohol-warning signs aimed at pregnant women. Molly Yard, president of the National Organization for Women charges that the legislation is a first step in setting up a "pregnancy-police state." (p. 52)

Letters to the editor, which soon appeared, also revealed mixed feelings among readers (Policing vs. Privacy, 1991). One writer, who described himself as a "dedicated civil libertarian," asked why it violates someone else's rights when a person disseminates useful information. Another writer, though, wondered what the reaction would be if a waiter refused to serve red meat or a rich dessert.

the job, social service professionals develop increased sensitivity to victims' plight. However, you may be thinking that the opposite could happen. Exposure to violent acts day after day leads professionals to become hardened to violence, and that only extreme or unusual victimization will elicit strong feelings. We have to remember that ceasing to experience strong emotional reactions to violence is not the same as judging the violence less seriously. Police officers and coroners may get used to seeing dead bodies, but this does not mean that they regard death with anything less than trepidation.

Luckily there have been some studies to sort out this question. Giovannoni and Becerra (1979) asked lawyers, pediatricians, social workers, and police officers to judge the seriousness of hypothetical acts of violence against children. Compared to their sample of laypeople, professionals overall did judge the acts less seriously. Giovannoni and Becerra (1979) attributed the difference, however, not to a general lessening of concern for violence among the professional community, but to the fact that professionals make finer distinctions among the types of violence portrayed in the survey. Professionals were less concerned than laypeople with parental behavior that deviated from cultural norms, such as a child being raised by a homosexual father. But the professionals were more concerned than laypeople with acts that could lead to dire physical consequences, such as banging a child against a wall or hitting with a stick. Social workers, police officers, and pediatricians tended to rate the acts more seriously than lawyers, which may reflect the fact that the lawyers are less likely to see the immediate consequences of violence (Giovannoni & Becerra, 1979).

The professionals' gender did not influence ratings of seriousness, suggesting that professional orientation and experience overrides any differences in attitudes that might be expected by gender (Giovannoni & Becerra, 1979). However, Saunders and Size (1986) found that police officers with traditional sex-role values were more likely to blame the victims of spousal violence and were less likely to suggest that arrests be made than were police officers with nontraditional values.

Variation Due to Characteristics of the Victim and Perpetrator

We have been talking about variations in attitudes that are attributable to characteristics of the people judging the violent act. How do the characteristics of the perpetrator and the victim affect people's judgments? Stereotypes about social class and gender, for example, affect professional and lay judgments. Both male and female Arkansas residents contacted through a telephone interview believed that aggressive conflict tactics were more wrong when used by a husband against his wife than when used by a wife against her husband (Koski & Mangold, 1988; see also Arias & Johnson, 1989). Abuse by mothers and by parents with higher incomes is regarded less seriously by emergency room personnel (Hampton & Newberger, 1985) and by laypeople (Herzberger & Tennen, 1985b), even though the consequences to the child are the same as when perpetrated by fathers and parents with lower incomes. Furthermore, sexual abuse (Finkelhor, 1984) and physical and emotional abuse (Herzberger & Tennen, 1985b) are regarded most seriously by laypeople when a father victimizes a daughter. Fathers presumably are bigger and seen as more aggressive in general than mothers, and, while sons can "take the heat" of violent punishment, "more gentle" daughters presumably cannot.

The Relationship between Attitudes and Behavior

Social psychologists study attitudes extensively because attitudes help to shape an individual's view of the world and provide a perspective through which a person evaluates and reacts to other people and events (Petty & Cacioppo, 1981). Of great interest to social psychologists are the conditions under which attitudes correspond to behavior. The relationship between attitudes and behavior is bidirectional (cf. Bem, 1972); sometimes we develop attitudes that correspond to the behavior we have engaged in, and other times our attitudes direct us toward one behavior versus another. It is also true that behaviors are rarely caused by a single attitude (LaPiere, 1934). We may decide to go to a certain party not only because we like the host, but because we are averse to staying home by ourselves and we like to be seen by others as having an active social life. Attitudes also vary in strength; accordingly, we should expect little correspondence between a weakly held attitude and the relevant behavior, or between behaviors and attitudes that are not very important to us (Sivacek & Crano, 1982).

One of the most helpful models of the attitude-behavior relationship was proposed by Ajzen and Fishbein (1980; Fishbein & Ajzen, 1975). Their *theory of reasoned action* proposes that an intention to behave in a particular way is determined by the person's expectations about the outcomes of the behavior and the value of these outcomes, and by the individual's beliefs about what others would think about the behavior. Thus, the individual takes into account the effects of his or her action in the social world.

Of interest to this book is whether attitudes about violence and aggression relate to violent behavior. There is not a lot of research on this relationship, but some support for a connection is found. Children who believe that aggression is wrong are much less likely to behave aggressively toward a peer (Boldizar, Perry, & Perry, 1989). Abusive men are more likely than other groups to believe that wife beating is justifiable and they feel less responsible for the violence (Saunders, Lynch, Grayson, & Linz, 1987). Groups for battering men offer programs that restructure the ways men think about women and violence, in addition to teaching men how to manage their anger (Jennings, 1987). Furthermore, parents of battered children are more likely to subscribe to violence as a means of producing social change (Blumenthal et al., 1975).

There is also indirect evidence of the connection between attitudes and behavior. The results of the Shotland and Straw (1976; see Box 2.2) study, for example, are consistent with the notion that family violence is viewed with less alarm than nonfamily violence. However, Shotland and Straw did not measure attitudes about violence, and it is quite possible that observers regarded a dispute between partners just as seriously as one between strangers, but that they held a stronger attitude against intervention in disputes among intimates. Thus, this study is an important reminder that multiple attitudes may be operating to determine behavior in any given situation.

Of course, we can also point to substantial evidence of a lack of correspondence between attitudes and behavior. In 1973 Ball-Rokeach tested for a subculture of violence in a nationwide survey. She found only a weak correspondence between attitudes and behavior in the general populace and no correspondence between the expression of machismo values and violence among prison inmates. Over 80 percent of the participants in Sigler's (1989) survey reported that hitting one's spouse is always wrong, but only 25 percent would report it to the police. Similarly, the behavior of parents towards children is predicted poorly by parental attitudes (Becker & Krug, 1965). Many parents use corporal punishment, not because they believe that this is the correct way to punish their child, but because they lose their temper.

It is quite possible then that much of what we do as parents, spouses, or third-party observers stems not from some belief system about violence being right or wrong, but from a host of attitudes about the consequences of one's behavior in violent situations. In addition, our behavior may stem from unthinking or unplanned responses to strong cues in the immediate situation and not have anything to do with attitudes (Fazio, 1986). Therefore, efforts to understand aggression must explore not only attitudes, but how we have learned aggressive modes of behavior, how we interpret other people's actions in ways that enhance or decrease the chance that we will respond aggressively, how our physiology promotes or inhibits aggressive responses, and how cues from the situation elicit action.

Concluding Remarks

Attitudes toward violence in the home vary substantially from one individual to the next. They vary predictably according to such factors as professional training, gender, and education. Attitudes also have changed over time, in correspondence with new information and the new focus of media attention. Generally, though, people are more accepting of violence toward family members than toward others.

You probably will have noticed that this chapter stayed away from discussions of "good attitudes" and "bad attitudes" about specific acts of violence. As the short section on cultural variations in attitudes demonstrates, there are few absolutes in this regard. At least to some extent, to understand what makes someone a good parent or a good spouse, we must understand the "cultural imperatives" that drive the individual's behavior (Ogbu, 1981) and consider the behavior in its social context. It is also the case that we need to be wary about allowing the alleged perpetrator's surface characteristics (e.g., gender, race) to influence our judgments about violence. Both professionals and laypeople show biases in their judgments that will lead to underestimates of violence among some groups and overestimates among others.

Social psychologists have not demonstrated a clear-cut linkage between attitudes about violence and violent behavior. We know that sometimes attitudes precede and may contribute to the violence, but other times attitudes may be formed as justifications for the violence that has already occurred. And many acts of aggression have nothing to do with the perpetrator's attitudes about violence. Thus, we must look for other causes of violence.

3

Victims' Reactions to Violence

CHAPTER OBJECTIVES

Victims' Beliefs about Themselves and Their Victimization
Causal Thinking
Learned Helplessness
Problem-Solving Abilities
Perceptions That Their Treatment Is Unusual
Are Victims Masochistic?
Decreased Sensitivity to Aggression

Why Do Abuse Victims Stay?
Fear and Dependence upon the Abuser
Lack of Support from Police and Social Services
Affection for the Perpetrator
Other Victim Reactions
Help-Seeking
Retaliation
Perpetrator Desistance: Which Strategies Work?
Concluding Remarks

Try to imagine a situation in which you feel completely secure and then you abruptly lose that feeling. Imagine being in the safety of your home, quietly reading or talking on the phone with a friend, when your partner (or your parent or sibling) rushes into the room and beats you. Afterwards, your relative is quite apologetic and loving. But two weeks or maybe two months later, the beating is repeated. Then, three months after that, it happens again. Do you know how you would respond?

Victims of crime and disasters of various sorts invariably suffer the common reactions of anger, shock, confusion, fear, and anxiety (Frieze, 1987). In fact, our view of the world may change dramatically. In a recent book, Janoff-Bulman (1992) notes that most of us, before suffering from trauma, believe that the world is benevolent and meaningful, and that we are "worthy" people (p. 6). Because of a need for stability in our world view, these assumptions are quite resistant to change. Yet, extraordinary events, especially ones that threaten our survival, force us to see the world and ourselves in a different way. In Janoff-Bulman's (1992) terms, our assumptions about the world are "shattered." When we are exposed to combat situations or we survive a tragic fire or an airplane crash, we may doubt that the world is basically good, that events occur for predictable reasons, and that we deserve a good fate.

Intimate violence may be particularly traumatic and mind-altering, given that the victim's place of refuge and safety now provokes anxiety (Janoff-Bulman, 1992). This can be especially true of child victims, who may not know of alternatives to staying in the violent home and may be completely dependent upon an abusive parent. Furthermore, because parents normally help children to interpret their experiences and to transform them into lessons about life, the child's sense of self and the world can be distorted easily by an abusive parent (cf. Belsky & Vondra, 1989; Janoff-Bulman, 1992). But adult victims of intimate violence also suffer from disruptions of their positive worldview.

In this chapter we will examine the reactions of child and adult victims of intimate violence and explore similarities in modes of thinking of both abuse victims and victims of other traumatic events. We also will investigate the circumstances under which victims escape from their maltreatment.

Victims' Beliefs about Themselves and Their Victimization

Causal Thinking

Human beings like to understand the causes of events. When something happens to us, we search for an explanation either within ourselves or in the world around us; or, in the absence of other explanations, we attribute the occurrence to luck. In general, people accept responsibility for the good things that happen to them, claiming that they are accountable for these fortuitous events (e.g., Lau & Russell, 1980). In contrast, people are more likely to attribute bad events to external forces. As Taylor and Brown (1988) report, exaggerated beliefs about our abilities to control beneficial events and an overly positive self-evaluation help us to respond well to setbacks and permit us to maintain a sense of mastery. Thus, these "illusions" are quite adaptive under normal circumstances.

This pattern does not occur with all people, however. Those experiencing low self-esteem or depression attribute bad events more frequently and perhaps more accurately to themselves (Abramson, Metalsky, & Alloy, 1988; Alloy & Abramson, 1982). Moreover, those with low self-esteem view negative feedback about the kind of impression they make on others as more accurate than positive feedback, while people with high self-esteem believe the opposite (Swann, Griffin, Predmore, & Gaines, 1987).

Victims of family violence often experience low self-esteem and depression (Friedrich & Einbender, 1983; Walker, 1984). While some victims suffer from these qualities prior to the abuse, the abuse often initiates a change in self-perception. Being subjected to violence and the verbal derogation that often accompanies it contributes to a sense of despair and a negative view of oneself (Browne, 1987). Consider the words of one abuse victim:

> I came to feel like I was no good . . . he was constantly repeating . . . 'you're no good,' or 'you should feel guilty.' And, after a while . . . I was accepting the punishment, along with being afraid to fight back. . . . What he said were the only words I heard. And there were no good ones. He became my conscience in a way. (Blackman, 1989, pp. 44–45)

Given that victims of violence suffer from a poor self-concept, it is not surprising that they report a feeling of responsibility for their victimization. Blackman's study (1989) found that 60 percent of victims of intimate violence blamed themselves, while 22 percent blamed the perpetrator. As one male victim of spouse abuse said, "Of course, I feel responsible. . . . I was the cause of it because there was something that I did that provoked her" (Blackman, 1989, p. 121). Similarly, Frieze (1979) interviewed sixty-eight battered women about their first episode of violence from a spouse. Asked why their husbands became violent, 25 percent of the women blamed their husbands, while 32 percent blamed themselves and 6 percent blamed both. But when Frieze described a hypothetical battering to a group of battered women, she found that the majority blamed the husband and only a few blamed the wife.

Sophisticated distinctions about cause and responsibility, of course, may not be possible with child victims (cf. Celano, 1992). Preschool and young school-aged children, for example, have little sense of self (e.g., Livesley & Bromley, 1973) and would be unlikely to attribute events to their personality or character. But they also believe in ''immanent justice,'' that bad things that happen are the consequence of something they did wrong (Piaget, 1965). Children often blame themselves for their parents' divorce or they may believe that if they fall out of a tree and break an arm, it is because they stole cookies the day before. Thus, children overattribute events to their behavior.

Young children also look to their parents as the moral authorities on how to react to an event (Piaget, 1965). Accordingly, an abusive mother or father has considerable power over the child's causal thinking. To the extent that parents demean their children and in various ways suggest that the child is responsible for the violence (cf. Larrance & Twentyman, 1983), young children may adopt this perspective.

As children get older, their reactions become less tied to parental reactions and their dependence upon parental authority for moral judgments is lessened (Piaget, 1965). Children's experience with peers and their families and with media portrayals of families provides comparative information that further distances the child's perspective from the perspective ''taught'' by an abusive parent.

However, whether parental messages have enduring effects or whether children learn to attribute responsibility through another means, we know that children, like their adult counterparts, often attribute responsibility for their ill treatment to themselves. This viewpoint is illustrated in interviews with twenty-four boys who were removed from their homes either because of abuse or because of other family problems such as alcoholism or instability (Herzberger, Potts, & Dillon, 1981). The boys, who resided in a group home and who had all received counseling for emotional traumas, had all been hit by parents at one time or another, but only some of them were considered physically abused. They discussed why their parent hit them and whether this treatment was deserved. As you can see from Table 3.1, almost all of the boys, both abused and nonabused, believed that their parent hit them because they did something bad. The boys were relatively unwilling to attribute their treatment to their parent's bad

TABLE 3.1 Percentage of Yes Responses to Questions about Attributions for Parental Punishment

| | % of Children with | | | |
Question	Nonabusive Mother	Abusive Mother	Nonabusive Father	Abusive Father
A. When your mother/father hit you, was it because you did something bad?	100	91	86	100
B. When your mother/father hit you, was it because she/he was mean?	11	36	14	57*
C. Do you think your mother/father felt bad about (hitting you)?	100	46**	77	67
D. Do you think you deserved to be treated that way (by your mother/father)?	100	27**	43	57

*Difference was significant at $p < .10$
**$p < .01$

Source: Adapted from Herzberger, S. D., Potts, D. A., & Dillon, M. (1981). Abusive and nonabusive treatment from the child's perspective. *Journal of Consulting and Clinical Psychology, 49*, p. 87. Copyrighted 1981 by the American Psychological Association. Reprinted by permission.

character. Over 60 percent of the boys abused by their mothers and over 40 percent of the boys abused by their fathers denied that their ill treatment was due to their parent being "mean."

We have to be careful, however, in interpreting findings from both adult and child interviews. Claims of responsibility for maltreatment seem to vary with the way the questions are worded. In Blackman's (1989) study, for example, 58 percent of the victims were willing to attribute the "cause" of their victimization to the perpetrator, a much greater percentage than was willing to attribute "blame." More neutral language evoked more willingness to shift responsibility back to the violent person. When we look at the victim's own words, we see that the victim often distinguishes between doing something wrong that provoked the perpetrator's reaction and incurring responsibility for the magnitude of the reaction (Miller & Porter, 1983). In Blackman's (1989) study, for example, 77 percent of the victims said they did not deserve to be abused. Open-ended responses in the interview study by Herzberger et al. (1981) revealed that even children could articulate this distinction. One child said, "Child abuse isn't a good thing to do to a person when they just do something little" (p. 87), and another child reported, "I wasn't no angel, neither. I did things wrong, you know. . . . they had like three quarters of the reason to hit me, but not that hard" (p. 86). Thus, self-blame for severe victimization has its limits.

We also must recognize that self-blame or feelings of personal responsibility are not uncommon among people explaining ordinary, nonviolent altercations with a partner. Blackman's (1989) interviews with individuals not involved in a violent relationship revealed that, like their victim counterparts, they tended to assume responsibility for the conflict experienced with a partner. Thus, the tendency to hold oneself responsible is not restricted to victims.

Some researchers believe that there are distinct advantages to assuming personal responsibility for being victimized (Janoff-Bulman, 1979). Attributing responsibility to oneself provides some comfort in that it allows people to feel that they have at least partial control over events. But this may only be true if the aspect of oneself that caused the problem is regarded as malleable.

Consider an example that should be familiar (Dweck, 1975). If you find no relationship between the amount of effort you expend on a course and your course grade, you might stop trying. You might also stop trying should you believe that your lack of ability, something that cannot be changed, is keeping you from succeeding in the course. On the other hand, if you attribute a poor grade to something about you that can be changed, such as a lack of effort, you may be motivated to try harder.

Janoff-Bulman (1979) identified the implications of this distinction for the case of a rape victim:

> If the rape victim engages in behavioral self-blame and attributes her victimization to a modifiable behavior (e.g., I should not have walked alone . . .), she is likely to maintain a belief in the future avoid-ability of a similar misfortune, while simultaneously maintaining a belief in personal control over important life outcomes. If, on the other hand, the rape victim blames herself characterologically (e.g., . . . I'm the type of person who attracts rapists), she . . . may perceive herself as a chronic victim. (p. 1802)

Research findings on this topic are mixed. Some research touts the benefits of behavioral self-blame and the detrimental effects of characterological self-blame (Janoff-Bulman, 1992). But other research (Meyer & Taylor, 1986; cf. Taylor & Brown, 1988) finds no adaptive benefit to claiming behavioral responsibility for victimization and, in fact, finds self-blame associated with lowered self-esteem and depression (Meyer & Taylor, 1986).

Furthermore, when applied to the situation of recurrent family violence, we can see that attributing responsibility to oneself can be dangerous. Behavioral self-blame may encourage unrealistic assessments about the future and may discourage victims from seeking help from others or leaving the abusive situation. Instead of seeking help victims may alter their behavior in ways that they perceive will decrease the likelihood of abuse. Battered wives, for example, might ensure that the kids are quiet when their husband is due home from work, or they might leave the husband by himself when he drinks. But, as Walker (1989) points out, these efforts to control the abuse usually fail in the long run because, even if the violence is triggered by things that the wife does or does not do, the violence is not *caused* by the wife's behavior. Thus, behavioral self-blame in family violence situations may prolong the abusive relationship.

Learned Helplessness

Some people, such as Walker (1984), compare victims of family violence to subjects of experimental research on *learned helplessness*. This term became familiar to social psychologists following research by Seligman (1975) on dogs that were exposed to uncontrollable, noncontingent shocks. The dogs learned over time to be "helpless" and, when subsequently provided with an opportunity to escape from the shock, remained in the painful situation.

Walker (1984, 1989) notes the parallels of the situation faced by the experimental subjects of learned helplessness and victims of recurrent, rather unpredictable family violence. Most pertinent, perhaps, is the fact that many of the battered women she studied had not escaped from the violent situation. However, the chronically battered women did perceive a connection between their own actions and what happened to them, and they tried to adapt their behavior to minimize the pain they would experience (Browne, 1987; Walker, 1984). As noted above, they engaged in strategies that would decrease the incidence of violence in a given circumstance, even though in the long run the violence recurred.

Efforts to control the likelihood of receiving abuse have also been noted among children. Early case studies (Flanzraich & Dunsavage, 1977) report on the behaviors of "parental children" who assume responsibilities normally reserved for parents.

> Cathy, a . . . 12-year-old . . . gets her seven brothers and sisters ready and off to school while her mother sleeps. If the mother is disturbed she gets angry with Cathy. . . .
>
> Terry, a 3½-year-old illustrates role reversal in an important way. Rather than eating her food, Terry frequently hoards it, then wraps it up and takes it home to her mother. Terry has learned early to make her needs subservient to her mother's. (Flanzraich & Dunsavage, 1977, pp. 14–15)

Role-reversal activities are an adaptive mechanism that allows the child to comfort the adult and thereby perhaps forestall violence. Other studies (cf. Crittenden & DiLalla, 1988) describe the abused child as often inhibiting anger and manifesting "compulsive compliance" in interactions with an abusive parent, presumably for the same purpose.

These studies suggest that people who suffer from family violence are in many ways not "helpless." They do, after all, change their behaviors in an attempt to minimize the suffering that they experience. But the studies also suggest that many victims of violence fail to take the most helpful step in preventing future violence—that of leaving the abusive situation.

Problem-Solving Abilities

One measure of helplessness is an inability to find effective solutions to problems (Abramson, Seligman, & Teasdale, 1978). A number of studies have suggested that victims of family violence show deficiencies in this ability, which may prevent their escape from abuse (e.g., Launius & Lindquist, 1988). One such study (Launius & Jensen, 1987) asked college women to report possible solutions to a number of interpersonal problems, half involving abuse or threatened abuse and half involving nonabusive situations (e.g., someone asking to cut in line at a theater). Three groups of women were compared: women who had been repeatedly, physically abused by a partner; those who had received counseling, but who had not experienced abuse; and those with no counseling and no abusive background. Abused women generated fewer possible solutions and fewer "effective" solutions to both types of problems than did women in the two other groups. The abused women also were less likely to choose an effective solution for use in the problem situation.

We do not know whether abused women or other victims suffer from problem-solving deficits prior to their victimization, or whether abuse contributes to the problem. We do know that fear suffered during and after victimization reduces one's ability to think clearly.

Crime victims, for example, often focus on the weapon used during the event and fail to note important characteristics that will help police to identify the criminal (Tooley, Brigham, Maass, & Bothwell, 1987). For victims of family violence, such a reaction may be more generalized. "Severe, recurrent, life-threatening violence seems likely to put victims in a state of perceptual alert, in which their abilities to think beyond the immediate situation may be sharply curtailed" (Blackman, 1989, p. 75). All of the victim's effort, then, may go towards immediate survival and not to producing long-term solutions to the problem of battering.

Perceptions That Their Treatment Is Unusual

If people believe that their experiences are common, they may be more likely to accept them and to consider them normal. This kind of thinking sometimes underlies parental unwillingness to control sibling or peer aggression (Pagelow, 1989). "Kids will be kids" and "boys will be boys" are routinely heard expressions. But what about severe forms of family violence? Do victims believe that violence is normative in family situations?

Blackman (1989) found that 74 percent of victims interviewed and 41 percent of the nonvictims believed that violence of one sort or another was common (i.e., that it affected at least half of the populace). Thus, while people in general appear to believe that we live in a violent society, victims are particularly apt to share this perspective. At the same time, however, victims view the particular behavior to which they are subjected as unique. For example, in Blackman's (1989) study 86 percent of adults, looking back on their abuse by a parent or a partner, regarded their treatment as atypical. One adult said

> "It must have been when I started school that I realized not all daddies act like my daddy does . . . some love and play with their kids." (p. 129)

This recognition does not just emerge in adulthood. When the abused children in Herzberger et al.'s (1981) study were asked whether their families were the same as or different from other families, 70 percent of them said "different" and the differences centered on parental treatment. One 9-year-old reported,

> "Very different. I don't think other families whoop their kids with extension cords. I don't think they would put their children outside with no shoes on." (p. 87)

Are Victims Masochistic?

One of the most common beliefs about abuse victims, particularly battered women, is that they are masochistic—that they do not really want the abuse to end. This explanation purports to account for victims' failure to report their abuse to the proper authorities or to leave the home (cf. Goolkasian, 1986). There is little evidence, however, to support this claim. While masochism itself has not been studied, research suggests few personality differences between women who have suffered abuse and those who have not, and most of these are generally assumed to be consequences of the abuse, not antecedents (Hotaling & Sugarman, 1986).

Another argument against the masochism myth lies with the pattern of violence in intimate dyads. The vast majority of abused women experience no violence from their partner until marriage or living together (Browne, 1987). Before the violence occurs, the partners' behavior is seen as attentive, friendly, and caring (see Box 3.1 for an example). Thus, abused women do not necessarily foresee that their new relationships will turn violent and therefore cannot be accused of seeking such a relationship. It is only with hindsight that women recognize that the acute attention they experienced was a sign of the partner's possessiveness and need for control that fueled his violent behavior.

There is just no evidence that abuse victims enjoy their treatment. One of the reasons why this myth is so pervasive is that people who have been victimized before *are* likely to be victimized again. Lewis (1987) states, for example, that 34 percent of the battered women's shelter residents she surveyed reported being the victims of child abuse, while only 7 percent of women sampled at a health clinic experienced child abuse. In addition, one quarter of the abused women reported abuse from a previous partner, while fewer than 10 percent of the health sample reported abuse by a partner. The suggestion, then, is that victims seek out relationships with people who are prone to violence.

However, women who have been abused as children are quicker to leave violent marriages than those who have not (cf. Pagelow, 1984). It is quite possible that revictimized women show up in shelters precisely because they desire to escape from further violence. Then, because many of the studies of revictimization use shelter populations (including Lewis, 1987), the proportion of repeated-abuse victims will be overestimated.

An alternative explanation has been offered for the disproportionate number of revictimizations. Russell (1975) suggests that one's

Browne (1987) describes the case of "Molly" and "Jim." An interview with Molly conducted after she was charged with murder demonstrates how battered women often are deceived by the early support and attentiveness of their violent mates.

> Jim's interest in Molly began at their first meeting and never abated. He was dependable and attentive, rearranging his schedule to be with her and dropping other activities and even former friends with whom she felt uncomfortable.
>
> In the following months, Jim was with her every moment Molly would allow. He occasionally spent time away from her and went drinking with old friends, but when he came back he was as gentle and considerate as ever and he never drank heavily around her. (p. 38)

Many months after their wedding Jim started being violent. He had lost his job and they eventually moved out of their apartment and were living in their van. Even then, following bouts of violence, Molly held out hope for an improved relationship:

> . . . Jim was always cold sober by morning—quiet and depressed and terribly sorry. He would apologize and stroke her face, and drink less and spend more time with her for the next several days. Molly prayed he'd find work soon. She kept telling herself things would be alright once he got a job. . . . (p. 39)

But Jim continued the systematic and repeated abuse that culminated in his murder.

status as a victim provokes further victimization from those who see the woman as "damaged merchandise," and therefore "fair game." Remember the studies cited in chapter 2 revealed a lack of empathy for victims, particularly ones who display their suffering (Coates et al., 1979; Perry et al., 1990).

Decreased Sensitivity to Aggression

As noted above, there is no evidence that victims of abuse are masochists who enjoy and perhaps seek out victimization. There is substantial evidence, however, that many people who have experienced victimization view some forms of violence less seriously than do non-victims (e.g., Arias & Johnson, 1989; but see Box 3.2 for research on social service professionals' reactions to victimization). In one study (Herzberger & Tennen, 1985a) college students were asked to read vignettes about parental handling of a disciplinary encounter with their child. The vignettes ended with the child being moderately punished (e.g., spanking, or forcing the child to acknowledge the wrong-doing at the dinner table) or severely punished (e.g., banging the child against the wall several times, or screaming at the child for twenty minutes and calling the child obscene names). The students judged the seriousness and appropriateness of the parent's action and the degree to which the action would likely result in positive or negative changes in the child's behavior and emotional state. Then the students were asked whether they had ever experienced similar treatment from parents. Generally, those who reported that they were treated similarly believed that the parental behavior was less serious, more appropriate, less likely to be labelled as abuse, and was more of the child's responsibility (see Table 3.2). Those who were treated similarly as children also viewed the parental action as leading to less emotional harm and to greater improvements in the child's behavior than those who were not treated similarly.

These results do not suggest that victims see violence as enjoyable or even innocuous: despite significant differences from nonvictims, victims still judged violence as inappropriate and serious (Herzberger & Tennen, 1985a). Victims do accommodate *somewhat* to the violence they experience, though; perhaps they, better than nonvictims, recognize that those who have suffered can heal and move on with their lives.

TABLE 3.2 Judgments Made by Individuals Who Did Not Experience (Not Similar) and Who Did Experience (Similar) Similar Treatment

Vignette Type	Severity		Appropriateness		Abuse		% Child's Responsibility	
	Not Similar	Similar	Not Similar	Similar	Not Similar	Similar	Not Similar	Similar
Emotional—moderate son (77,62)	3.48	3.05*	3.78	4.85****	12.99	1.61***	45.20	51.95*
Emotional—moderate daughter (84,54)	4.09	3.06*****	3.24	4.83****	11.90	0.00***	37.94	52.50*****
Emotional—severe son (123,14)	6.10	6.00	1.36	1.86	83.47	64.29*	19.40	19.86
Emotional—severe daughter (123,15)	6.24	5.87	1.32	1.60	75.61	73.33	20.07	22.47
Physical—moderate son (35,104)	3.91	3.23***	3.11	4.46****	14.71	7.69	40.57	46.01
Physical—moderate daughter (44,92)	3.80	3.20***	3.25	4.24****	16.28	4.35**	42.16	48.45
Physical—severe son (124,14)	6.56	5.86**	1.44	2.36**	88.62	57.14**	21.39	36.54**
Physical—severe daughter (123,15)	6.71	5.87***	1.24	2.40***	97.56	80.00	18.87	30.67**

Note: The numbers in parentheses represent the number of participants who did not receive similar treatment and the number who received treatment, respectively, as a child. Severity and appropriateness were rated on a 7-pt. scale (with 7 indicating "extremely severe" or "perfectly appropriate"). Figures in the remaining columns indicate the percentage of respondents who judged the depicted act to be "child abuse" and the percentage of responsibility for the act attributed to the child.

*p < .10.   ***p < .01.
**p < .05.   ****p < .001.

Source: Adapted from Herzberger, S. D. & Tennen, H. (1985a). The effect of self-relevance on moderate and severe disciplinary encounters. *Journal of Marriage and the Family, 47,* p. 314. Copyrighted 1985 by the National Council on Family Relations, 3989 Central Ave. NE, Suite 550, Minneapolis, MN 55421. Reprinted by permission.

Kelder, McNamara, Carlson, and Lynn (1991) replicated the Herzberger and Tennen (1985a) results, but suggested limits to the connection between maltreatment and judgments of appropriateness. They found that people who were disciplined severely in childhood and adolescence rated physical punishment as more appropriate than those who were less severely disciplined. However, those who experienced the most extreme physical discipline accompanied by physical injury were likely to reject the use of physical punishment as inappropriate. Kelder et al. speculate that it is just this group that may be most sensitive to society's rejection of child abuse.

Why Do Abuse Victims Stay?

> A man left his home and walked down the block to the bus stop. He got into an argument with a stranger and proceeded to hit him several times. When told of this encounter, we ask, Why was he so violent? The man then returned home and got into an argument with his wife. He hit her several times. We ask, Why did she stay? (Fagan & Wexler, 1987, p. 5)

This apocryphal story nicely sums up a common reaction to cases of family violence. We find it hard to understand why victims of abuse remain to experience more violence. In an effort to understand the puzzle, we shift some of the burden of blame onto the victim: after all, "If she didn't like it, why didn't she leave?"

Fear and Dependence upon the Abuser

It is hard for many of us to understand why, when violence emerges, victims of family violence stay in the home. Why do they not get help? Abused children often are not aware of solutions to their plight, and abused women, while they are aware of possible solutions, may not feel capable of seeking them. Women and children are often economically dependent upon the abuser and cannot imagine how they will support themselves once leaving home (cf. Frieze & Browne, 1989).

Families in which abuse occurs are also likely to be isolated and, therefore, less frequently come into contact with others whom they believe might render support (Straus et al., 1980). Abused children are more likely to reside far away from other relatives and may move more frequently than other children (cf. Pagelow, 1984). Abuse victims also may have been threatened about the repercussions of telling others and now fear that disclosure will endanger their own lives or those of other family members (Pagelow, 1984).

Lack of Support from Police and Social Services

Victims' fears that departure will escalate violence are compounded by a belief that they may receive little help outside the home. Until recently police and social service agencies have provided little support and assistance to victims of family violence who wish to leave the home, and victims were well aware of this (Frieze & Browne, 1989; also see Chapter 9). Police handled domestic violence by urging the violent partner to take a walk to cool down or by staying in the residence until the couple seemed to have gotten over "their conflict" (Sherman & Berk, 1984). This treatment suggested to victims that police would not intervene to protect them and reinforced the viewpoint that this was a matter to be handled privately within the family.

Affection for the Perpetrator

Victims of family violence often still love the perpetrator. About half of the spouse abuse victims in recent surveys (cf. Pagelow, 1984; Saunders & Size, 1986) say that they love their spouse and hope that the marriage will improve. As in the example of Molly and Jim (Box 3.1), this hope is nurtured by the perpetrator's contrition and extreme remorse after the violence (e.g., Browne, 1987; Walker, 1984).

The perpetrator's contrition may lead the victim to redefine the violence, to see it less seriously and to deny its relevance to the future (Frieze & Browne, 1989). Battered women often redefine the violence by pointing to a characteristic in their partner that they believe to be ephemeral. For example, many women blame their victimization on their partner's drinking (Browne, 1987) and think that when the drinking stops, so will the abuse. But, while alcohol and other drug use are implicated in the incidence of violence (Frieze & Browne, 1989), they are likely not to be the sole cause of the aggression. Moreover, abusive partners may drink or use drugs to provide an excuse for the violence or to build up their courage to aggress against another person (Frieze & Browne, 1989). Thus, redefining the violence in a manner that minimizes its seriousness is counterproductive and potentially lethal. Similarly, trying to control the circumstances of the abuse by changing one's own behavior may ameliorate the violence, but it is unlikely to promote permanent solutions to the problem (Hilberman & Munson, 1978).

These explanations, plus the added burdens of poor problem-solving ability, low self-esteem, and a causal thinking pattern that promotes feelings of personal responsibility, all contribute to the continuation of violent relationships. Perhaps, then, instead of being so puzzled about why victims of abuse stay, we should turn our attention to questions of how some of them manage to leave, or at least how they manage to get help.

Other Victim Reactions

Is there a way of looking at one's victimization that promotes escape from the maltreatment? And are there certain characteristics of the victimization that just will no longer be tolerated? These are important questions, but we have to remind ourselves of the limitations to the correspondence between how we think and how we act (Miller & Porter, 1983). A woman who attributes the cause of the abuse to her spouse may still believe that she needs the income he provides; therefore, she may stay in the relationship. A child who knows she does not deserve the maltreatment and believes that she cannot take it anymore, still may have nowhere else to go. What then does prompt people to take action and what kinds of action are successful?

Help-Seeking

Some victims recognize that more than just conformity to the perpetrator's wishes or waiting for the perpetrator to change is necessary to break the violent pattern. They often seek help from the police or the social service community (Frieze & Browne, 1989). Others go to shelters or seek various forms of support from family and friends. Some, especially those who blame themselves for their victimization, undergo psychotherapy, and through this channel become aware of opportunities for a change in life circumstances (Frieze, 1979). Adolescents often respond to the abuse by running away (Pagelow, 1984); if they are fortunate, they are then helped by a social service agency. Often, however, teenage runaways are seen as troublemakers who deserve to be punished.

Women who are most likely to seek outside help tend to blame their partner more for the abuse, have less hope of controlling the violence, or have been raped in addition to beaten (cf. Frieze & Browne, 1989). Other women report leaving their partners and seeking shelter when they perceived that the partner might hurt their children (Walker, 1978). Miller and Porter (1983) suggest that the more serious the victimization, the more the victim is assured that the cause of the violence resides in the perpetrator, not in the victim (see also Kelder et al., 1991). This recognition may provide victims with the self-confidence to call attention to their plight.

Retaliation

Some victims fight back. Adolescents who kill an abusive parent generally do so after prolonged and brutal victimization and often in an effort to protect other family members (cf. Newhill, 1991).

Browne (1987) identified key characteristics that predict which battered women will seriously harm or kill their abusive partners. She reports that alcohol and drug use by the perpetrator, frequent violence, severe injuries, actual or threatened sexual assault, threats by the perpetrator to kill the woman, and her own threats to commit suicide predicted a woman's severe retaliation.

Women who fight back are not generally aggressive (Browne, 1987). While men who commit homicide almost inevitably have had a history of violence, most women who kill their partners do not. Like the abused adolescents, abused women who kill their partners do so in response to extreme provocation.

Perpetrator Desistance: Which Strategies Work?

Not many studies have been done to test the effectiveness of victims' various options available to stop the abuse. But one study by Bowker (1983) examined women's beliefs about what worked in their abusive situation. Bowker recruited women from the Milwaukee area who had once been victims of abuse before the offender ceased his violence. Bowker asked women to report strategies that worked the most and the least in helping them to dissuade the offender from further violence. Table 3.3 shows the women's responses.

The most effective strategies were to fight back, disclose information about the violence to friends and relatives and to seek help from a social service agency or women's group. Thus, both informal social sanctions and formal legal sanctions worked for these women. Trying to talk with the offender about his violence or getting him to promise to stop were regarded as almost completely ineffective.

A close look at the statistics, however, reveals substantial variation in the effectiveness of most strategies. For example, almost as many women reported that formal legal sanctions worked least well as reported that they worked best (we will discuss why this might be in Chapter 9). But when asked what enabled the women to force their

TABLE 3.3 Self-Reports of What Worked "Best" and "Least" in Ending Battering in the Last Incident

Factors	What Worked "Best" (Percentage of Cases)	What Worked "Least" (Percentage of Cases)
Talk husband out of abuse	3	7
Get husband to promise cessation	–	14
Threats (nonviolent)	12	3
Hiding	3	2
Passively defending self	1	1
Aggressively defending self	10	5
Talking to own relatives	7	3
Talking to in-laws	3	4
Talking to neighbors	3	1
Talking to friends	14	1
Talking to anyone else	3	1
Taking shelter	8	–
Calling the police	5	11
Contacting a social-service agency	9	5
Contacting a women's group	10	1
Contacting the clergy	3	3
Contacting a lawyer or D.A.	5	8
Other	2	–
Nothing	1	32
Total	102[a]	102[a]

Note: [a]Percentages do not sum 100 due to rounding.

Source: Adapted from L. H. Bowker (1983), *Beating wife-beating*. Lexington, MA: Lexington Books, p. 122. Adapted by permission of the author.

husbands to stop the battering, almost 30 percent said that they had just "had enough" and "decided to act" to end it; half of the women interviewed indicated that they acted after a supportive family member or agency official gave them the confidence to act. The women also reported that 30 percent of the men stopped the violence out of fear of the possibility of a divorce, and 21 percent stopped because of fear of legal sanction.

This study highlights the diversity of offender reactions to strategies used by victims. The same strategies will not work with all violent offenders. The study suggests, however, that calling outsiders' attention to the violence and receiving outside support may be more effective than trying to handle the abuse oneself. Of course, Bowker (1983) did not study the specific circumstances under which each strategy worked or did not work. It could well be, for example, that some women found that disclosure of the abuse did not work because it brought support to the offender from neighbors or relatives who approved of the violence. It could also be that the women who regarded legal interventions as ineffectual received little support from the police or criminal justice system. The study also lacks an appropriate control group of women whose abuse continued. It would be valuable to see the proportion of women in the latter group who also tried each strategy, but failed to alter the course of their victimization.

Concluding Remarks

As this chapter makes clear, victims of violence are not the masochistic people that they are sometimes portrayed to be. They generally reject the violence they experience and try strategies to reduce its frequency and severity. However, often the victims retain hope for saving the relationship and this hope may prevent them from viewing the situation as seriously as an outsider might.

Victims also often manifest a deficit in problem-solving ability and they hold themselves at least partially responsible for their victimization. While they recognize that their treatment is atypical, many regard it less seriously than observers would. All of these characteristics may decrease the likelihood of leaving the relationship. When the seriousness and inevitability of the violence becomes apparent to adult victims, though, they often will make an attempt to leave or to get help. We know almost nothing about the circumstances under which children seek help.

The Dynamics of Family Life

CHAPTER OBJECTIVES

The Social System of the Family
Parent-Child Relations
  Parent Factors
  Child Factors
  The Interaction between Parent
    Factors and Child Factors
  Relationship to Other Family
    Subsystems
Spousal or Partner Relations
  Perpetrator Characteristics
  Victim Characteristics
  Couple Characteristics
  Inequality

  Relationship to Other Family
    Subsystems
Sibling Relations
Adult Child-Elderly Parent
Relations
Family System and Social
Environment Influences
  Economic and Social Stressors
  Lack of Social Support
  Societal Norms
Concluding Remarks

Family life is complicated. A person's relationship with a parent, sibling, or child is affected by and, in turn, affects relationships with others in the family. Work and social relationships outside the family influence what goes on in the home as well. The primary purposes of this chapter are to study the interrelated influences within and outside the complex social system known as the family and to recognize the multitude of factors that distinguish violent families from nonviolent ones.

This overview of family life will help us to begin to think about the processes through which some families become violent. We may derive hints about patterns of thought and behavior that permit and even elicit anger and violence. However, the view of violent families presented in this chapter is largely a static one that does not address the process by which families begin to be violent. Later chapters will discuss theories of violence and begin to differentiate the causes of violence from its effects.

The Social System of the Family

Families are complex social systems that comprise subsystems of individuals such as parent and child, siblings, and husband and wife (Minuchin & Fishman, 1981). Families also are components of larger systems, such as communities, workforces, and society itself. To truly understand the family then, we need to explore the personalities of the individuals, the workings of the family subsystems and their interrelationship with the family as a whole, and the extra-familial environment through which family relationships develop and change.

This complicated network of family life is exemplified in part by Figure 4.1, which shows Belsky's (1984) process model of parenting. The figure displays the interrelationships among the factors that influence the parent-child subsystem. According to Belsky, parenting is a compilation of one's personality, work environment, social life, marital relations, and the characteristics of the child. Many of these factors interrelate: one's personality, for example, both is determined by and determines one's work environment, social life, and marital relations. Thus, to fully understand parenting we must examine a complicated network of interrelationships.

Similar diagrams or models can be constructed to depict the complex interactions of other family subsystems. Minuchin and Fishman (1981), trying to make this point, have characterized people in the family as relating ''kaleidoscopically'' to others. A son relating to his father creates a different subunit than when relating to his sibling. While part of the son's behavior will be consistent across these subunits, part of it will be modified and take on characteristics dictated by each interrelationship.

Keeping this multifaceted view of the family in mind, let us now discuss the influences on family life in more depth, starting first at a subsystem level. We will study parent-child, spouse or partner,

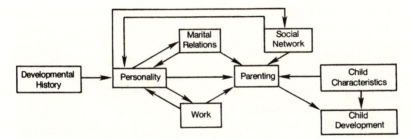

FIGURE 4.1

The determinants of parenting: A process model

Source: Belsky, J. (1984). The determinants of parenting: A process model. *Child Development, 55,* 84. © 1984 by the Society for Research in Child Development, Inc. Reprinted by permission.

sibling, and then adult child-elderly parent subsystems. We will examine which kinds of behaviors characterize successful relationships and which correspond to violent ones.

Parent-Child Relations

We need to be careful when we identify the components of healthy parent-child relations. One of the primary tasks of parenting is to provide an environment that supports the development of "competent" children who will be prepared to take on a variety of social and economic roles. But competence and the socialization mechanisms that foster it cannot be defined universally (Ogbu, 1981). Ogbu notes that characteristics of children that would be valued in one culture might be devalued in another. Take independence and individualism, for example. Societies that depend economically and socially upon personal initiative and competition would reward independent and self-promoting children. Those that depend upon cooperation and a stable social environment might see such children as a risk. Keeping this caveat in mind, let us examine how effective parent-child relations are usually defined by contemporary American writers.

Parent Factors

The emphasis in most writings about good parent-child relations is upon the parent's responsibility to the child. Beneficial parenting occurs when the parent is nurturant, attentive to the child, sensitive to his or her needs and capabilities, and promotes good social and cognitive development (Clarke-Stewart, 1973; Rutter, 1989). Good parents are consistent in their discipline and set limits for the child's behavior, but they are not excessively or harshly punitive (Baumrind, 1971). These parenting behaviors promote healthy socioemotional development and self-esteem, cooperation, and cognitive growth (e.g., Baumrind, 1971; Coopersmith, 1967; Hoffman, 1970).

But these characteristics represent the *ideal* parent. What distinguishes families in which parents exhibit abusive parenting from those which do not? Kaufman and Zigler (1989) present an overview of characteristics of child abusing families and the cultural supports for abuse (see Table 4.1). They note that parental characteristics such as low intelligence, lack of physical attractiveness, low self-esteem, poor interpersonal skills, and a poor relationship with one's own parents may be associated with a propensity to engage in violence. High levels of anger and impulsivity are characteristic of abusive parents as well (Wolfe, 1987).

Another distinguishing feature of abusive parents is their inappropriate expectations about the child's behavior (Wolfe, 1987). Parents who understand child development are less likely to misinterpret a child's behavior or to exaggerate his or her ability to perform a difficult task (Dix, 1991). For example, parents recognize that with age children become more responsible for their misbehavior and that their misbehavior is more intentional; consequently, older children's misdeeds are more upsetting to parents than younger children's misdeeds (Dix & Grusec, 1985). Parents who misjudge the maturity level of their children are more susceptible to anger and violence.

Because abusive parents often have inappropriate expectations about their child's behavior, they have been known to interpret their infant's cries as intentionally motivated to disturb the parent (Pollock & Steele, 1972; Wolfe, 1987). They also attribute a child's inability to perform certain tasks to the child's stubbornness or ignorance.

While there is some support for these differences between abusing and nonabusing parents, some writers (e.g., Starr, 1988) warn that few differences in personality or social skill consistently emerge. Furthermore, although psychological disturbance underlies some types of bad parenting (e.g., Conger, McCarty, Yang, Lahey, & Kropp, 1984; Phares & Compas, 1992), one need not be classified as neurotic or psychotic to display poor parenting behaviors. And at this point there is no evidence that severe psychological maladjustment is more prevalent among abusive than nonabusive parents (O'Leary, 1993). Thus, we need to study factors other than personality to truly understand the abusive situation.

TABLE 4.1 Determinants of Abuse: Compensatory and Risk Factors

Ontogenetic Level	Microsystem Level	Exosystem Level	Macrosystem Level
Compensatory Factors			
High IQ	Healthy children	Good social supports	Culture that promotes a sense of shared responsibility in caring for the community's children
Awareness of past abuse	Supportive spouse	Few stressful events	Culture opposed to violence
History of a positive relationship with one parent	Economic security/ savings in the bank	Strong, supportive religious affiliation	Economic prosperity
Special talents		Positive school experiences and peer relations as a child	
Physical attractiveness		Therapeutic interventions	
Good interpersonal skills			
Risk Factors			
History of abuse	Marital discord	Unemployment	Cultural acceptance of corporal punishment
Low self-esteem	Children with behavior problems	Isolation; poor social supports	View of children as possessions
Low IQ	Premature or unhealthy children	Poor peer relations as a child	Economic depression
Poor interpersonal skills	Single parent		
	Poverty		

Source: Adapted from Kaufman, J. & Zigler, E. (1989). The intergenerational transmission of child abuse. In D. Cicchetti & V. Carlson (Eds.), *Child maltreatment: Theory and research on the causes and consequences of child abuse and neglect* (p. 139). Cambridge: Cambridge University Press. Copyright © Cambridge University Press 1989. Reprinted with the permission of Cambridge University Press.

Child Factors

Parent-child relations are bidirectional (Lewis & Rosenblum, 1974). As Table 4.1 illustrates, they are a function not only of the parent and his or her background, but of the characteristics presented by the child. Although we should not blame children for parental mistreatment (see Box 4.1), children who are regarded by parents or others as "difficult" or who present physical anomalies or illnesses elicit more negative parenting styles than "easy" children. Parents teach difficult children (or at least difficult boys) less than other children (Maccoby, Snow, & Jacklin, 1984) and they report feeling less effectual in their childrearing activities (Sirignano & Lachman, 1985). Premature infants who emit aversive high-pitched cries and are unresponsive to parental caregiving efforts may be especially likely to become targets of harsh parental treatment (Frodi, Lamb, Leavitt, Donovan, Neff, & Sherry, 1978). Mentally or physically handicapped children also incur more maltreatment (Friedrich & Boriskin, 1976).

The Interaction between Parent Factors and Child Factors

Perhaps just as important as the child's and the parent's characteristics is the coherence or disjunction in the characteristics of the parent-child pair (Thomas, Chess, & Birch, 1968). Parents who are quiet and sedentary may not look with favor upon children who are especially active and require constant stimulation. Parents who enjoy cuddling with their infant may be disappointed with a more independent child who resists being picked up. The interaction of stress-invoking child characteristics and debilitating parent characteristics especially presages poor parenting (cf. Bugental, Mantyla, & Lewis, 1989). Mothers and fathers with little child care experience and knowledge react less well to a problem child than do mature, skilled parents (see also Holden, 1988).

These findings are a reminder that the distinctions between parental and child contributions to any parent-child relationship are arbitrary and exaggerated. Parenting is a social event and it is affected by the personalities and preferences of both interactants. Also, parent-child relations do not hinge upon an isolated event; the relationship develops and evolves continuously from birth. How children present themselves on any occasion may be due to earlier parental behavior, and how parents present themselves on any occasion may be due to earlier child behavior. For example, Patterson's research (1980) has

BOX 4.1

At this point a cautionary remark is in order that applies to our understanding of parent-child relations and can be extended to understanding spousal relations or others within the family. People have worried that research on the characteristics of children that elicit harsh or inadequate parenting will lead to blaming the victim. That is, if we admit that difficult children are more likely to be maltreated, should we also then hold the child responsible for the abuse and exonerate the maltreating parent?

To most, the answer would be *no*. We can understand the conditions under which certain people may be more or less likely to be poor parents without assigning responsibility for such parenting to the child. Parents, unless emotionally disturbed or cognitively incapable, must assume responsibility for their parenting practices. They are, after all, the parent and charged with rearing a healthy child.

shown that children who are unresponsive to parental demands elicit more coercive parental control attempts, which in turn elicit more child noncompliance. Thus, while at any given moment we might trace a parent's action to a behavior by the child, or vice versa, we cannot claim to know all the proximal or distal causes of the parent's behavior.

Another illustration of this phenomenon comes from observations of both abusive parents and their children (Reid, Taplin, & Lorber, 1981). Reid et al. find that children of abusive parents exhibit much higher rates of hitting, threatening, whining, and teasing than children from nonabusive homes and higher rates than other oppositional, but not abused, children. Likewise, as Table 4.2 shows, abusive mothers exhibit higher rates of mildly (e.g., disapproval, teasing) and seriously aversive behaviors (e.g., threats, hitting) than do other mothers (Reid, 1986). When disciplining, abusive mothers also use a higher proportion of abusive or highly aversive behaviors.

These statistics show that the behaviors of both parent and child in abusive homes seem to create a distressful, uncomfortable home environment. But it is important to recognize that most of the home life in abusive families is identical to that in nonabusive families

TABLE 4.2 Mean Rates at Which Mothers Were Observed to Emit Generally Aversive and Highly Aversive Behaviors in the Homesetting

Measure	Group 1[a]	Group 2[b]	Group 3[c]	Differences between Group Means
Total aversive behavior per minute[d]	.12	.38	.75	Group 1 < 2; $p < .10$ Group 2 < 3; $p < .05$ Group 1 < 3; $p < .01$
Total abusive behavior per minute[e]	.003	.02	.08	Group 1 < 2; $p < .15$ Group 2 < 3; $p < .01$ Group 1 < 3; $p < .01$
Proportion of all aversive behavior that was abusive[f]	.01	.05	.11	Group 1 < 2; $p < .10$ Group 2 < 3; $p < .05$ Group 1 < 3; $p < .01$

Note: [a]Nondistressed.
[b]Referred for child management problems; no known child abuse.
[c]Referred for child management problems; admitted to child-abusive behavior.
[d]Including command, disapprove, high rate, negative, tease, whine, threat, destructive, humiliate, ignore, noncomply, hit, yell.
[e]Including threat, humiliate, hit, yell.
[f]Total abusive behaviors divided by total aversive behaviors.

Source: Adapted from Reid, J. B. (1986). Social-interactional patterns in families of abused and nonabused children. In C. Zahn-Waxler, E. M. Cummings, & R. Iannotti (Eds.), *Altruism and aggression: Biological and social origins* (p. 249). Cambridge: Cambridge University Press. Copyright © Cambridge University Press 1990. Reprinted with the permission of Cambridge University Press.

(cf. Reid, 1986). Reid reports that 95 percent of the interactions of parents and children in abusive and nonabusive households are characterized as positive or neutral.

Relationship to Other Family Subsystems

We must remember that the quality of the parent-child relationship corresponds to relationships with other family members as well. Parenting practices, for example, relate to the quality of the marital relationship (cf. Belsky & Vondra, 1989). Good marriages may serve to buffer the stresses of parenting; they also may be an indication of the parents' healthy personality characteristics. Sears, Maccoby, and Levin (1957) report that women who respect their husbands direct more praise towards their children. Elder, Caspi, and Downey (1986) studied parenting practices, marital relations, and child development across four generations of a group of families. They found complex networks of intra- and inter-generational processes in which family instability, marital tension, parental hostility towards children, and child behavior problems repeat themselves in successive family groupings.

When spouses are violent or divorce, children suffer (cf. Grych & Fincham, 1992). Boys who come from homes with a substantial amount of marital conflict are more likely to fight both at home and at school (Loeber & Dishion, 1984). Men who are violent toward wives are not only less involved in parenting, but when involved show more irritability toward their children (Holden & Ritchie, 1991). Abused mothers experience more stress than nonabused mothers, which may decrease their sensitivity to children's concerns (Holden & Ritchie, 1991).

Spousal or Partner Relations

Attempts to describe the characteristics of a successful marriage or partnership are fraught with the same difficulty as attempts to characterize good parenting. Couplings come in all shapes and sizes, from those in which the partners argue incessantly and loudly to those in which the partners rarely disagree. Some couples are vitally interested and involved in each others' professional and personal lives; others lead substantially independent lives.

Good marriages, however, meet each partner's needs for love, esteem, and material and psychological support (Minuchin & Fishman, 1981). As with any social organization, when both members of the couple feel that resources and rewards are justly distributed, resentment and conflict are mitigated (cf. Gelles, 1983; Teichman & Teichman, 1989). In contrast, couples who experience less marital satisfaction criticize each other and express anger more often (Gottman, 1979). Distressed partners also engage in more negative behaviors or more often reciprocate the negative behavior of the other (cf. Biglan, Lewin, & Hops, 1990).

Perpetrator Characteristics

Of course, people who are distressed with their marriage do not all become violent and in contrast, some people who otherwise report being quite affectionate and satisfied with their marriages do become violent (Lloyd, 1990). What distinguishes violent partners from non-violent ones? Perhaps surprisingly, very few reliable differences in personality or social background have been found (Hotaling & Sugarman, 1986). O'Leary (1993) has summarized some of the factors that do appear to make a difference (see Table 4.3). O'Leary distinguishes between the factors related to physical aggression and verbal aggression, the mild forms of which characterize almost all partner relationships. He further demarcates mild physical acts and severe physical aggression.

O'Leary and others (Hotaling & Sugarman, 1986) note that less severe forms of physical aggression are related to the use of alcohol, holding attitudes that support violence, and having witnessed or experienced aggression as a child or adult. Less education and lower occupation levels have also been shown among violent partners (Hotaling & Sugarman, 1986).

Hotaling and Sugarman (1986) find that perpetrators of violence do not consistently suffer from poor self-esteem. O'Leary (1993) suggests, though, that a poor self-image does characterize those who engage in severe aggressive acts. Furthermore, the same group manifests other serious personality disorders, such as sadism or antisocial personality (O'Leary, 1993). Again, people who engage in milder partner violence are not distinguishable from nonviolent people in psychopathology.

Batterers also tend to be less assertive than non-battering partners (Hotaling & Sugarman, 1986). Thus, they may get frustrated over perceived injustices, but be unable to resolve disputes in a reasoned manner. Lloyd (1990) found that violent couples were more likely to attack each other verbally during conflicts and were less likely to engage in *squabbles,* in which conflicts remained calm and relatively short in duration. Squabbles help to clear the air and let one partner know how the other feels about some issue. Violent couples, Lloyd (1990) suggests, may not use squabbles to their benefit and instead continue to argue vehemently.

Victim Characteristics

Victims of spouse abuse are practically indistinguishable in personality and social characteristics from nonvictims (Hotaling & Sugarman, 1986), although some studies suggest that victims have lower self-esteem. The only consistent factor that distinguishes victims from nonvictims is the formers' witnessing of violence during childhood. As of 1986 this factor had been shown to relate to victimization in 73 percent of the fifteen studies that had examined this relationship (Hotaling & Sugarman, 1986).

TABLE 4.3 The Continuum of Aggressive Behaviors in Intimate Relationships

Verbal Aggression ─────→	Physical Aggression ─────→	Severe Aggression ─────→	Murder
Insults	Pushing	Beating	
Yelling	Slapping	Punching	
Name-calling	Shoving	Hitting with object	

Causes

Need to control[a] ──────────────────────────────────────→

Misuse of power[a] ──────────────────────────────────────→

Jealousy[a] ──→

Marital discord ──→

Accept violence as a means of control ───────────────────→

Modeling of physical aggression ─────────────────────────→

Abused as a child ───────────────────────────────────────→

Aggressive personality styles ───────────────────────────→

Alcohol abuse ───→

Personality disorders ───────────→

Emotional lability ──────────────→

Poor self-esteem ────────────────→

Contributing factors: job stressors and unemployment

Note: Need to control and variables on the left are associated with all forms of aggression; acceptance of violence and variables in the middle are associated with physical aggression, severe aggression, and murder. Personality disorders and the variables on the right are associated with severe aggression and murder.

[a]More relevant for males than for females.

Source: O'Leary, K. D. (1993). Through a psychological lens: Personality traits, personality disorders, and levels of violence. In R. J. Gelles & D. R. Loseke (Eds.), *Current controversies on family violence* (pp. 7–30). Newbury Park, CA: Sage Publications. Copyright, 1993. Reprinted by permission of Sage Publications, Inc.

Couple Characteristics

The way spouses or partners think about each other also plays a role in their relationship. As would be predicted, people who view problems in their relationship as global, or generalizable to other situations, experience more dissatisfaction than those who view problems as isolated events (Bradbury & Fincham, 1990).

Some people make "relationship-enhancing" attributions about their marriage, while others make "distress-maintaining" attributions (Holtzworth-Munroe & Jacobson, 1985). Relationship-enhancing beliefs attribute negative behaviors by a partner to external factors not under the control of the partner or to the partner's temporary or unintended characteristics. In contrast, distress-maintaining attributions contend that the partner's personality is responsible for the action, or that the action is due to some intended and stable characteristic of the partner. As expected, spouses involved in distressed marriages are more likely to make distress-maintaining attributions, while nondistressed spouses are more likely to make attributions that enhance the relationship. Furthermore, when couples are taught to avoid "blaming attributions" and to accept their partners' positive efforts, they report improved marital satisfaction (Margolin & Weiss, 1978).

Incompatibility within the couple also sets the stage for marital problems. Women who practice their religion more than their partner are especially vulnerable to violence (Hotaling & Sugarman, 1986). And, consistent with the notion that the marital subsystem interrelates with other subsystems, Edleson et al. (1991) report that conflict over child rearing styles and responsibilities significantly relates to physical violence between spouses.

Inequality

One of the most interesting aspects of incompatibility in partner violence pertains to discrepancies in the occupational or economic attainments of men and women. When women's occupational achievements are either relatively low or relatively high compared to their husband's, the risk of violence increases (Hornung, McCullough, & Sugimoto, 1981). Similarly, Yllo (1983) compared states where the status of women across economic, educational, political, and legal realms was judged low, moderate, or high relative to men. Severe wife abuse occurred in states where women's status was either low or high (see Figure 4.2). Yllo (1983) suggests that greater violence against women may be used in low status states to keep women

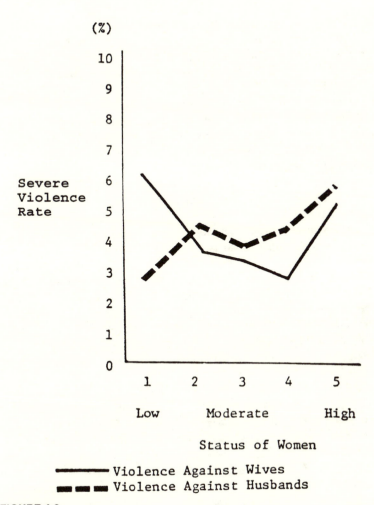

(%)

Severe
Violence
Rate

Status of Women

━━━━━ Violence Against Wives
■ ■ ■ Violence Against Husbands

FIGURE 4.2
Violence against wives and violence against husbands by the status of women

Source: Yllo, K. (1983). Sexual equality and violence against wives in American states. *Journal of Comparative Family Studies, 14,* p. 77. Copyright 1983. Journal of Comparative Family Studies, Department of Sociology, University of Calgary, Calgary, Alberta T2N 1N4, Canada. Reprinted by permission.

''in their place''; the lack of options for women then assures that this strategy works. In high status states men may respond with violence to the threat of enhanced power for women in general or to the threat that may stem from their own wife's changing social circumstances.

A different relationship between women's status and violence occurs when we examine abuse of husbands. Here the likelihood of severe husband abuse increased as the indices of women's status increased. Thus, when women hold positions of high power, they may be more likely to use violence, just as men do, to reinforce their dominance. It is also possible that in high status states women may be more conscious of their rights and the privileges granted to other women. If they are not then accorded high status within the family, conflict and abuse may emerge (see Coleman & Straus, 1986). Yllo (1983) warns us that the pattern may also reflect women's enhanced ability to retaliate against the violence of a husband in high status states. Consequently, we would expect to see more mutual violence in these places.

The relationship between spouse abuse and the distribution of power in the household also is apparent from the 1976 nationwide interview study conducted by Straus et al. (1980). The interviewers tallied responses to questions about who in the household had the final say in such matters as buying a car, having a child, and the food budget and compared the answers to rates of spouse abuse in the home (see Figure 4.3). Democratic households where men and women shared power had the least violence, and husband-dominant households had the most, with wife-dominant households also showing increases in violence.

This cross-sectional view of the relation between power and violence does not permit us to sort out whether the power differential contributed to the abuse or was a consequence of it (see Box 4.2), but the finding that both spouses were more likely to be beaten when one of them held more decision-making power suggests that violence may be a tactic used by both the powerful and the powerless. Frieze and McHugh (1992) concur with this view. They found that wives who are beaten by their husbands use a more diverse array of strategies in attempts to influence their spouses than do wives who are not beaten, including verbal and physical aggression.

Straus et al. (1980) suggest that inequality "may initiate a chain reaction of power confrontations running throughout the family" (p. 193). In support of this idea, Straus et al. found that children also were slightly more likely to be abused in families where power was distributed unequally between the spouses.

Cross-cultural work reiterates the importance of power differentials in predicting violence. Levinson's (1989) study of small-scale societies reveals that in cultures where men control the couple's wealth and property, violence against wives is more likely. However,

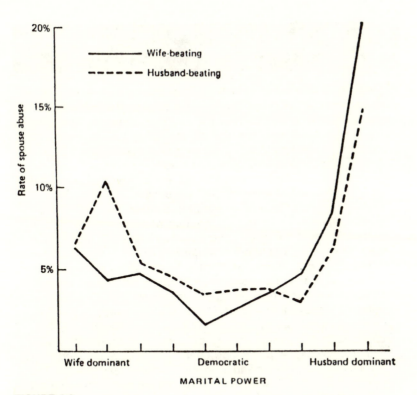

FIGURE 4.3

Marital violence by marital power

Source: Straus, M. A., Gelles, R. J., & Steinmetz, S. K. (1980). *Behind closed doors: Violence in the American family* (p. 194). New York: Anchor/Doubleday. Reprinted by permission.

this relationship is mediated by men's decision-making authority in the household and the difficulty of divorce. When men make most of the household decisions and women have little ability to escape marriage through divorce, economic inequality most strongly predicts the wife's victimization.

Cross-cultural studies have also found that women who work outside the home are less likely to be victims of aggression than those whose work is restricted to the home setting (cf. Levinson, 1989). This may be partly attributable to the fact that

> women who stay at home contribute less to family subsistence and are consequently valued less than women who work outside the home. In any wife-beating incident there is always a risk to the husband that he

Most of the research on family violence uses cross-sectional designs. That is, the researcher obtains data from a sample of individuals at one point in time. This method informs us about the relationships among a set of static variables, such as gender or educational background and experience with violence, but does not permit conclusions about the causes of violence or its effects. For example, through cross-sectional research we may learn that people who value traditional sex-role behaviors are more likely to tolerate violence against family members (e.g., Greenblat, 1985). While this finding can generate numerous intriguing hypotheses about the relationship between these two factors, the data do not speak to whether traditional values may encourage tolerance of aggression, or whether tolerance for aggression is a cause of sex-role behaviors, or indeed whether both sex-role traditionalism and tolerance for aggression are a function of some third factor that was not identified in the study.

An improvement over cross-sectional, retrospective, and archival research designs is the prospective longitudinal study, which follows a sample of individuals over time, measuring their involvement in violence and assessing factors that preceded, occurred concurrently with, and were consequent to the violent events. This research design provides information about the process through which violent and nonviolent relationships unfold, and provides opportunities to study the causes and effects of violence in families. This design is expensive because large numbers of people must be tracked. Thus, it is employed rarely, even when the behavior under investigation is more common and less sensitive than family violence (e.g., divorce).

will anger his wife to the point that she leaves him. This is more costly to men whose wives contribute directly to subsistence. (Levinson, 1989, p. 57)

The same kind of thinking may account for at least part of Yllo's (1983) findings about the incidence of husband abuse in states where women in general have high status. Women who can afford to live apart from their husbands due to higher wages and a better education may not be inhibited by the thought that an abused husband will leave.

Relationship to Other Family Subsystems

Earlier we discussed the strong links between parent-child and spousal relations, especially in families where parents are undergoing a divorce or are involved in violence. A review by Easterbrooks and Emde (1988) suggests that, while children may influence marital relations and even spark severe disagreements between spouses, most evidence points to the causal direction going the other way. That is, lousy marriage partners do not make the best parents. Easterbrooks and Emde note that marital harmony leads to positive emotions, which influence the parents' views of the child and their parenting behaviors. Spouses who are unhappy with each other, in contrast, may feel emotionally drained and will not have the energy or enthusiasm with which to tackle parenting tasks.

Sibling Relations

Siblings have positive and negative effects on each other. Children with younger siblings assume caretaking responsibilities and thus practice the roles they will adopt as parents (Bryant, 1989); in turn, older children's caretaking provides younger children with knowledge of the values, rules, and challenges of life in their society (Ervin-Tripp, 1989). Younger siblings greatly admire their older brothers and sisters (Buhrmester & Furman, 1990). Older siblings do not return the compliment; they report less admiration of younger siblings and more quarreling and antagonism towards them. But older siblings are more nurturant and are perceived to be so by their younger siblings (Buhrmester & Furman, 1990).

Sibling relations are often characterized by conflict and, not infrequently, by violence. As we know from Chapter 1, sibling relations may be the most volatile of any family relations. However, some people believe that sibling conflict contributes positively to children's social development. Bank and Kahn (1982) suggest that conflicts with siblings provide a social laboratory through which children learn how to resolve conflicts. They also suggest that conflicts may promote feelings of loyalty between siblings and provide an acceptable target for aggressive urges. Children's conflicts also teach them about the similarities and differences among people and help children to define their own individuality (Hartup & Laursen, 1993).

Antagonism between siblings decreases as children get older and is more common between siblings close in age (Buhrmester & Furman, 1990). Same-sex siblings tend to experience more conflicts than opposite-sex siblings (Minnett, Vandell, & Santrock, 1983), but they may also feel closer and have warmer relations overall (Furman & Buhrmester, 1985). While boys may inflict more injury upon siblings than girls, girls employ a wide range of aggressive behaviors towards siblings and mild acts of aggression may be perpetrated equally often by males and females (Felson, 1983; Goodwin & Roscoe, 1990). Children who exhibit little or at least "normal" levels of aggression tend to have conflicts of relatively short duration, while truly aggressive siblings engage in prolonged fights (Loeber & Tengs, 1986; Patterson, 1984).

Underlying all sibling relationships, except between twins, is an asymmetry of power (Furman & Buhrmester, 1985; Sutton-Smith & Rosenberg, 1968). As with other family relationships, power differences manifest themselves in negative ways, such as when older children dominate and boss their younger siblings. However, power differences are associated with positive interactions as well, such as when the older sibling nurtures the younger child. Also, younger siblings typically create ways to reduce the negative effects of the power imbalance. They are much more likely to appeal to an adult to resolve conflicts, or at least to threaten to do so, than their older sibling (Sutton-Smith & Rosenberg, 1968).

Parents strongly influence sibling relations. Children notice the manner in which parents interact with their siblings in comparison to themselves (Dunn, 1992). Rivalry is an important dimension of sibling relations (Furman & Buhrmester, 1985) and children are attentive to perceived or actual parental partiality.

Parental involvement in their children's conflicts often complicates sibling relationships. Interviews with college students who recollected their relations with siblings revealed that mothers who intervene in sibling conflicts tend to have children who fight more (Felson, 1983). The increased fighting may stem from younger siblings' attempts to win the conflict by appealing for parental mediation or support. When parents rarely intervene, younger siblings are more likely to comply with the older sibling's wishes and overt conflicts may be less frequent.

Research has also shown that parents of aggressive children tend to ignore many of the deviant behaviors of their offspring, attending only to extreme problems (Bank & Kahn, 1982; Patterson, 1984). When the parents do discipline the aggressive child, their punishment tends to be ineffective for the severe problems shown (Patterson, 1984).

Children understand when aggression will produce negative consequences, such as punishment by parents, and this information shapes conflict situations. Research on *peer* conflict shows that boys expect to incur less parental disapproval and to feel less guilt from aggressive activities than do girls (Perry, Perry, & Weiss, 1989). Boys also value the potential positive consequences of aggression (e.g., achieving control) more than girls do and are less concerned with the potential negative consequences (e.g., retaliation, victim suffering; Boldizar, Perry, & Perry, 1989). These differences in expectations and values may explain boys' greater involvement in aggression against peers. However, as shown in Table 1.2, fewer behavioral differences between boys and girls emerge in sibling conflicts (Goodwin & Roscoe, 1990). Correspondingly, boys and girls perceive similar consequences for aggression against siblings (Herzberger & Hall, 1993a, 1993b).

In Chapter 1 we learned that violence often manifests itself within more than one subsystem within the family. This may be especially true when sibling violence is considered. In their 1975 national survey Hotaling and Straus (1989) found that 37 percent of children from nonassaultive families severely abused a sibling. But when both spouse abuse and child abuse were present in the family, 100 percent of the children assaulted a sibling.

Adult Child-Elderly Parent Relations

Much of the writing on abuse of the elderly has focused upon the stresses that stem from assuming new responsibilities for a dependent, elderly family member (e.g., Gelles & Cornell, 1985; Pagelow, 1989). These writers point to the strain caused when a person must now take care of an elderly parent or relative, just at a time when he or (more typically) she has been relieved of child rearing responsibilities and might be expected to turn attention to personal needs and goals. Caring for an elderly relative might also mean reallocation of resources and space within a household, which might entail further hardships, including lessened privacy. Most families that assume responsibility for helping an elderly relative, however, do so without becoming violent. Thus, recent research has attempted to discover the factors associated with violent versus nonviolent caretaking.

Victims of abuse are likely to be women and members of the older generation of elderly, above 70 (Pagelow, 1989; Wolfe & Pillemer, 1989). Women are also more likely to live to this age; so their overrepresentation as victims may be a function more of their availability than any other characteristic. The majority of cases of elderly abuse also are found among the middle class (Pagelow, 1989). Middle-class elderly perhaps lack both the financial resources of wealthier people to secure good live-in help and the access to social services available to the poor.

Researchers have found that abuse of the elderly takes many different forms and appears to stem from different family circumstances (Wolf & Pillemer, 1989). For example, the dependent, needy elderly person described in the above scenario is more likely to be subject to neglect than to suffer physical abuse (Wolf & Pillemer, 1989). The physically abused elderly are no more physically impaired than the nonabused elderly (Wolf & Pillemer, 1989). They do tend to have fewer contacts with friends and relatives and to be less satisfied with their contacts than nonabused elderly (Wolf & Pillemer, 1989). This provides a situation in which abuse may be more difficult to detect, but sometimes the victim is too embarrassed to have people visit and actually enhances the degree of isolation.

Some people suggest that the focus of attention should be on the perpetrator, not the victim, if we want to understand abuse of the elderly. While we tend to think about an elderly relative who moves into the home as taking resources from the rest of the family, Wolf and Pillemer's (1989) research suggests that the opposite may be closer to the truth. The abuser often depends financially on the victim and, if not already living with the elderly person, might move in to be closer to the source of support. Furthermore, a high proportion of violent perpetrators are found to be suffering from a personal crisis, such as alcoholism (Pierce & Trotta, 1986) or from various forms of mental illness (Tomita, 1990; Wolf & Pillemer, 1989).

It has also been suggested that the earlier ill treatment of his or her own child may redound to the detriment of the elderly parent. While some studies have found supportive evidence for this (Pierce & Trotta, 1986), others have not (Wolf & Pillemer, 1989).

Family System and Social Environment Influences

Surrounding the parent-child, spousal, sibling, and adult-child elderly subsystems are a wealth of factors that may detract from good relationships or buffer emerging problems. Perhaps the most studied environmental contributor to family violence is stress, especially that due to economic and social problems.

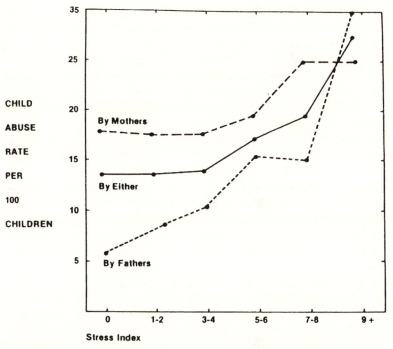

FIGURE 4.4
Stress and child abuse

Source: Straus, M. A., & Kantor, G. K. (1987). Stress and child abuse. In R. E. Helfer & R. S. Kempe (Eds.), *The battered child* (4th Ed., p. 51). Chicago: University of Chicago. © 1987 by the University of Chicago. Reprinted by permission of the University of Chicago.

Economic and Social Stressors

Unemployment, poverty, and other poor living conditions are known to undermine the quality of parenting. For example, a longitudinal study of Californians growing up during the 1930s revealed that economic hardship led fathers to display greater rejection of their daughters, particularly daughters judged to be unattractive (Elder, Nguyen, & Caspi, 1985). In this study economic circumstances did not affect mothers' behavior. However, a study (Garbarino, 1976a) of child abuse rates in New York State found that the factors predicting stress upon mothers (e.g., percentage of working women with dependent children, median income in single-parent, female-headed households) were those most predictive of the incidence of child abuse (see also Burgess, 1994).

Straus and Kantor (1987) studied the cumulative effect of a variety of stressors in a nationwide sample of adults. They assessed the adults' experience with events such as employment, financial, or health problems and their use of various conflict tactics in interactions with children. Figure 4.4 demonstrates that, as the number of stressors experienced during the previous year increased, the rate of child abuse increased as well, particularly among fathers. However, in a reminder that stress is not the whole explanation for violence, the authors note that many people escaped from the pressure and did not violate others. Even among the extremely stressed individuals, the child abuse rate was lower than 40 per 100 children.

As we have seen, economic stress has been implicated in cases of abuse against the elderly (Wolf & Pillemer, 1989) and may influence relationships between adult partners as well. As Hotaling and Sugarman's (1986) review demonstrates, higher family income and higher social class decrease the risk of spouse abuse, and men who are unemployed or only partially employed are substantially more likely to beat their wives than are fully employed husbands (e.g., Gelles & Cornell, 1985).

Lack of Social Support

One of the factors that mediates the relationship between stress and family violence is social support, which is available through a variety of sources. Parents in Straus and Kantor's (1987) study, for example, who attended religious services regularly and who were involved in a number of social or civic organizations had child abuse rates about half those of other parents. Numerous studies have shown similar beneficial effects of social support on parental levels of depression, parental punitiveness, and attentiveness to children's needs (cf. Belsky, 1980; Belsky & Vondra, 1989). And one of the primary goals of self-help organizations, such as Parents Anonymous or battering men's groups, is to provide emotional support for members who seek alternatives to violent lives (Jennings, 1987; Katz, 1981).

Rutter (1988) suggests a variety of mechanisms through which social support may enhance social interactions of family members. He asserts, for example, that a supportive marriage partner may enable a spouse to feel more comfortable when faced with new situations, just as young children explore their environment more when they have formed an appropriate emotional attachment to a parent (Bowlby, 1969). Social support may be important by itself, or it may buffer the stress derived from other aspects of the environment

(Rutter, 1988). Knowing that someone else understands the problems that a parent endures may reduce the anxiety the parent experiences.

Of course, social support is not always welcome or helpful. While many studies have shown a positive relationship between good intra-family relations and a strong network of friends and family (cf. Belsky & Vondra, 1989), other research shows that inappropriate "support" may be counterproductive. As Levinson (1989) states,

> I think the problem here is a misunderstanding of what life is often like in extended families. Rather than being free and easy with little stress and much mutual support, extended-family life can be quite stressful. (p. 55)

Straus and Kantor's (1987) research revealed that parents with many relatives within an hour's drive were much more likely to maltreat their children. As the authors suggest, social networks may elicit antisocial tendencies if they are not emotionally supportive, if they draw upon the resources of parents rather than contribute to the resources, or, as might be the case with parents, if they encourage harsh discipline of children.

In a similar vein, many writers (Bowker, 1983; Dobash & Dobash, 1979; Fagan, 1989) have cautioned against undue optimism about efforts to change men who batter their partners. In societies or subcultures where domination of women by violence is acceptable or at least "understood," women who seek relief from friends and relatives may be surprised at the lack of support they receive. Furthermore, efforts to change the batterers will be hampered if the men remain in an environment that promotes violence.

Most studies, however, point to isolation from social networks as one of the key characteristics of abusive households (O'Leary, 1993; Walker, 1984). Women living with abusive partners report getting together with neighbors about half as frequently as women living with nonabusive partners (Walker, 1984). The former group report moving about three times as often as well (6.2 times during the relationship versus 2.2 times for nonbattered women). Those responsible for the abuse might promote isolation of the family as a means of keeping the violence a secret, but it may also be that a lack of social networks contributes to the abuse. And, as Walker (1979) has shown, some victims may withdraw from social situations out of embarrassment or in an effort to minimize conflicts with a partner.

> Women who have great difficulty in dealing with this kind of social battering tend to isolate themselves further. Many of them report that the tension surrounding the manipulative behavior spoils the pleasure

they might have gotten in attending a party. They do not go out as frequently as they would like, and slowly cut themselves off from others. They fear accusations of jealousy that result from social events. They begin to turn down all invitations, and eventually the invitations stop coming. (Walker, 1979, p. 172)

Societal Norms

We can also look to the larger society, or the *macrosystem,* for risk factors that contribute to violence in families (e.g., Dobash & Dobash, 1979). Levinson (1989) suggests several models describing the manner in which culture influences violent family life. Similar to Dobash and Dobash (1979), Levinson first suggests that societal norms that value domination of men over women and adults over children foster an ethos that promotes coercion to achieve domination. This model he calls the *cultural consistency* model. The *cultural spillover* model suggests that whenever society approves the use of aggression to achieve goals (e.g., to enforce orders in cities or in schools), it risks spillover of the use of aggression in family settings where aggression is not normally approved. The *culture pattern* model suggests that cultures vary in the degree of violence manifested, and that in violent cultures violence is generalized across settings and relationships.

Levinson's (1989) cross-cultural analysis of ninety small-scale societies around the globe provides partial support for each model. Some societies are more generally violent than others. Spouse and child abuse are unrelated to patterns of warfare between communities, but they relate to patterns of aggression towards nonfamily members in the same community. Harsh punishment of criminals, painful female initiation ceremonies, and fighting among women and among men characterize societies where wife beating is prominent. Harsh punishment of criminals and painful female initiation ceremonies also characterize societies using physical child punishment.

Concluding Remarks

This chapter provided an overview of the forces that influence family life. We saw that families can be divided into subsystems, and that each subsystem affects and, in turn, is affected by other subsystems within the family. Thus, to understand family violence we not only have to examine the characteristics of the perpetrator and victim, but examine as well relationships between other family members.

Environmental and cultural forces external to the family also strongly influence family relationships. Such factors as stress, poverty, inequality, and social support alter rates of victimization. As this shows, family violence may be due to a multiplicity of factors that affect various aspects of family interaction.

This chapter gave us a static view of healthy and unhealthy family life. In the next few chapters we will explore how families attain their violent or nonviolent state. In doing so, we will study how violent behavior is nurtured by the environment in which we live and how family members' actions may contribute to our learning to be aggressive. We will investigate especially how one's experience as a child in the family influences one's subsequent family relationships. We will also study how our nature as biological beings contributes to violence. The next chapter, though, prepares you to think about the causes of aggression, and urges caution about concluding that violence in the family is caused by any one factor.

5

Theories of Aggression

CHAPTER OBJECTIVES

Thinking about the Causes of Violence
An Illustration from the Cyclical Hypothesis Literature
Concluding Remarks

> I try to control myself, but eventually my temper just builds up and I get into a rage and lash out at my wife. Sometimes I hurt her. This is exactly what my parents did to each other.

> My neighbor beats her son so badly that I sometimes hear the child screaming from our yard. One time she told me that her parents beat her too, and she has just carried on the tradition.

> Listen, I know it's not right to hit my little brother. But I see my parents fighting this way, and they are older and should know better.

> It is little wonder that he is violent; he inherited these tendencies from his father.

> She must be sick. One moment she's calm and then all of a sudden she lashes out. Maybe she's on drugs or something.

> You know, human beings, like other animals need to be aggressive for their own survival.

Thinking about the Causes of Violence

If you talk with people about why violence occurs in families, you might hear explanations such as these. It is natural for human beings to try to understand events and, in doing so, they attend to well-remembered events or some other salient cue to explain the behavior they observe.

There are several problems in settling upon an explanation for behavior in this casual way, however. First, it is doubtful that any one factor sufficiently accounts for the existence of family violence. As we saw in the last chapter, when aggression occurs in the family often a complicated, interrelated set of family relationships and circumstances will be present as well. Attributing the violence to one cause, then, is inevitably risky. Furthermore, we also learned that many people who are violence-free lead lives filled with multiple sources of stress known to be associated with aggression. Others manifest few or none of the known correlates of aggression; yet they are aggressive towards a family member. These results should warn us that some causes of violence (and some inhibitors) may be invisible to a casual observer.

Second, the causes of violence operate *probabilistically.* We can identify factors or constellations of factors that increase or decrease the chances of violence, but we cannot say with certainty that any given person who possesses the characteristics will be violent. Social psychologists, utilizing what they know about the causes of violence, can predict which groups of people are more likely to be aggressive than other groups, but they cannot identify the specific individuals within the group who will act in accordance with the prediction and those for whom the prediction is inaccurate (see Box 5.1).

Third, people usually do not conduct a thorough search for the causes of events (Fiske & Taylor, 1991). For example, a woman who claims to have learned her violent parenting at her mother's knee (or, more accurately, from her hand) does not objectively sift through the evidence in favor of and against each plausible explanation. Instead, she latches onto a reasonable explanation for her behavior and often is satisfied. Less salient, but perhaps equally plausible explanations, will be overlooked in this process.

An Illustration from the Cyclical Hypothesis Literature

An example from literature on the *cyclical hypothesis of abuse* will further describe problems in explaining behavior. One of the most pervasive beliefs about family violence is that we pass on to our children the conflict tactics, discipline techniques, and styles of family interaction that we learned from our own parents. Families engaged

One study that illustrates the difficulty of predicting violent be-havior was conducted by Lidz, Mulvey, and Gardner (1993), who studied psychiatric patients entering the emergency department of a hospital. Attending clinicians were asked to judge the like-lihood that the patient would commit a violent act in the next six months. Follow-up interviews were then conducted with the pa-tient and someone else who knew the patient well. Each patient who was predicted to commit an act of violence was paired with a patient of the same sex, race, and admission status (admitted to the hospital or not), and roughly the same age, but who was predicted not to be violent. The patients' involvement in violence over the next six months was then monitored. The two groups were not matched on diagnosis (for example, the group predicted to be violent had more substance abuse problems), nor were they matched on violent history. The "predicted" group had more than twice the history of violence as the comparision group.

During the six-month follow-up period, 36 percent of the com-parison group and 53 percent of the predicted group was re-ported to have been violent. The researchers calculated the *sensitivity* and the *specificity* of the clinician's predictions (see Box Table 5.A). Sensitivity refers to the percentage of violent

BOX TABLE 5.A Occurrence of Violent Incidents for Predicted and Comparison Patients: Counts of Matched Pairs

Was Comparison Patient Violent?	Was Predicted Patient Violent?		
	No	Yes	Total (%)
No	111	117	228 (63.9)**
Yes	56	73	129 (36.1)
Total (%)	167 (46.8)	190 (53.2)*	357 (100.0)

*The positive predictive value of clinical judgments of violence.
**The negative predictive value of clinical judgments that patients will not be violent.

Source: Lidz, C. W., Mulvey, E. P., & Gardner, W. (1993). The accuracy of predictions of violence to others. *JAMA, 269*, p. 1009. Copyright 1993, American Medical Association. Reprinted by permission.

(continued on next page)

BOX 5.1
(Continued)

people who were accurately identified (the ratio of *true positives*—those predicted to be violent who were violent, to the total number of violent people, summing both true positives and false negatives). The clinicians' sensitivity index was 60 percent, indicating a significant improvement in accuracy over a prediction based upon chance. Specificity refers to the percentage of nonviolent people who were accurately identified (the ratio of *true negatives*—those predicted to be nonviolent who were nonviolent, to the total number of nonviolent people, summing both true negatives and false positives). The clinicians' specificity index was 58 percent, also a significant improvement over chance.

The researchers found that the accuracy of clinicians' predictions was not affected by the age or race of the patient, but was substantially affected by the patient's gender. As Box Table 5.B shows, clinicians greatly underestimated women's propensity for violence, and they predicted both violence and nonviolence with no more accuracy than had they flipped a coin to render a

BOX TABLE 5.B Occurrence of Violent Incidents for Predicted and Comparison Patients: Gender Differences

Gender	Was Comparison Patient Violent?	Was Predicted Patient Violent?		Total (%)
		No	Yes	
Women	No	39	40	79 (55.2)**
	Yes	27	37	64 (44.8)
	Total (%)	66 (46.2)	77 (53.8)*	143 (100.0)
Men	No	72	77	149 (69.6)**
	Yes	29	36	65 (30.4)
	Total (%)	101 (47.2)	113 (52.8)*	214 (100.0)

*The positive predictive values of clinical judgments of violence in each gender.
**The negative predictive values of clinical judgments that patients will not be violent.

Source: Lidz, C. W., Mulvey, E. P., & Gardner, W. (1993). The accuracy of predictions of violence to others. *JAMA, 269,* p. 1010. Copyright 1993, American Medical Association. Reprinted by permission.

judgment. The sensitivity and specificity indices involving male patients, however, were 63 and 60 percent, respectively, and revealed an accuracy rate significantly above what would be expected by chance.

An important question to ask is whether the clinicians' judgments offer any improvement over a prediction based solely upon knowledge of the violent history of the patient. The answer is mixed. Using just history of violence to predict future behavior produces a higher sensitivity index (69 percent), but the specificity index is lower (48 percent).

This study tells us that, if you want to ensure that you identify people who will be violent, you would be better off making a judgment just from knowing their history of violence than by using other clues derived from clinicians' interviews. But, if you want to ensure that you do not falsely predict violence, you should rely upon more evidence than just the person's history. The study also demonstrates that psychiatrists and other clinicians may underestimate women's potential for violent acts and may use improper clues for predicting aggression among women.

This study reveals more accuracy in the clinical judgment process than most previous investigations. But the authors suggest that, even considering the better than chance accuracy for predictions of men, clinicians made a substantial proportion of errors and that the use of clinical judgment to predict violence is still a matter for debate.

in violent activities are said to perpetuate a cycle of violence by inculcating violent norms within each succeeding generation.

Despite the attention this belief has received, until quite recently there has been little good research on this issue and the research brings mixed results (Herzberger, 1990; Kaufman & Zigler, 1989; Widom, 1989a). Let us look at some of the findings. The first controlled study of the cyclical hypothesis was done by Straus, Gelles, and Steinmetz (1980), who surveyed a random sample of adults in the United States. In a summary of their findings Straus (1979a) reports that those who have been physically punished twice or more a year as teens were more likely than those who were physically punished less often to have abused their own children. Table 5.1 shows their findings,

TABLE 5.1 Child Abuse Rates of a National Sample of Adults Who Had or Had Not Experienced Physical Punishment as a Teenager

Physical Punishment		Abuse Own Child	
		No	*Yes*
By mother	No	88.2	11.8
	Yes	81.5	18.5
By father	No	86.8	13.2
	Yes	83.3	16.7

Source: Adapted from Straus, M. A. (1979a). Family patterns and child abuse in a nationally representative American sample. *Child Abuse and Neglect, 3,* p. 220. Copyright 1979, with kind permission from Pergamon Press, Ltd., Headington Hill Hall, Oxford OX3 OBW, UK.

separated for those who experienced physical punishment by a mother versus a father. Those punished by mothers were almost 60 percent more likely to abuse their own children. Fathers' physical punishment less strongly related to child abuse in the next generation.

Let us think about what these statistics signify. If you interpret these data the way most people do, you will focus on the increased percentage of abuse cases among those who were physically punished as a teenager and you will conclude (perhaps accurately) that such treatment as a teenager substantially increases the likelihood of being an adult abuser. Thus, you will find that the data offer compelling support for the cyclical hypothesis.

Another way to look at the results (also perhaps accurately) suggests that the cyclical hypothesis is largely incorrect. After all, over 80 percent of the adults who experienced physical punishment as a teenager did not grow up to abuse their own children.

Later studies have confirmed that some people mimic their parents' disciplinary styles, but as Straus et al. demonstrated, the cycle is not as pervasive as many believe. Depending upon the methodology employed, researchers find that from 18 to 70 percent of abusive parents experienced abuse (Kaufman & Zigler, 1989). Studies of high-risk samples, such as known abusers, discover a higher incidence of abuse history (e.g., Egeland, Jacobvitz, & Papatola, 1987) than studies using surveys of a randomly drawn sample (e.g., Straus, Gelles, & Steinmetz, 1980). And studies that broadly define abuse or measure "the potential to abuse" (e.g., Milner, Robertson, & Rogers,

1990) also find more support for the cyclical hypothesis. Researchers claim that the results in general accord with the notion that "aggressive parenting furnishes children with a script for the parent role that they enact with their own children" (Simons, Whitbeck, Conger, & Chyi-In, 1991, p. 169).

The literature on spouse abuse also consistently demonstrates the cyclical phenomenon (Hotaling & Sugarman, 1986). Again, however, the effect is weak (O'Leary, 1993), especially among samples not drawn from people in therapy (e.g., Caesar, 1988). One of the studies (Kalmuss, 1984), using a nationally-representative sample of married or cohabiting adults, found that when neither spousal nor parent-child hitting was present in the adult's childhood history, the probability of using severe violence against a partner was low. In this case, only 1 percent of the men and 2 percent of the women were likely to hit their partners. But, if the interviewees reported violence in their childhood history, the likelihood of violence noted in their current lives increased. Then, 6 percent of men and 8 percent of women hit their partners.

We conclude from this literature that adults sometimes display the violence that they observed or experienced during childhood. However, latching onto the conclusion that we engage in the behavior that is passed to us by our parents is too simplistic (Herzberger, 1983; Kaufman & Zigler, 1989). The reviewed studies demonstrate that more than just this obvious factor must be responsible for the presence or absence of violence; otherwise, why is the effect generally restricted to such a small proportion of the people who have childhood histories involving abuse? And, how would we account for the people who spontaneously seem to engage in abuse in the absence of an abusive history?

Additionally, just because a person repeats violence that he or she observed or experienced as a youth does not mean that the violence was "taught" or "learned" in the sense that we normally use these words. Observing the parent's action may even be irrelevant to a person's own violence. Instead, the similarities between a parent and child may stem from being exposed to common cultural norms originating outside the family, or from the parent passing along his or her aggressive tendencies through genetic inheritance (Rowe, 1994). It is hard to put aside such a readily available, salient explanation for violence as "learning from one's parents," but the findings are consistent with other explanations as well. These explanations tend to be less obvious, and neither laypeople nor researchers have been diligent about ruling out such explanations before rendering judgments about the causes of family violence.

There is one final way in which this literature demonstrates problems of causal thinking about violence. Because it is widely believed that early parent-child interactions predict future violence, some experts have suggested that we use information about a person's history to distinguish people who might have a proclivity toward abuse from those who do not (e.g., Milner et al., 1990). Such information would then be used to identify people who would be appropriate candidates for preventive intervention programs such as parent education and other supportive services.

Just as efforts to predict violence among psychiatric patients have been criticized (see Box 5.1), efforts to prevent child abuse through identification of "potential abusers" are widely rejected (Albee, 1980). Critics fear that more people will be identified and labeled than will ever commit assault against a child. While some people may assert that this is a drawback that we must live with in our efforts to save children, others warn that applying the label "potential abuser" may stigmatize the parent, enhance stress and anxiety, and even create a self-fulfilling prophecy that increases, rather than decreases, the risk of abuse. People do not always act in accordance with how we expect them to act or in accordance with an applied label (Hilton & Darley, 1985), but they often do, particularly when they are unsure about whether the label is incorrect (Swann & Ely, 1984). Unfortunately, given the widespread belief that people who have been abused are likely to be abusers themselves, many victims worry that they will ultimately fulfill this prophecy.

Let me give you an example. In 1979, two of my colleagues and I delivered a paper in which we summarized the lack of support for the cyclical hypothesis and criticized its wholesale acceptance by the professional community (Potts, Herzberger, & Holland, 1979). Portions of the paper were soon published in newspapers and read on radio stations around the country, and shortly afterward, parents sent in letters, thanking us for providing them with hope that they could be good parents, even though they had been abused. They were thrilled that someone thought that they could conquer their past and were not closet abusers.

Exaggerated public beliefs about the causes of violence might make these parents ripe candidates for confirming the expectations placed upon them by the label "potential abuser."

Concluding Remarks

The cyclical hypothesis has intrigued researchers for decades and the myth of a pervasive cyclical pattern has tainted the thinking of lay-people for just as long. It fits with our beliefs that parents are the primary socialization force for children and that they instill in children traditions that are passed from generation to generation. Furthermore, the cyclical hypothesis fits memories of parental behaviors that we now see in ourselves. We may notice a mannerism that reminds us of our father, or we may see a connection between our quick temper and our mother's. While disciplining a child, it is common for parents to murmur, "When I was a child, I always swore I would never say or do this to my children. But, look at me now!"

The statistics presented in this chapter, however, should convince you that influence across generations is greatly exaggerated. While cross-generational violence occurs, it is even more likely that it will not occur. Some of the consistency across generations may be due to a child learning from a parent, but some of it may just as well have come from other sources.

The way we think about the cyclical pattern of abuse has important repercussions. Many researchers have commented on the undue influence of the cyclical hypothesis (cf. Gelles & Straus, 1988; Potts et al., 1979). And those of us who question its ability to account for the wealth of violent incidents are disturbed by the staunch belief in this causal factor.

This short chapter was designed to make readers cautious about thinking about causes and to recognize that any instance of violent behavior probably was caused by a wealth of contributing factors. In the next three chapters we will study influential theories of aggression and explore the extent to which the theories help us to understand violence in families.

In the next chapter we will investigate social and cognitive influences on family violence, and the factors that promote or inhibit the behavior we have adopted from our social environment. The following chapter will explore biological theories of aggression, covering genetic, hormonal, and temperamental contributions to violence. We will also discuss theories about the role of evolution in violence against family members. Finally, an upcoming chapter will address empathy and alcohol and drug use, which are thought to relate to family violence through both biological and social pathways.

6

Learning to Be Aggressive

CHAPTER OBJECTIVES

How Is Behavior Learned?
Is Family Violence Learned?
What Are the Mechanisms through Which Family Violence May Be Learned?
  A "Direct" Path to Aggression
  The Role of Alternative Disciplinary Methods
  Assertiveness and Problem-Solving Skills
  Social Cognitive Information Processing

  Cognitive Appraisal of Violence
  Emotional Support
Who Is Susceptible to Learned Aggression and Who Is Immune?
  Victimization versus Observation
  Gender of Parent and Child
  Age of Onset of Abusive Treatment
Concluding Remarks

There is no question that learning plays a role in violent behavior (Bandura, 1973). Decades of extensive research on aggression have demonstrated that people can learn to be violent and can learn to be nonviolent. In this chapter we will review social and cognitive mechanisms through which aggression is learned, and then study how these mechanisms are applied to understanding the development of violence within the family.

How Is Behavior Learned?

Learning occurs through a variety of mechanisms (Bandura, 1973). One mechanism is through rewards and punishments experienced following initial aggressive behaviors. Behavior increases if it is followed by positive consequences or by the removal of noxious consequences; conversely, behavior decreases if it is followed by punishment (Skinner, 1969). This form of learning is called *operant conditioning*. If children achieve desired goals by being aggressive with peers, for example, they learn that aggression is beneficial. In contrast, if children are shunned by peers and generally experience more punishment than reward following aggressive activity, then they will be prompted to learn more prosocial means of interaction.

What may be most disconcerting to those who hope to reduce aggression are findings that witnessing or participating in aggression may be self-reinforcing (cf. Blanchard & Blanchard, 1986). Studies of extremely violent prison inmates (Toch, 1969), as well as ordinary male college students (Sebastian, 1978), show that aggression against others leads to self-satisfaction and feelings of excitement. Thus, aggression sometimes brings its own reward.

Another form of learning, *classical conditioning*, takes place when a previously neutral stimulus is paired with a stimulus known to provoke a response and the neutral stimulus eventually provokes a similar response. The classic example of this form of learning is that of Pavlov's (1927/1960) dog. The dog learned to salivate in response to a bell because the bell's sound was quickly followed by the dog's food, which by itself caused salivation. The bell thus became a signal that the food was about to arrive. Classical conditioning is believed to account for emotional reactions to seemingly innocuous characteristics or events. Suppose, for example, you have been assaulted repeatedly during your childhood by members of a gang known as the "Stripes," named for their red and white jackets. When as an adult you meet a person wearing red and white stripes, you may take an immediate disliking to him or her. You may not even be aware of the association you have made between your childhood experiences and your current reaction.

Social learning theorists have shown that people need not directly experience rewards and punishments to learn how to act (Bandura, 1986). We learn vicariously from watching others' experiences, even from the experiences of people far removed, such as those on television. Viewing violent programs primes individuals to interpret ambiguous cues in violent ways (cf. Linz, Donnerstein, Bross, & Chapin,

1986), and repeated exposure to media violence provides a script that subsequently can be used as a guide to behavior during conflict situations. Phillips (1983) has graphically illustrated the copycat effect of media portrayals of suicide and assaults. He showed, for example, that immediately after heavyweight prize fights broadcast during the years from 1973 to 1978 the homicide rate in the United States increased substantially. And the more well-publicized the prize fight, the more homicides that occurred over the next few days.

Vicarious learning is enhanced through rewards and punishments experienced by a model (cf. Bandura, 1986). People are more likely to imitate the behaviors that earn others reward and avoid behaviors that bring others censure. As predicted by social learning theory, while unpunished violence (e.g., as might occur during a prizefight) increases the propensity of others to act aggressively, punished violence (e.g., execution of a prisoner) diminishes this propensity (Phillips & Hensley, 1984).

We may also imitate another's aggression because we want to develop the other's characteristics or want to be appreciated by the other. Models whom we respect or admire, such as parents, celebrities, and sports figures, are especially imitated. We believe that if we act like them, we can be like them. Because of their availability and their nurturing qualities (Yussen & Levy, 1975), family members also are prime sources of imitation.

Watching other people engaged in aggression, whether in person or through news reports, TV programs, or movies, also *disinhibits* us (Bandura, 1973; Liebert, Sprafkin, & Davidson, 1982). Repeated exposure to violence may lead us to believe that violence is normative and, therefore, acceptable behavior. It also desensitizes us to the consequences of aggression (cf. Donnerstein, Linz, & Penrod, 1987; Linz et al., 1986). We become more inured to commonly featured injuries and deaths, showing less and less physiological arousal and emotional distress.

Another route through which aggression may be spurred is through learning to interpret violence as a legitimate and appropriate response to provocations. We saw in Chapter 2 that attitudes toward violence sometimes relate to violent actions. People who feel that violence is not really inappropriate may be less inhibited from using violence in certain situations.

A recent study by Bebber (1994) illustrates this phenomenon. Bebber examined the rates of violent crime in the United States during the years following American military actions in the 1980s. Throughout this period American military personnel were sent to conflicts in Grenada (1983), Libya (1986), the Persian Gulf (1988), and Panama (1989). During the years following these conflicts, the rate of violent crime in the United States increased significantly. In comparison to the 32 percent increase in violent crime in each year immediately following an armed conflict, violent crime increased by 6 percent during the other six years of the decade. The changes in crime statistics were not associated with fluctuations in the economy, nor with the availability of drugs or guns, other factors thought to be associated with crime rates. Bebber's (1994) study does not link individual attitudes to participation in violent crime. But Bebber suggests that

> . . . (I)t is reasonable to conclude that acts of official violence during wartime, initiated by popular political leaders and widely sanctioned by the society at large, established a powerful exemplar for subsequent individual acts of murder, rape, and aggravated assault. (p. 115)

We also need to remember that human beings are not passive learners (Bandura, 1986). We select from among the learning experiences offered, add our own interpretations, and thereby alter the lesson learned.

> Self-directedness is exercised by wielding influence over the external environment as well as enlisting self-regulatory functions. . . . To be sure, self-regulatory functions are fashioned from, and occasionally supported by, external influences. Having some external origins and supports, however, does not refute the fact that the exercise of self-influence partly determines the course of one's behavior. (Bandura, 1986, p. 20)

We can turn to Bebber's (1994) study again for an example of this idea at a societal level. Bebber demonstrated that the largest increases in the rate of crime following armed conflict occurred in states whose citizenry strongly supported Reagan and Bush in the preceding national elections. Thus, the individual's predisposition to support or disagree with leaders moderates the effect of information gleaned from national policies.

The theoretical propositions that suggest that aggression is learned are therefore quite straightforward. However, efforts to study whether behaviors of one sort or another are learned are confounded by the fact that people are exposed to many different models throughout their lives and the various models are not always consistent in their teaching. Parents, siblings, peers, teachers, and the media all influence an individual's behavior and one person's influence will often conflict with another's. Furthermore, any given model may not always act consistently (cf. Bandura, 1986). One study (Grusec & Dix, 1986) showed, for example, that mothers offer assorted feedback to their children in play groups. Sometimes mothers reinforced prosocial activities through complimenting the child, but often the mothers ignored the child's behavior. Finally, learning signifies both the acquisition of new behavior and its performance (Bandura, 1973, 1986). Human beings acquire information about all sorts of aggressive acts that, unless motivated to do so, they would never perform.

For these reasons tracking the learning process is difficult. We should recognize that the person produced from the learned experiences will be an amalgam of a diverse array of teachers, whose messages have been mixed with the person's own perspectives, and that he or she may never manifest the learned behaviors. With these caveats in mind, let us turn to the question of whether family violence is learned.

Is Family Violence Learned?

The previous chapter provided much evidence that some people manifest violence in their current families that they observed or experienced in their family-of-origin. These results are consistent with the notion that family violence can be transmitted through learning from one family subsystem to another and from one generation to the next. However, most studies that demonstrate the cyclical pattern do not try to eliminate biological or other explanations for the behavior, and these explanations are often just as credible (Rowe, 1994). After all, the parents who are around to model aggressive actions have also passed along their genes to the offspring who observe the aggression. This means that attempts to study social influences are usually confounded by biological influences.

One way to eliminate this confounding is to randomly assign people to different learning experiences and then to examine whether different behaviors result. It is through many such studies that we feel confident about the role of learning in the development of aggression in general (Bandura, 1986). However, we cannot randomly assign wives to husbands and children to parents, nor can we deliberately expose certain people to violence from a relative. For these reasons we need to be cautious about concluding that the violence in the family is transmitted through learning that takes place in the home environment. In this chapter, though, we can demonstrate the extent to which the literature is consistent with the notion that family violence is learned and we can elucidate some of the mechanisms theorized to account for such learning.

What Are the Mechanisms through Which Family Violence May Be Learned?

A "Direct" Path to Aggression

As noted at the beginning of this chapter, learning transpires through many different processes. Simons et al. (1991) tested several of these processes on a sample of parents. The first process is termed a *direct* path. While Simons et al. do not specify the mechanisms through which the learning might transpire, they hypothesized that "harsh parenting might result in the person learning a set of aggressive disciplinary behaviors that are used in a reflexive, rather unthinking way" (p. 167). Learning through imitation or through rewards and punishments are examples of this direct path, although these mechanisms do not always occur in the absence of reflection.

The cycle of violence might also take an *indirect* path. For example, harsh parents may transmit to their offspring a parenting philosophy that favors harsh discipline or a hostile personality that fosters aggressive behavior. Finally and even more indirectly, children may "inherit the social class of their parents with its accompanying stressors and life-style" (p. 167), and it is these factors that produce the conditions under which violence may be elicited. According to the latter hypotheses, aggression is not directly learned, but is a by-product of other characteristics passed along by one's parents.

Simons and his colleagues (1991) tested these hypothesized paths using a sample of seventh-graders and their parents, all of whom were Caucasian and residing in rural areas. They found that both indirect and direct explanations received at least minimal support and that the social class explanation did not. Furthermore, after controlling for indirect paths, support was still found for the direct modeling approach to the cycle of violence. "Mothers' harsh parenting of sons and daughters and fathers' harsh parenting of sons were related to the parenting practices of the grandmother" (p. 168). In addition, fathers' harsh parenting of their daughters related, albeit less strongly, to the grandfathers' parenting style. Thus, despite other possible routes to aggression within the family, this study suggests that violent parenting is adopted directly by the next generation.

When Simon et al. (1991) talk about a direct path to aggression, they do not imply that the child perfectly mimics the behavior of the parent, such that, for example, a parent who used a belt to beat a child would produce a child who likewise uses a belt. In fact, it is aggressive *styles* of interaction that are adopted, not just specific behaviors.

One feature of learned behavior is that behavior learned in one context often generalizes to other contexts, especially those situations similar to the original (cf. Bandura, 1986). Stimuli that evoke the behavior can vary from the original stimulus as well, as we see in the case of Pavlov's dog (Pavlov, 1927/1960). Generalization was shown when different bell tones were played and still salivation recurred before food was presented.

Generalization of this type has been seen in cases of family violence. Children who have witnessed one parent beating the other are more likely to be violent towards their siblings and their parents (Hotaling & Straus, 1989). The majority of studies also show that abusive spouses and their victims are more likely to have a history of abuse by their parents (cf. Hotaling & Sugarman, 1986). Thus, witnesses and victims of family violence appear to generalize their learning about acceptable targets of violence across family members.

Children who are exposed to family violence are also more likely to aggress against nonfamily members. We have already seen examples of this in reviews of the 1985 National Resurvey data (see Table 1.5; cf. Hotaling & Straus, 1989). In another well-controlled investigation, Widom (1989b) found that young adults who had been physically abused or neglected were significantly more likely to have been arrested for a violent crime than youth in the control group. And adults who were abused as children, particularly men, have shown an increased propensity to aggress against nonfamily members (Malinosky-Rummell & Hansen, 1993).

People who are exposed to violence may also become self-destructive (Widom, 1989a). Green (1978) found that 41 percent of a sample of abused children in New York City revealed such self-destructive behaviors as biting, cutting, and burning oneself, or banging one's head against a wall. In contrast, 17 percent of a sample of neglected children and 7 percent of children from a control group manifested this type of behavior.

These studies suggest that violent methods of family interaction may be taught to other family members and that the methods will likely generalize to a variety of relationships and situations. It would be helpful to be able to draw a model of the specific conditions under which exposure to violence influences the various relationships the individual has. For example, are children who witness spouse abuse most likely to manifest violence in conflicts with their future spouse, whereas children who have been abused are most likely to become abusive parents? If so, then it would appear that the child associates violence with particular *relationships*. Another scenario is that the child best learns to associate violence with particular *targets*. In this case, children who have been abused may think of children as an appropriate target for violence and hence, as children, direct aggression toward peers and siblings and, as adults, toward their own children.

Unfortunately, we do not know the answers to these questions. Studies are rarely longitudinal; researchers do not follow individuals to assess their involvement in violence throughout a reasonable portion of their lifetime to sort out the patterns of influence. Furthermore, few researchers simultaneously study more than one or two types of violent family situations (e.g., spouse abuse and child abuse and sibling violence); thus they cannot distinguish among the separate and interconnected effects of each form.

We do know, however, that the more forms of violence to which children are exposed, the more likely they will manifest violence themselves either in their youth or in adulthood (Hotaling & Straus, 1989; Kalmuss, 1984). Yet, at best we are stuck with a vague conclusion that violence in the home begets violence in and out of the home, and the more violence in the first home, the more likely is violence in successive ones.

The Role of Alternative Disciplinary Methods

Some people have suggested that occasional and moderate physical aggression may neither harm children nor promote their aggressive behavior. Parke and Slaby's (1983) review of the literature, for example, suggests that only high intensities of physical punishment operate destructively. Baumrind (1971) and others suggest that it may not be the physical aggression itself that damages the child, but corresponding parental characteristics. Abusive parents employ reasoning less often as a disciplinary tool, more frequently display anger, and less often vary their discipline in accordance with the child's misbehavior (e.g., Trickett & Kuczynski, 1986). Thus, these parents not only model violence and anger, but they fail to teach more pacific conflict resolution strategies. Consequently, during subsequent conflicts children exposed to violence may fall back on the only tool learned.

TABLE 6.1 Preadolescents' Mean Aggression toward Parent by Spanking Frequency and Discussion Frequency[a]

Parental Discussion Frequency	Spanking Frequency		
	Min.	*Mod.*	*Freq.*
Minimal	0.11	0.65	3.19
Moderate	0.00	0.70	0.97
Frequent	0.50	0.18	0.73

[a]Cell sizes range from 16 to 61. Total sample size was 348.

Source: Larzelere, R. E. (1986). Moderate spanking: Model or deterrent of children's aggression in the family. *Journal of Family Violence, 1,* p. 32. Reprinted by permission of Plenum Publishing Corp.

Larzelere (1986) suggested that parents who reason with children and calmly discuss conflicts provide alternative models of resolving disputes and thus decrease the likelihood that more aggressive conflict strategies will be employed. By reanalyzing the national survey data collected by Straus et al. (1980), Larzelere found support for this hypothesis. As Table 6.1 shows, preadolescents and adolescents who received frequent spankings, but infrequent rational discussion, displayed the most aggression towards a parent. Rational discussion, however, was limited in its effectiveness in reducing aggression. It did not moderate the levels of aggression displayed by younger children, nor did it moderate the levels of aggression displayed by adolescents towards siblings.

There is another reason why occasional or moderate aggressiveness is not as innocuous as it may seem. Important thinkers from Aristotle to Freud have touted the value of letting off steam through mild aggression or intense emotional experiences. Freud (1948) believed that the "catharsis" that resulted from such experiences prevented larger, more violent outbursts in the future. The evidence, however, largely disputes this proposal (Geen & Quanty, 1977). While it is true that mild aggression may produce a dampening of physiological arousal and therefore may make the aggressor feel calmer, the derived physiological and emotional benefits actually may reinforce future aggressiveness. If it feels good to aggress, why not do it again? Furthermore, in the absence of punishment for mild aggression, social restraints against behaving in an aggressive way may be lowered.

Reid's (1986) study, discussed in Chapter 4, illustrates the problems of ignoring mild aggression. You will recall that aversive behaviors such as commanding, disapproving, and threatening were much more common among abusive families than among other families. Abusive parents were much more frequently irritated with their children and often feared that eventually they would lose control. Parents who get used to expressing anger and disapproval of their children are in danger. As Reid (1986) remarks:

> . . . (C)hild abuse in such families is inevitable . . . For a parent who reports spanking his or her child on the average of once every three days (and spanking for that parent typically means something more serious than spanking on the bottom with an open hand), who makes a practice of using threats in his or her attempts to control the behavior of their children, it is simply a matter of time before a discipline confrontation will escalate into violence. (p. 247)

For this reason, Reid urges that intervention programs focus their efforts not only upon ridding the parents of abusive behaviors, but of the lower-level aversive actions that may be precursors of violence.

Assertiveness and Problem-Solving Skills

Another plausible mechanism through which family members learn to be violent is through lack of exposure to beneficial problem-solving skills. Violent spouses (Maiuro, Cahn, & Vitaliano, 1986), their abused partners (Launius & Jensen, 1987), and abusive parents (Hansen, Pallotta, Tishelman, Conaway, & MacMillan, 1989) often show deficits in problem-solving skills. Maiuro et al. (1986) found that, while violent men refused requests in a manner comparable to nonviolent men, the former lacked the skill to assert their rights in a positive way and to make legitimate requests of others. The lack of knowledge about how to assert oneself, when combined with the men's generally high anger and hostility, contributed to explosive home situations. Hansen et al. (1989) tested a small sample of abusive, neglectful, and control parents on a variety of problem situations. They found that abusive parents showed the greatest deficit in deriving effective solutions to a range of interpersonal, financial, and stress-related concerns.

To the extent that children learn strategies for solving problems from their parents, those exposed to poor problem-solving will be disadvantaged in subsequent relationships and, again, may turn to violent tactics.

Social Cognitive Information Processing

The Simons et al. (1991) study showed only minimal support for the notion that people learn to be violent through developing a hostile personality in response to parental aggression or through adopting a philosophy that promotes violence. However, other research provides more support for indirect paths to violence. Dodge, Bates, and Pettit (1990), for example, tracked over 300 4-year-olds from the time they pre-registered for kindergarten until well into the kindergarten year. Through interviews with the mother they determined whether the child had experienced physical harm by an adult. They also observed the child's aggressive behavior in school and secured ratings of the child's aggression from his or her teacher and classmates.

Dodge and his colleagues determined that children who had been harmed were less likely to attend to relevant social cues in interpersonal contexts, less likely to suggest competent solutions to problems, and more likely to attribute other's behavior to hostile tendencies. Although children who were harmed were also more likely to display aggression in the school setting (see Figure 6.1), the connection

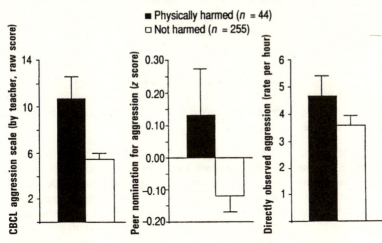

FIGURE 6.1
Teacher-rated, peer-rated, and directly observed aggressive behavior in groups of physically harmed and not harmed children
Note: Bar represents the group mean with the standard error.
Source: Dodge, K. A., Bates, J. E., & Pettit, G. S. (1990, 12 Dec.).
Mechanisms in the cycle of violence. *Science, 250,* p. 1681. Copyright 1990 by the AAAS. Reprinted by permission.

between early harm and later aggression was explained by these social cognitive deficits. In other words, when the child's style of thinking about interpersonal situations was taken into account, the relationship between early harm and later aggression was no longer significant.

The findings suggest that "early physical harm has its effect on a child's aggressive behavioral development largely by altering the child's patterns of processing social information" (Dodge et al., 1990, p. 1682). Lack of attention to relevant cues and inappropriate concern over others' possible hostility may prime children to falsely expect aggression from others and actually may stimulate the development of aggressive conflict. For example, people who expect attack will be on the lookout for signs of imminent aggression in otherwise ambiguous circumstances and may then adopt an aggressive posture as others approach (Dodge, 1986). Others may notice this posture and therefore prepare for aggression, and a cycle of violence may be set into motion.

Cognitive Appraisal of Violence

Earlier we discussed the relationship between crime and exposure to "legitimate" violence such as war (Bebber, 1994). One's perspective on violence has been shown to relate to family violence situations as well. Parents or spouses who feel anger at the aggression that they witnessed or experienced in their youth are less likely to engage in maltreatment towards family members (Caesar, 1988; Hunter & Kilstrom, 1979; Trickett & Susman, 1989). Caesar (1988) compared a small sample of violent men to their nonviolent counterparts and found that the former were more likely to rationalize their violent pasts. One batterer reported:

> Once when I was 13 or 14, I played hooky. My sister snitched. My dad beat me every day for about a week or two weeks. Every morning I had to kneel down . . . My dad was a great big strong dude . . . I seen him hit men and almost shatter faces. Knock 'em through doors. He loved to fight. He was bad. I say it with a sense of pride because I know he shouldn't have hurt those people, but he was all right. But you've got to understand my dad. When he was 11 years old, they threw him out of the house. He had a stepmother and they lived on a ranch. And they used to make him sleep on a porch. He got treated bad. He got beat bad. I got beat bad, but my dad, his beatings were more severe than my beatings. (Caesar, 1988, p. 56)

In contrast to the man quoted above who sympathized strongly with his attacker, people who repudiate their relative's treatment may be more able to break the cycle (see also Egeland, Jacobvitz, & Sroufe, 1988). Through interpreting violence as an aberration or as an unacceptable response to conflict, some people who are exposed to violence as a child or as an adult may learn not to be violent. This cognitive structuring may take place on one's own or in response to an intervention such as therapy (see Chapter 10).

Emotional Support

Many researchers point to the absence of emotional support and love in the childhood histories of abusive people (Egeland et al., 1987; Herrenkohl, Herrenkohl, & Toedter, 1983), which suggests that emotional abuse combined with physical maltreatment may be one key to the transmission process. "Not only the negative model provided by harsh discipline, but also the lack of a positive parenting model and lack of positive support for the growth of self-esteem contribute to problems of parenting" (Herrenkohl et al., 1983, p. 315).

Abused children who are shown love by someone experience the positive emotions associated with good relationships and may be more likely to view abuse as an aberration, rather than as a proper means of rearing children. They also may have a more sanguine picture of what family life can be. Milner et al.'s (1990) study of how abusive backgrounds affect child abuse potential confirms this. College students who reported being nurtured often by an adult or friend as a child scored significantly lower in the Child Abuse Potential inventory. Also, Kruttschnitt, Ward, and Sheble (1987) found that "abuse-resistant youth," those who were abused but did not become involved in violent criminal behavior, were more likely to report having close relationships with siblings or involvement in team sports through which support may have been derived.

Even when nurturance and emotional support is missing from one's childhood history, support during adulthood may inhibit aggression. Quinton, Rutter, and Liddle (1984) studied mothers who as children were removed from their home and placed in a group home for children whose parents could not "cope with" child rearing. The quality of their own parenting was measured through interviews and observations. The authors also assessed whether the mothers had a supportive spouse and whether the spouse evidenced psychosocial problems, such as drug or alcohol problems, criminality, or psychiatric disorders. As Table 6.2 illustrates, the mothers with supportive spouses and those married to husbands without serious psychosocial difficulties were much more likely to be regarded as good parents.

TABLE 6.2 Spouse's Characteristics and Quality of Mother's Current Parenting

	Quality of Parenting			Statistical Significance		
	Good (%)	*Intermediate (%)*	*Poor (%)*	X^2	*df*	*p*
Spouse support						
Nonsupportive (N = 13)	0	38	62	10.07	2	0.01
Supportive (N = 21)	52	19	29			
Spouse deviance[a]						
With problems (N = 16)	6	19	75	14.53	2	0.001
Without problems (N = 17)	53	35	12			

[a]Deviance rating was not known for one spouse in this group.

Source: Adapted from Quinton, E., Rutter, M., & Liddle, C. (1984). Institutional rearing, parenting difficulties and marital support. *Psychological Medicine, 14,* p. 115. Copyright © Cambridge University Press 1984. Reprinted with the permission of Cambridge University Press.

Who Is Susceptible to Learned Aggression and Who Is Immune?

We must remember that many people—maybe as many as 80 percent of those abused—escape from imitating the violence exhibited in their families, and thus bring the cyclical pattern to an end. As Rutter (1989) has said, "(I)ntergenerational discontinuities are at least as striking as continuities . . ." (p. 321). In this section, let us look at who is most likely to be caught in the cyclical pattern and who is not.

Victimization versus Observation

Given that it is hard to understand why abused children would abuse another person, it is surprising that more research has not examined whether being a witness to family violence is more likely to spur violent tendencies than being a victim. After all, observing violence teaches the child new behaviors and modes of conflict resolution, without the punishment from pain or infliction of injury. We know from years of research on the influence of television that children readily adopt the violent behaviors they view (e.g., Liebert et al., 1982). Also, Widom's (1989a) review of the literature on the cycle of violence suggests that children of battered women develop aggressive and other problem behaviors.

Is there any evidence that children who witness violence will display the same level of aggression as those who experience it? This question cannot be answered satisfactorily at this point. Several studies measure both the child's witnessing of spousal assault and experiencing of abuse by a parent and then they measure whether the person as an adult abused his or her own spouse. These studies (Caesar, 1988; Kalmuss, 1984) show that observing spousal assault is associated more strongly than experiencing child abuse with spouse abuse in the next generation.

The national surveys of Straus and his colleagues (cf. Hotaling & Straus, 1989) provide different results. Table 1.4 in Chapter 1 showed that being the child of spouse abusers and the victim of child abusers both increase the likelihood of engaging in violence against siblings, although child abuse appears to have the stronger influence. Also, Milner et al. (1990) measured college students' ''child abuse potential'' (CAP) and their history of witnessing and being the victim of abuse. A person's CAP is measured on a self-report questionnaire that taps rigidity, unhappiness, and family and other interpersonal problems that are believed to promote abusive behavior (Milner, 1986). These characteristics have been shown to distinguish between abusive and nonabusive individuals. Milner et al. (1990) found that CAP scores were more highly correlated with being a victim of abuse than an observer.

However, it is difficult, if not impossible in today's world, to isolate the unique contributions of different ways of learning to be violent. Remember that if one form of violence exists in a family, often multiple forms do (Hotaling & Straus, 1989). Furthermore, people are exposed to violence outside family relationships as well. Research demonstrates that these multiple sources of learning have a cumulative effect. Kalmuss (1984) found that spouses who were most likely to exhibit violence had childhoods in which they both witnessed and experienced violence. A provocative study by Heath, Kruttschnitt, and Ward (1986) examined the self-reported television viewing habits of violent male criminals and nonincarcerated men. Those who reported watching aggressive television during childhood and early adolescence *and* who experienced parental abuse demonstrated the most violence as adults.

Gender of Parent and Child

In general, boys have more opportunities and sources both inside and outside the home through which to learn to behave aggressively. Boys also more readily imitate the aggression they observe in others and may do so in a wider variety of situations; girls, in contrast, refrain from imitating, unless explicitly informed that aggressive behavior is acceptable (Bandura, 1973). Proportionate to their involvement in aggressive activities, boys are neither rewarded nor punished for aggression more than girls are (Maccoby & Jacklin, 1980), but the increased frequency of boys' involvement may mean that they do learn different messages. For example, boys expect to feel less guilt and to receive less parental disapproval for aggression than girls (Perry, Perry, & Weiss, 1989).

Consistent with the above research, research on the consequences of family violence has found that girls from violent homes experience more somatic symptoms and become more withdrawn and dependent than boys (Jaffe, Wolfe, & Wilson, 1990). Boys are more likely to act out the aggression they witness.

Because of boys' wider sphere of learning opportunities for aggression, some theorists (cf. Caspi & Elder, 1988) have suggested that kin relationships more strongly influence girls' behavior than boys'. However, the characteristic effects of experiencing or witnessing violence appear in both boys and girls (Hotaling & Straus, 1989). Boys are much more likely to receive abusive treatment (Simons et al., 1991) and, consistent with a learning hypothesis, they engage in more aggression both towards family and nonfamily members than do girls (Hotaling & Straus, 1989). But girls who experience violence in the home or witness it among other relatives will display more aggression in the home than girls who do not, just as boys do. It is just that girls' level of aggression tends to be lower.

We might expect to see more parity between the sexes in situations in which no societal support for aggression exists (e.g., child-to-parent violence) and in situations in which support for aggression by both genders exists (e.g., parent-to-child violence). In fact, as suggested in Chapter 1, reliable differences in child abuse by mothers versus fathers have not been found. Similarly, no differences are evident in the proportion of girls versus boys who assault their parents (Paulson, Coombs, & Landsverk, 1990).

Are mothers and fathers equally influential in regard to violence training, or are children affected more by the violence of one particular parent? Straus et al. (1980) found that fathers' physical punishment of teenagers led to more abuse overall against spouses and children in the succeeding generation than did mothers'. Other research found the opposite trend. Simons et al. (1991), for example, showed that mothers' harsh parenting had stronger effects than fathers' on the next generation. Both groups of researchers, however, studied parents whose own mother and father performed different family roles, with the mother generally serving as the full-time homemaker and the father employed outside the home. Perhaps the results would be different in families where mothers and fathers pursue more egalitarian parenting roles (Lamb & Oppenheim, 1989). In households where both parents engage in similar amounts of caretaking and other parental responsibilities, children may adapt their own parenting to the styles of both their mother and father.

Do boys and girls learn better and more from one parent versus another? Straus et al. (1980) found that frequent punishment by the father was more strongly associated with the son's abusive fathering, while physical punishment by mothers more strongly related to the daughter's abusive parenting. These results appear to be unusual, however. Maccoby and Jacklin's (1985) review of the socialization literature found, in general, that the correlations between parental behavior and child behavior were no stronger among same-sex pairs than opposite-sex pairs, and children show no strong inclination to imitate a parent of the same sex. Also, Kalmuss (1984) finds no specific effect of the sex of the parent in her study of spouse abusers.

Age of Onset of Abusive Treatment

Children who experience violence in early life appear to be more maladjusted than those whose abuse began later (Erickson, Egeland, & Pianta, 1989). One of the primary developmental tasks of infancy and toddlerhood is learning about attachment, and children whose parents do not permit them to feel secure in relationships with the parents and the environment will suffer (Ainsworth, 1980). Erickson et al. (1989) found that children who were abused in infancy exhibit less confidence and assertiveness in school and less creative initiative than children whose abuse began during the preschool years or later. Of course, this finding does not test the contention that the earlier the maltreatment, the more likely it is that children will become abusers, but remember that problem-solving skills do relate to aggressive behavior and to the potential to abuse (see earlier discussion in this chapter).

While most studies have examined violence against infants or young children, some have explored the consequences of violence against adolescents. Like their younger counterparts, abused adolescents experience low self-esteem, aggression, and other characteristics associated with maltreatment (Garbarino, 1989a). However, individuals whose onset of abuse occurred in adolescence are less likely to have parents who experienced abuse themselves than individuals whose onset occurred earlier. This suggests that adolescent maltreatment may often stem from causes other than parental learning experiences and that those who learned poor parenting in childhood may exhibit poor parenting practices early in their parenting career.

Concluding Remarks

We have seen that there are a host of mechanisms through which violence may be learned and thereby enter into the family. Holden and Zambarano (1992) suggest that there also are a host of mechanisms that might stop people from engaging in aggression and, particularly, from "passing the rod" from one generation to the next. It might be helpful to think of violent parenting or violent marital or sibling relations as predisposing the exposed individual to exhibiting aggression, but the circumstances of the person's current life may determine whether this predisposition is evoked or inhibited.

Because many people exhibit violence toward family members even when no history of family violence preceded their aggression, we need to examine other ways in which violence is learned. Obvious targets for our attention might be the media or peer group norms. But again, the family is a prime filter through which material learned outside the home passes. When one's family situation is violent, the influence of outside forces, such as violent television, may be compounded.

We can conclude this chapter by noting that there is evidence that some people learn to be violent from other family members; others learn not to be violent, even when they have been exposed to violence in their youth. But there are other sources of violence. In the next chapter we will examine the role of biological contributors to violence.

7

Biological Contributions to Family Violence

CHAPTER OBJECTIVES

The Evolution of Family Violence
  The Relationship between Natural Selection and Wife Beating
  The Relationship between Natural Selection and Child Abuse
  Final Thoughts on Evolutionary Explanations

Genetics and Family Violence
Hormonal Contributions to Aggression
Temperament and Physiological Reactivity
Other Biological Relationships
Concluding Remarks

In this chapter we will examine biologically-based theories of aggression, concentrating on three topics. The first part of the chapter pertains to our evolutionary history. Human beings have evolved behaviors that presumably allowed us to adapt to life circumstances and to survive; some of these behaviors may promote aggression. The second part presents the genetics of violence and the extent to which genetically encoded characteristics are passed on to offspring, thus creating a predisposition for aggression in subsequent generations. The final part of the chapter will review hormonal contributors to aggression and the role of temperament and physiological reactions to life events. We will investigate whether each of these mechanisms helps us to understand and predict the incidence of violence in the home.

Biosocial or evolutionary explanations of human behavior often bring vociferous criticism from people who worry that the theorist is suggesting that "biology is destiny" and that deviation from our evolutionary history is unwise. Goldsmith (1991) addresses this criticism directly:

> Let me now head off one reaction that is probably inevitable in today's social climate. This is not a political essay. In invoking evolutionary biology . . . I trust I will not be saddled with the view that because something is "biological" it is *necessary* or *appropriate* or *right* for human society or that I am defending any social or economic status quo. Quite the contrary, there are a number of aspects of human behavior—regardless of what their origins may be—that may be maladaptive or culturally inappropriate in the technologically complicated world in which we now live. Unarguably, homicide, rape, and a host of other forms of violence and exploitation are deplorable, yet despite both moral and legal sanctions they remain disturbingly ubiquitous. I have argued . . . that in order to address biological and social problems we must accept the inherent complexity of what is meant by the word "cause." In short, where there is a problem, there is much to be said for trying to understand it before attempting to solve it. (p. 67)

The Evolution of Family Violence

Evolutionary theory proposes that human beings, like all species of plants and animals, have evolved through a continuous process of *natural selection*. Evolutionary biologists do not claim that all aspects of our character that have evolved are necessarily beneficial in today's world (see Box 7.1). Nonetheless, throughout evolutionary history the *fittest* members of the species were those most likely to survive. Survival, in an evolutionary sense, also means to pass on one's genes through one's progeny (Borgia, 1980). Thus, fitness connotes not only the ability to fight off predators, but to compete for scarce resources, as well as for mates (Buss & Schmitt, 1993; Feingold, 1992). Such competition is not a characteristic reserved for males; low status female members of several primate species are less likely to secure a mate, to procreate, and to rear offspring successfully than high status female members of the species, and aggressiveness confers higher status (Floody, 1983).

Aggressive members of the species are predicted by evolutionary theory to be most likely to survive and to procreate (Borgia, 1980). In this view, harming other human beings is not the goal, but the ability to attack others provides an economical means of securing control over resources.

Paradoxically, human beings also may have evolved altruistic behaviors, which involve self-sacrifice to increase the fitness of another person (Wilson, 1975). However, this altruism does not seem to generalize to all situations and toward all people. Like other animal species, we are more likely to behave altruistically towards those who share our genes, and the closer the relation the more altruistic we will be. We will help our children more than we help other relatives, and will help relatives more than we help members of our social group, who theoretically share some of the gene pool. This characteristic pattern of altruistic behavior has led theorists and researchers to claim that the ultimate goal of altruistic behavior may be the *selfish* act of ensuring the survival of one's own genes (Wilson, 1975).

Because of the importance to individuals of passing on their genes, selecting a mate and rearing children are especially significant tasks (Burgess & Draper, 1989; Goldsmith, 1991). Child rearing for human beings is an intensive and lengthy commitment. Human infants and young children are relatively helpless; thus, parents exert enormous efforts to raise a child to adulthood. Now, consider that in some time periods and some locales resources were limited; also consider the fact that some children are more likely to live and to procreate than others. This situation suggests that, from an evolutionary perspective, not all children are equally worthy of parental commitment of time and resources (Trivers, 1972). This recognition has generated the concept of *parental investment,* which refers to "any investment by the parent in an individual offspring that increases the offspring's chance of surviving (and hence reproductive success) at the cost of the parent's ability to invest in other offspring" (Trivers, 1972, p. 139).

Parental investment also depends upon *parental certainty* (Trivers, 1972). According to this concept, parents may not invest time and resources in children who are not biologically related to them. Thus, children whose paternity is in doubt may elicit less paternal investment than those whose paternity is certain, and step-children and adopted children may be treated differently than are genetically-related offspring.

Because of the importance of ensuring paternity and, ultimately, of ensuring the survival of one's genes, courtship rituals and male sexual jealousy may be seen as adaptive evolutionary mechanisms (Goldsmith, 1991; Trivers, 1972). Women may have evolved behavior that promotes the selection of a mate who has more potential to invest in their offspring (Buss & Schmitt, 1993; Feingold, 1992) and more interest in doing so (Goldsmith, 1991). An extended period of courtship among humans permits a woman to look for signs that a man will provide adequate resources for their offspring and that he will be monogamous (and, hence, will not divide his attention between her children and those of another woman). Goldsmith (1991) provides an example of this process in birds:

> . . . (T)he males stake out territory sufficient to support the young, start building nests, and announce their presence with songs and bright feathers before mating. This process also serves the female by increasing the male's parental investment, a tactic that is effective if it involves him until it is too late in the breeding season to seek another mate. (p. 51)

Of course, some ways of testing a mate's investment potential may not require a ''breeding season.'' Feingold (1992) describes such a test found in the personal ads placed in newspapers by people seeking dating partners. Summarizing studies of personal ads, he found that about one-quarter of ads placed by women mentioned income or occupational requirements, whereas only 7 percent of men's ads had such stipulations. Women were also more likely than men to mention a requirement that potential partners be sincere, honest, or understanding (36 percent to 21 percent, respectively).

As Feingold's (1992) research suggests, a man's selection interests may be different from those of women and may reflect their different approaches to reproduction (Buss & Schmitt, 1993; Goldsmith, 1991). The more healthy children they produce, the more their genes survive. Thus, procreation with multiple partners may be beneficial, as long as the resources are available to support all the children. In societies or in species where pairings are stable and largely monogamous, men may be especially careful to assure that their sole partner produces their own children. Thus, they will be alert for signs that their mate is sexually interested in other men. In the absence of such signs, men will be freer to invest in the offspring produced by the couple's relationship.

Some authors have deduced from these principles of evolutionary theory that violence in families should occur less frequently than violence outside of families. They point to evidence that, even though inequality or asymmetries produced by sex or age foster aggression of the stronger against the weak in many species, family members have evolved complementary roles that function to satisfy the needs of each member and thereby reduce the potential for violence (Sprey, 1988; Troost, 1988). Furthermore, comparative research with a variety of vertebrate species (Lore & Schultz, 1993) suggests that mechanisms have evolved that enable human beings and other animals to employ aggression when it will further the organism's interests, but to inhibit aggression when it will not. Given that the need for family harmony and cooperation is biologically fruitful, these inhibitory mechanisms may gain precedence over aggression within the family setting. Finally, the smaller physical size of women and children, along with behavioral characteristics that make them seem ''weaker,'' serve the purpose of appeasing the man, thereby rendering aggression unnecessary to accomplish his aims (Sprey, 1988). Similarly, the weaker child may not provoke as much aggression from parents.

Other authors, however, examine the same evolutionary principles and see in them the seeds of substantial aggression within the family, at least in contemporary society. Let us look at this perspective.

The Relationship between Natural Selection and Wife Beating

Burgess and Draper (1989; see also Burgess and Garbarino, 1983) suggest that the cross-species tendency to protect and proliferate one's genes creates the potential for family violence. They contend that a set of social arrangements may have evolved to complement the natural selection process. In the majority of societies around the world living arrangements are largely determined by men and households are grouped around related men. Younger women then are brought into groups as newcomers through marriage, and older women who have resided in the groups for some time usually have a greater commitment, either through biological relationship or interest, to the husband than the new wife. Authority and decision-making, then, usually rests with men.

Remember that it is just this type of inequitable living situation that increases the chance of violence against women (cf. Levinson, 1989), but for the reasons given above the potential for violence may not translate into violent behavior. Furthermore, most of these societies also segregate the sexes to a large extent. Men do their work with other men and women work with groups of other women. Thus, although the women are ostensibly under the control of men, their everyday life tasks are conducted relatively independently of male companions. Burgess and Draper (1989) propose that this arrangement fosters male parental certainty and, consequently, male parental investment. Sex segregation and the monitoring of young women by older women ensures greater monogamy. Sexual jealousy is thus reduced and violence against women for suspected or actual philandering is avoided. The decreased contact between husband and wife and the support system offered by other women also buffers women against potential violence. In societies with female-work groups wife-beating is rare, despite the fact that other aspects of the culture promote male domination (Levinson, 1989).

The picture that is painted by Burgess and Draper is of cultures that have evolved a social organization to handle simultaneously the evolutionarily-driven need for parental certainty and parental investment and the unequal distribution of power and decision-making that might prompt violence. But they ask us to contrast this picture with what we know about modern life in our culture (see also Burgess, 1994). Men and women increasingly are subject to integration of the sexes and less frequently are part of same-sex support groups. More than half of all mothers with young children are employed outside of the home (*Statistical Abstract of the United States, 1992*). Men and women work in the same organizations and hold similar jobs. Close contact between unrelated men and women is thus essential and unavoidable. Sexual philandering is common among women and men; from one-quarter to one-half of all married women and one-half or more of all married men have engaged in an extramarital affair (Lawson, 1988). We also live in a mobile society, where couples no longer reside near relatives and where strong relationships with neighbors and other potential sources of support are less common.

These societal changes mean that "some of the traditional 'safeguards' that simpler social systems have built into their institutions and that may buffer women from extreme male violence are no longer common" (Burgess & Draper, 1989, p. 84). Thus, we might expect higher rates of spouse assault in the contemporary United States and a host of other societies.

Of course, many aspects of this sociobiological view of spouse abuse need further explanation. First, if our goal as a species is to procreate and to ensure that our offspring procreate, why would men beat wives who are monogamous? Given that offspring require extraordinary effort to rear, it is unreasonable that men would increase their own parental burden by harming their mate and possibly rendering her unfit to parent. Earlier researchers (e.g., Gelles, 1974; Walker, 1984) reported that women recalled being pregnant at the time of at least some of their husband's beatings. This might be interpreted as support for evolutionary theory in that the violence might bring about a miscarriage and thus end an unwanted (by the husband, at least) pregnancy. But recent research suggests that an evolutionary connection between violence and pregnancy may be lacking. Gelles (1988) asked a nationwide sample of men and women to recall violent events during the previous year. When controlling for age of respondent, pregnant women were no more likely to be victimized than nonpregnant women. Also, other researchers (McFarlane, Parker, Soeken, & Bullock, 1992) found that beatings of pregnant women tended to concentrate on the woman's head, and were not focused on her body, where the danger to the developing child would seem to be greatest.

Second, the connection between sexual jealousy and violence against a partner is unclear. Researchers cite cases wherein men were extremely controlling and sexual jealousy seemed to be the basis for this behavior. In fact, virtually all of Walker's (1984) sample of abused women reported that their partner was jealous about the possibility of their having an affair with another man. Consequently, Walker notes, the women learned to walk in public with their eyes averted and rarely spoke to people. Studies such as this convince us that sexual jealousy is prevalent among batterers. However, in many other species the couple acts in unison to drive away other potential suitors (Burgess & Draper, 1989). This behavior not only helps to maintain monogamous relationships, but maintains good feelings between the spouses. So theorists must elucidate why humans vent their jealousy toward their mate instead.

The Relationship between Natural Selection and Child Abuse

Because parenting is time-consuming and depends upon the available resources, evolutionary theory predicts that it may be *natural* for parents to exert effort toward those children who will survive and procreate (Goldsmith, 1991). In addition, natural selection principles would encourage parents to moderate their fertility and their parenting behaviors in accordance with resource availability. Some behaviors that today have been termed "abusive" actually may have been adaptive at some time during evolutionary history (Burgess & Draper, 1989). For example, the severe weaning practices and early malnutrition of infants in some cultures may slow a child's development and lead him or her to be shorter in stature. Ultimately, the smaller child and adult will require less food, assuring more resources for the group. Longer breast-feeding of boys evident in some cultures also may be adaptive, given the normally higher mortality rate among boys (Burgess & Draper, 1989). The abrupt weaning of girls may lead to increases in their mortality rate, but may assure a more equal proportion of boys and girls.

These basic principles generate a number of testable hypotheses. First, we might expect that when resources are scant child abuse will increase. Consistent with the prediction, although child abuse is found in families of all socioeconomic classes, poor parents may be three times as likely to abuse children as wealthier parents (e.g., Reiss & Roth, 1993). Furthermore, children from large families are much more likely to suffer from abuse than those with fewer brothers and sisters (cf. Zigler & Hall, 1989). This makes sense from an evolutionary perspective, given that members of large households must compete more for available resources.

Of course, these results would best support the theory if a particular member of the household were "selected" for the abuse and if the selected member were the weakest one. Research findings are somewhat ambivalent on this issue. Often when one member of the family is abused, other family members are also likely to be victimized (Herrenkohl & Herrenkohl, 1979; Hotaling & Straus, 1989). Thus, it is not always the case that the weakest member is isolated for maltreatment. However, children who require more care because of physical or psychological disabilities are more likely to be abused. Infants, who because of their physical limitations require considerable care and add to parental fatigue and stress, are disproportionately likely to be abused compared to children of other ages (cf. Zigler & Hall, 1989). Premature infants are even more likely to be victimized, possibly because of the parent's greater caretaking responsibilities and also because of the premature infant's aversive cry (e.g., Frodi, 1981).

Once parents invest so much energy in the care of a child through the child's early years, it would be a waste of this effort and thus unwise for them to harm the older child. Homicide statistics accord with the theoretical predictions: 30 percent of all children killed by their mothers are murdered before their first birthday and three-quarters of the murdered children are younger than six (Silverman &

Kennedy, 1988). But statistics on abusive treatment short of murder contradict the predictions of parental investment. Maltreatment occurs to children at all age levels and infants are only slightly overrepresented among the victims (cf. Zigler & Hall, 1989).

And why would parents beat their children rather than kill them? Murdering a child may be adaptive when resources are low; but maiming or otherwise injuring a child only adds to the parental burden. Yet, proportionately few acts of abuse lead to the death of a child. Statistics from the National Center on Child Abuse and Neglect (1988), for example, reveal that in 1986 two of every 100,000 children received a fatal injury as a result of maltreatment and less than three of every 1,000 received an injury serious enough to be considered life-threatening or life-impairing.

Second, we would expect that women would be especially sensitive to wasted effort compared to men (Goldsmith, 1991; Trivers, 1972).

> For example, given heavy, 'obligate' maternal investment in women (gestation, parturition, lactation, and rearing) and the low reproductive potential of women in comparison to men, the prediction from comparative evolutionary ecology is that women will have a more conservative and tenacious attitude toward offspring than will men. It is also predicted that women will try harder to keep children alive but that they, too, will reach a point at which costs exceed benefits. In the language of fitness, a woman would have a high likelihood of curtailing investment in any offspring who impairs her ability to support other living children, unborn children, or both. (Burgess & Draper, 1989, p. 102)

While the high incidence of child abuse by mothers seems to contradict the notion of higher maternal investment, we need to attend to the latter part of the quotation. Even mothers, or perhaps most especially mothers, may perceive more demands from childrearing than they can handle, and in some circumstances the stress may overwhelm their tendency to protect their young. Child abuse or even child murder may then result.

From this perspective, abortion may be considered a preemptive method of population and resource control. In 1988 three out of every hundred women in this country between the ages of 15 and 44 had abortions (*Statistical Abstract of the United States, 1992*), or 401 abortions for each 1,000 live births. A disproportionate number of these were performed on poor people or teenagers who lack the resources for productive parenting. Many people have also worried about unwanted children whose mothers for one reason or another did not obtain an abortion (cf. Pagelow, 1984). A recent survey

(Williams & Pratt, 1990) estimates that 10.3 percent of births to women who were ever married and 25 percent of births to women who were never married were unwanted at the time of conception. Again, poor women are overrepresented among those who did not want their child. And children of poor, single mothers are thought particularly to be at risk of abuse (Olds & Henderson, 1989).

Third, evolutionary theory also leads us to predict that adults should invest energy and resources most in others who share close biological relationships. From this we might predict that parents will be more likely to reject and abuse stepchildren or adopted children than their own progeny. Research findings are consistent with this prediction (cf. Burgess & Garbarino, 1983; Garbarino, 1989a).

Final Thoughts on Evolutionary Explanations

It is important to note that, just as learning theories cannot by themselves explain family violence, neither can evolutionary proclivities such as parental investment and parental certainty. Evolutionary biologists suggest that these concepts best serve as background for understanding patterns of human behavior and its potential (Sprey, 1988). But knowledge of how the social system of the family may have evolved does not provide proximate explanations for any given case of violence. The theory provides little help in predicting the intensity and direction of individual behaviors (Sprey, 1988). Furthermore, biological views of family violence are really *biosocial;* that is, they propose underlying biological mechanisms that establish proclivities for violent behavior and then identify the social circumstances (such as stressful living) that elicit these natural proclivities (cf. Burgess & Draper, 1989). Thus, dual biological and social causal mechanisms are needed to explain the violence in any given family.

While it appears reasonable that biological and social causes coexist to produce violence, a test of this notion is difficult. Although we can find diverse social situations and track differences in behavior that seem to correspond to them, we cannot do comparable studies looking at a variety of biological adaptations. Human beings almost completely share an evolutionary history; it would be impossible to find groups of people who vary in the way they have evolved and so provide a test of the biological portion of the theory. Besides, the biological adaptations that may distinguish one culture from another coincide with environmental differences as well. Thus, tests of evolutionary influence on family violence are difficult, if not impossible, to conduct.

Another criticism of biosocial theories of family violence is that they provide explanations for virtually any finding, which renders their theoretical tenets relatively irrefutable (cf. Plomin, DeFries, & McClearn, 1990). An example is the biosocial theorist's predictions of both more violence and less violence in families than nonfamilies. Bleier (1984), a noted critic of sociobiology, rejects much of the theory as well for its underlying assumptions about the genetic basis for the human behaviors discussed:

> This logic makes a *premise* of the genetic basis of behaviors, then cites a certain animal or human behavior, constructs a speculative story to explain how the behavior (*if* it were genetically based) could have served or could serve to maximize the reproductive success of the individual, and this *conjecture* then becomes evidence for the *premise* that the behavior was genetically determined. (p. 17)

The theory is also criticized for androcentrism (Bem, 1993; Bleier, 1984). Take, for example, the assumption that it is evolutionarily wise for men to seek physically attractive partners and for women to seek intelligent ones (Buss & Schmitt, 1993; Feingold, 1992). Theorists do not explain how such valued female characteristics as "full lips" and "clear skin" communicate and actually relate to reproductive value, nor do they question why men would not take the genetically wise step of seeking an intelligent mother for their children. The theory thus is accused of providing a scientific veneer under which sexism is reinforced.

Genetics and Family Violence

Genetic research provides another opportunity to study the role of biological factors in family violence. People as diverse as dog breeders and researchers who study mice know that across generations aggression can be fostered or inhibited through selective mating between aggressive or nonaggressive members of the species (cf. Svare & Mann, 1983). Researchers are beginning to suggest that genetics may underlie observed patterns of family violence among human beings as well (DiLalla & Gottesman, 1991; Rowe, 1994).

In previous chapters you have discovered that, if one form of violence is present in the family, often another form is as well. You also discovered that violence is sometimes passed from one generation to the next (Kalmuss, 1984; Oliver, 1988; Simons et al., 1991).

Remember, though, that we could not definitively conclude that aggression is passed through learned behavior because, while family members share a similar learning environment, they also share genes.

Genetic research typically capitalizes on this confounding of influences. Monozygotic (MZ) twins share 100 percent of their genes, while dizygotic (DZ) twins (as well as non-twin siblings) share an average of 50 percent. Thus, a comparison of the behaviors of MZ and DZ twins provides a method of sorting biological from environmental influences. To the extent that the degree of ''concordance'' (i.e., the overlap) in the behavior of MZ twins matches that of DZ twins, environmental factors are held more responsible for the behavior under examination. However, if MZ twins display more similar behaviors than do DZ twins, biological influence on behavior is presumed. A *heritability* index is the ''proportion of the observed variance in a population that can be explained by genetic variance'' (Plomin et al., 1990).

Another way to study genetic contributions to behavior is through investigations of adopted children. Children adopted shortly after birth share the environment of their adopted parents, but the genes of their biological parents. We can thus compare the correlation of the behavior of adopted children with their biological parents to the correlation of the children with their adopted parents. The results of such studies must be viewed with caution because children are adopted into households that are probably healthier and more economically and psychologically stable than average. However, if comparisons of biological and adoptive contributions control for similar living circumstances, we may derive an estimate of the role of environment versus genetics (DiLalla & Gottesman, 1991).

Genetic contributions to behaviors in the family are well documented (Rowe, 1994). Across a host of characteristics, similarities in the behavior of family members are more attributable to shared genetic inheritance than to their shared environment. For example, monozygotic twins perceive more similarity in their parents' warmth than do dizygotic twins (Rowe, 1994). Adult monozygotic twins reared apart manifest more similarity in their own child-rearing styles than do dizygotic twins reared together or apart, accounting for about one-fourth of the variation (Plomin, McClearn, Pedersen, Nesselroade, & Bergeman, 1989). Plomin et al. (1989) also found that twins reared apart rate their family environments no more differently than twins reared together, suggesting that the shared rearing environment plays little role in developing a perspective on the family.

Although research has not specifically focused on genetic contributions to family violence, research abounds on the role of genetics in extra-familial criminality and juvenile delinquency. For example, Sigvardsson, Cloninger, Bohman, and von Knorring (1982) compared women who had been adopted from biological parents with criminal histories to those whose biological parents exhibited no criminal behavior. They found the highest rates of ''petty'' criminality (e.g., fraud, theft) among those who had criminal biological histories and who also had been exposed to *criminogenic* (i.e., crime-producing) circumstances after adoption (see Table 7.1). They found similar rates of criminal behavior among women who had either criminal biological parents or a criminogenic upbringing and found the least criminality among women exposed to neither genetic nor environmental influences.

It is also worthwhile to note that, compared to comparable men, the female criminals were more than twice as likely to have criminal biological parents (50 percent versus 21 percent) and to have parents who committed offenses repeatedly (Sigvardsson et al., 1982). These data suggest that, given society's expectations that ''boys will be boys'' and girls will behave properly, the biological predisposition for criminality among women who do commit crimes may be stronger than that for men who commit crimes.

Mednick, Gabrielli, and Hutchings (1984, 1987) studied all adoptions outside of the family between 1924 and 1947 in a northern European country, comparing the rates of conviction of adoptive and biological parents and the adopted individual. Because of the relatively low conviction rate of women, the study concentrated on male adoptees. Table 7.2 shows the percentage of male adoptees who were convicted of a crime in relation to the criminal histories of their biological and adoptive families. As demonstrated, sons with convicted biological and adoptive parents were most likely to commit a crime (1 in 4 chance) and those with convicted biological parents, but non-convicted adoptive parents had a 1 in 5 chance of committing a crime. Those with adoptive, but not biological criminal parents and those with no parental criminal history were dramatically less likely to commit a crime themselves.

Mednick et al. (1984, 1987) also found by studying siblings and half-siblings who had been adopted that the closer the degree of genetic relationship, the more likely that both siblings would display similar criminality. The criminal behavior of both siblings was especially likely if their biological father had also been convicted of a

TABLE 7.1 Cross-Fostering Analysis of Petty Criminality in Female Adoptees

Predisposition to Petty Criminality		Observed Female Adoptees	
Congenital	*Postnatal*	*Total No.*	*% with Petty Criminality*
No	No	566	0.5
No	Yes	209	2.9
Yes	No	93	2.2
Yes	Yes	45	11.1

*"Congenital" refers to variables about biologic parents, whereas "postnatal" refers to variables about rearing experiences and adoptive placement. Classification of predisposition depended on whether the set of background variables were more like the average characteristics of adoptees with petty criminality only (classified as high) or with no criminality and/or alcohol abuse (classified as low).

Source: Sigvardsson, S., Cloninger, C. R., Bohmen, M., & von Knorring, A. L. (1982). Predisposition to petty criminality in Swedish adoptees. III. Sex differences and validation of the male typology. *Archives of General Psychiatry, 39,* p. 1251. Copyright 1982, American Medical Association. Reprinted by permission.

TABLE 7.2 Cross-Fostering Analysis: Percentage of Adoptive Sons Conviction of Criminal Law Offenses

Have Adoptive Parents Been Convicted?	Have Biological Parents Been Convicted?	
	Yes	*No*
Yes	24.5 (of 143)	14.7 (of 204)
No	20.0 (of 1,226)	13.5 (of 2,492)

Source: Mednick, S. A., Gabrielli, W. F., Jr., Hutchings, B. (1987). Genetic factors in the etiology of criminal behavior. In S. A. Mednick, T. E. Moffitt, & S. A. Stack (Eds.), *The causes of crime: New biological approaches* (p. 79). Cambridge: Cambridge University Press. © 1987 Cambridge University Press. Reprinted with permission of Cambridge University Press.

crime. Also, the more recidivism among biological parents, the more likely it was that an adopted son would commit a crime against property.

While these results suggest some genetic contribution to a son's risk of criminal behavior, remember that, as is typically the case with adoption studies, adoptive households differed from biological households. In this case, adoptive parents were substantially less likely to be convicted of crimes and even less likely to be repeat criminals than were biological parents. Thus, there was more opportunity to show a relationship between the biological parent's and the son's criminality.

Furthermore, these findings (Mednick et al., 1984; 1987) do not necessarily speak to the transmission of violent criminality. Cloninger and Gottesman (1987) reviewed twin and adoption studies of a variety of antisocial behavioral disorders (e.g., truancy or fighting in adolescence; marital or job instability in adulthood) and found that people who commit crimes against persons are quite different in character than those who commit crimes against property. They conclude that "there is no significant genetic overlap between the liabilities to crimes against persons and crimes against property only" (p. 100). Thus, we need to look specifically at the transmission of violent crime.

Convictions for violent crime were assessed in the Mednick et al. (1984, 1987) study and no significant relationship was found between the biological parent's overall criminality and the adopted son's violent criminal behavior (see Figure 7.1; Mednick et al., 1984).

However, Cloninger and Gottesman (1987) found a strong genetic contribution to violent crime in their analysis of data about male twins. While the heritability for property crime was higher (.76), that for violent crime reached .50.

Again, support is mixed for a genetic contribution to juvenile crime. Genetic contributions are minimal to the commission of juvenile delinquency (DiLalla & Gottesman, 1991; Cloninger & Gottesman, 1987), and do not appear to explain mildly aggressive behaviors among children in a study by Plomin et al. (1990). Yet Jary and Stewart (1985) found evidence for a genetic contribution among children diagnosed with aggressive conduct disorders. Some of their sample had been adopted; others remained with their biological parents. None of the adoptive parents exhibited antisocial traits, but 11 percent of the adoptees' biological mothers and fathers exhibited such

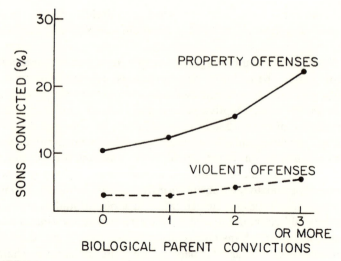

FIGURE 7.1

Percentage of male adoptee property offenders and violent offenders by biological-parent convictions.

Source: Mednick, S. A., Gabrielli, W. F., Jr., & Hutchings, B. (1987). Genetic factors in the etiology of criminal behavior. In S. A. Mednick, T. E. Moffitt, & S. A. Stack (Eds.), *The causes of crime: New biological approaches* (p. 81). Cambridge: Cambridge University Press. Copyright © Cambridge University Press 1987. Reprinted with the permission of Cambridge University Press.

characteristics. Fourteen percent of a sample of nonadoptees' biological fathers also manifested an aggressive personality (but none of their mothers did).

Thus, while strong support has been found for a genetic role in the commission of property crimes, the role of genetics in violent assault is more ambiguous. This research, however, reiterates the importance of testing both genetic and social models of the transmission of behavior (DiLalla & Gottesman, 1991; Rowe, 1994).

Hormonal Contributions to Aggression

In contrast to the paucity of research on genetic contributors to family violence, many studies have examined the role of biochemical, physiological, and neurological factors. We will review some of the conclusions about the most commonly studied factors, beginning with hormonal contributions.

Testosterone, a sex hormone produced in males in greater quantities than in females, has long been implicated in some forms of aggressive behavior in animals. We know, for example, that male rodents commit more infanticide than do female rodents, and administration of testosterone to the females increases their rate of infanticide (cf. Gandelman, 1983). However, variation in the level of testosterone does not distinguish rodents that kill young members of the species from those that do not. This suggests that, while testosterone may be one necessary factor in aggression among animals, it is not sufficient and at best plays an indirect role (Gandelman, 1983).

The connection between aggression and hormones is less prominent among animals higher in the phylogenetic scale (Gandelman, 1983) and is not always manifest in human beings (Mazur, 1983), but some studies do show a relationship. Olweus (1987), who studied males between 15 and 17 years old, found that verbal and physical aggressiveness, as measured by self-report, related to testosterone levels measured one or two months later. Provoked aggression showed the closest relationship to testosterone. Adolescents with high levels of testosterone tended to be those who agreed with such statements as "When a teacher criticizes me, I tend to answer back and protest" and "When a boy is nasty with me, I try to get even with him." In contrast, unprovoked aggression (signified by responses to "I really admire the fighters among the boys") was unrelated to testosterone level. Among the boys who also exhibited low tolerance of frustration, however, the relationship between testosterone level and unprovoked aggression was high.

Another well-cited study is by Ehrenkranz, Bliss, and Sheard (1974), who investigated three groups of prison inmates. They found that chronically aggressive inmates had the highest levels of testosterone, while "socially dominant," but nonaggressive inmates had slightly lower levels and nonaggressive, nondominant inmates differed significantly from the other two groups. Unfortunately, the chronically aggressive group may have also displayed considerable social dominance; therefore whether aggressiveness or social dominance is related to testosterone cannot be determined.

Dabbs's (1992) review of the literature reveals that men with high testosterone are more likely to have unsuccessful family relationships and become more easily angered. Booth and Dabbs (1993), in a study of former servicemen, found that men with high testosterone levels were more likely to answer yes to the question, "Did you ever hit or throw things at your wife?" Twenty-nine percent of those with high testosterone admitted to engaging in these behaviors, compared with 23 percent of those with low testosterone.

We need to be cautious about concluding from the results of cross-sectional studies that high testosterone levels cause aggression.

Studies with rhesus monkeys, for example, find that changes in the relative social status of monkeys precede changes in their level of testosterone (Rose, Bernstein, & Gordon, 1974). Monkeys placed among stronger monkeys show reduced levels of testosterone, whereas those placed among weaker monkeys show higher levels. Thus, behavioral and environmental changes can bring about concomitant biological change. This result is also seen among humans. Male tennis players, wrestlers, and just graduated medical doctors show changes in their testosterone levels following such events as winning, losing, and graduating (Mazur, 1983), and these changes can last as long as two months (Dabbs, 1992).

Although research with other animal species suggests that hormones have less effect upon female behavior (e.g., Svare & Mann, 1983), human males are not the only ones influenced by hormones. Variations in the levels of the sex hormones, estrogen and progesterone, which are more prominent in women than men, relate to behavioral changes in women. The massive hormonal changes following delivery of a child, for example, are implicated in the postpartum depression experienced by roughly one-fifth of all new mothers (Hopkins, Marcus, & Campbell, 1984). Such mothers experience anxiety over child rearing, irritability, and rapid mood changes. A much smaller proportion of women, perhaps one of every 5,000, experience postpartum psychosis, during which thoughts about infanticide are common (Hopkins et al., 1984).

Several studies have focused upon the consequences of hormonal variations throughout the menstrual cycle. Floody's (1983) review of the literature suggests that approximately 10 percent of women experience severe irritability during or preceding menstruation, and perhaps 20 percent experience moderate levels of irritability. Correspondingly, aggressiveness tends to peak at the time of menstruation and is manifested least at the time of ovulation (Floody, 1983).

Again, we need to be careful about cause-and-effect conclusions and about thinking that hormones directly and simply relate to behavior (cf. Mazur, 1983; Widom & Ames, 1988). Antisocial behaviors by women may precede hormonal changes and even act to bring them about (Horney, 1978). In fact, stress due to an accident, travel, or change of job also affects the onset of menstruation (Horney, 1978).

Furthermore, the myths and folklore that are taught to us about behavior during menstruation may elicit or may serve as an excuse for socially expected behaviors. By early adolescence both males and females are well aware of the stereotypical reactions anticipated in women during menstruation (Clarke & Ruble, 1978). And there is evidence that expectations influence women's perceptions of the symptoms they experience (Parlee, 1987). Ruble (1977) found that women who were led to believe that they were in the premenstrual phase of their monthly cycle reported feeling more symptoms that stereotypically are associated with this phase than women who (inaccurately) thought that they were in the middle of their cycle. Similarly, Floody (1983) reports that studies in which women retrospectively provide judgments about menstrual symptoms they experienced find more mood changes than studies in which women record their symptoms daily. Thus, researchers need to assess the role of expectations as a contributor to whatever aggression is displayed by women during the menstrual cycle.

Temperament and Physiological Reactivity

A variety of factors that pertain to one's temperament and reactivity to events also have been explored as possible explanations for violence. *Difficult temperament* in the family violence literature usually signifies infants or children who are hard for their parents to handle. Bad temperament can also describe adults who are moody or irritable and who react quickly and adversely to frustrating events.

While some instances of irritability undoubtedly can be attributed to environmental factors, genetic contributions to temperament have been found (Goldsmith & Gottesman, 1981). Also, research on violent offenders finds that low levels of the serotonin metabolite 5-hydroxyindoleacetic acid (5-HIAA) in the cerebral spinal fluid may render some people easily angered and prone to aggress against themselves and others (cf. Reiss & Roth, 1993; Virkkunen, DeJong, Bartko, & Linnoila, 1989).

The connection between genetic or biochemical correlates of temperamental difficulties and aggression within families is yet to be demonstrated. However, Caspi, Elder, and Bem (1987), using archived longitudinal data, found that ill-tempered children became ill-tempered adults and that their temperament directly and indirectly influenced the quality of their family life. Ill-tempered men were more likely than other men to be divorced, to have an erratic work life, and to be regarded by their spouses as inadequate parents. Ill-tempered women were more likely than other women to marry men in lower status occupations than their fathers, to be divorced, and to be regarded by both husbands and children as ill-tempered parents.

Caspi et al. suggest two patterns through which this early personality characteristic leads to problems in adulthood. First, a child's ill-tempered actions may limit success in school and then in work situations, thus increasing the likelihood of frustration and further displays of ill-temper. Second, the child's irritability may frustrate caregivers, who give in to tantrums and therefore reward the child. The child may then learn that this kind of behavior pays off and may develop this as an interaction style.

Physiological reactivity is another characteristic that has been linked to aggression, conduct disorders, and adult and juvenile criminality. Adrenaline excretion, which is an indicator of fear or perceived threat and leads to increased heart rate, is lower among aggressive individuals (cf. Olweus, 1987) and among those who show the motoric restlessness and lack of concentration characteristic of hyperactivity (Magnusson, 1988). Furthermore, these individuals show little change in adrenaline levels from nonstressful to stressful conditions. Thus, it is possible that the body's feedback system that is designed to warn of impending trouble does not function as well among people who are prone to problem behavior.

Lower physiological reactivity is also characteristic of those who seek stimulation through exciting and sometimes dangerous activities such as drug use, gambling, parachuting, and sex with a variety of partners (Widom & Ames, 1988; Zuckerman, Buchsbaum, & Murphy, 1980). Thrill-seeking may be viewed as a way to raise physiological arousal to optimal levels. Interestingly, studies with twins show a genetic contribution to most behavioral and physiological indicators of "sensation seeking" (Zuckerman et al., 1980).

Physiological reactivity has been implicated in a number of studies of abusive parents' reactions to children's behavior. Pruitt and Erickson (1985), for example, found that adults with a high potential to abuse children (as measured by the *Child Abuse Potential Inventory,* Milner, 1986) revealed greater physiological arousal during a videotaped presentation of an infant crying and smiling than did adults with a low potential to abuse. Frodi and Lamb (1980) found similar results among a sample of abusive and nonabusive parents.

Other Biological Relationships

The literature on biology is rife with other possible routes to explore the concomitants of family violence. Left-hemisphere dysfunction has figured prominently among the characteristics of violent individuals (cf. Nachson & Denno, 1987), as have abnormal EEG patterns and tumors in the temporal lobe and other areas of the limbic system (Moyer, 1987). Damage to the brain may spontaneously elicit hostile behaviors or may disrupt the mechanisms that are responsible for maintaining a high threshold for anger-induced aggression. It is also possible that the damage may preclude rational assessment of the person's social environment. If an individual cannot adequately reason about the extent to which he or she has been provoked or cannot discern the difference between an accidental or intentional slight, then aggression may follow.

Concluding Remarks

This chapter has introduced us to evidence of biological underpinnings of violent behavior. Although the evidence in favor of an evolutionarily-driven propensity for family violence is not strong, this theory has received many adherents and proposes to explain why so much violence may be evident in modern society. Evidence has also accumulated regarding genetic, hormonal, and other physiological contributors to aggression.

One idea that should be apparent from this chapter is the reciprocal interplay between biological systems and environmental stimulation. Magnusson (1988) states this relationship well:

> . . . (I)ndividual subsystems of cognitions, emotions, physiological factors, and conduct are in a constant, reciprocal interaction, influencing each other with developmental consequences for all systems involved. During development both the psychological and the biological subsystems change, not only as a result of maturation, but also as a result of the interaction among the subsystems; as a result of experience this interaction among subsystems within the individual depends on the nature of the environment in which the individual is developing. Given this view, the interpretation of results in terms of cause and effect is not self-evident. (p. 143)

While Magnusson (1988) was urging caution in assessing the role of adrenaline in producing violence, his thoughts apply as well to almost any biological or environmental factor that shows a relationship to aggressive behavior. In Chapter 4, the topic of family dynamics began with a discussion of the complex, multifaceted set of systems that influence family members' behavior. This chapter complements that view and demonstrates that, even at the level of the individual, aggression is multiply determined. A quote from a National Institute of Justice report (Goolkasian, 1986) reinforces this perspective. When testifying about whether an inability to handle stress should be considered a *cause* of violence, one respondent noted:

> It is not his impulses. Clearly, he doesn't beat up his boss. He doesn't beat up his secretary. He doesn't, you know, beat up the kids on the block. (Goolkasian, 1986, p. 4)

The paucity of biological research specifically on family violence also bears notice. While some of the factors known to influence non-family violence appear to affect family violence as well, we cannot assume that all do. Nor can we assume that biological factors found to affect violence in families extend their influence outside. The family presents a much different social and biological system than that which confronts the individual in the external world. Thus, much more research needs to be done to extend our knowledge about biological contributors to crime in general to family violence.

We also need to recognize that should biological factors be prominent contributors to violence in the family, we need not look only to biological solutions, just as environmental contributors need not demand environmental solutions. Human beings can learn to overcome a biological propensity, just as medication or other medical intervention can overcome a characteristic stimulated by the environment.

In the next chapter we will examine two more factors that have been implicated in the expression of violence in the family. Both factors, lack of empathy and use of alcohol and other drugs, have been studied from biological and social perspectives and both show the importance of an integrated view of the contributors to aggression. Thus, the next chapter exemplifies what has been promoted during this discussion on the causes of violence.

Nature and Nurture
on Display

CHAPTER OBJECTIVES

Empathy
  Relationship to Violence
  Biological Determinants of
    Empathy
  Social Determinants of
    Empathy
  Interaction between Biological
    and Social Determinants

Alcohol and Drug Use
  Relationship to Violence
  Biochemical Determinants
  Social Determinants
  Alcohol or Drug Use by the
    Victim
Concluding Remarks

In the previous chapters we reviewed many of the important contributors to violence in families. We noted that violence is multiply determined and may be a function of both biological and social causes. In this chapter we will study two more factors that have been linked to family violence: lack of empathy and alcohol or drug use. Both of these factors have been studied from biological and social perspectives and therefore present good examples of the multifaceted approach to understanding violence. Furthermore, both empathy and alcohol or drug use provide examples of how biological and social forces may interact to produce aggressive behavior.

Empathy

The term *empathy* is usually defined as knowing how another person is responding to an event, feeling at least to some extent what the other person feels, and behaving appropriately, usually with compassion, in response to the other's experience (Levenson & Ruef, 1992). Empathy is often regarded as a key to altruistic behavior (Davis, 1994). Seeing a person in distress, imagining how the person feels, and feeling it oneself may prompt an individual to alleviate the other person's suffering.

Relationship to Violence

People who are aggressive toward strangers or acquaintances are more likely to lack empathy than individuals who are not so aggressive (Davis, 1994; Rushton, Fulker, Neale, Nias, & Eysenck, 1986). This holds true as well for perpetrators of violence in the home (Feshbach, 1989; Newberger & White, 1989). You might recall that victims of violence are also less empathic than nonvictims. College students who have been abused regard the similar treatment of others somewhat less severely than their nonabused counterparts (Herzberger & Tennen, 1985a). Abused children also generally display less empathy than nonabused children (Feshbach, 1989; Straker & Jacobson, 1981). Abused toddlers, for example, fail to show concern when a peer is distressed. While a nonabused toddler will seek help or show dismay under these conditions (Wallach & Wallach, 1983), the abused toddler is likely to react with physical aggression or fear, or may alternate between comforting and attacking the peer (Main & George, 1985). This phenomenon extends to people who have witnessed abuse of others in the family (Hinchey & Gavelek, 1982). Preschoolers who witnessed spousal assault showed less competence on measures of empathic ability than their counterparts who had not witnessed assault.

These findings may be counterintuitive and they certainly lead to an intriguing question: Why would anyone who has been abused victimize another human being? Given the injury, pain, humiliation, and depression suffered, why would the person not instead turn away from violence? Now let us examine what might account for this and for variations in empathy in general.

Biological Determinants of Empathy

Empathy has been examined by sociobiologists, geneticists, and others interested in exploring biological contributions to behavior. As noted in the previous chapter, sociobiologists such as Wilson (1975) have suggested that human beings have evolved altruistic behaviors to increase the likelihood that those who share our genes will survive, will procreate, and will thus perpetuate our gene pool. The theory has been modified by others to suggest that we may also behave altruistically to non-relatives who share characteristics about ourselves that we value (Dawkins, 1976).

The evolutionary origins of empathy and altruism are, as noted previously, difficult to test (Bleier, 1984; Davis, 1994) and do not explain how any given individual becomes empathic while another does not. However, there is substantial evidence that empathy is part of our biological heritage. First, the fact that newborns display empathic reactions, such as crying, to other people's distress (Sagi & Hoffman, 1976) suggests that empathy is innate. Second, changes in our physiology, such as blood pressure or heart rate, often accompany empathic distress and the more similar the physiological reactions between a suffering person and an observer, the more likely it is that the observer will characterize accurately the negative emotions experienced by the sufferer (Levenson & Ruef, 1992).

Third, studies such as one by Rushton et al. (1986) reveal a substantial genetic contribution to empathy and altruism. Correlations between monozygotic twins on measures of empathy and altruism were more than twice as strong (.54 and .53, respectively) as between dizygotic twins, and about 50 percent of the variation in empathy was attributable to genetic influence.

Social Determinants of Empathy

While the evidence for a biological contribution to empathy is strong, some theorists such as Feshbach (1989) see roots of empathy in the environment in which the person develops. Empathy may be learned from parents (or others) who demonstrate sensitivity to the emotions of others and responsiveness to social cues. This type of learning is associated with the use of *inductive reasoning* as a discipline technique (Barnett, 1987). Inductive discipline teaches children how their misbehavior affects others adversely. Children who are not trained in this way may not become empathic adults. Then, when placed in a situation in which they might engage in violence, they may not appreciate the potential victim's feelings. Feshbach (1989) suggests that empathy is not merely emotional responsivity to another's pain or suffering. Individuals who lack empathy merge their own feelings and those of others and are narcissistic in their interpretations of others' suffering.

Predictably, then, research has shown that abused children are less able to take the perspective of others by stepping outside of their own experience (Barahal, Waterman, & Martin, 1981). They are less able to imagine themselves in roles played by another, which may make them less sensitive to the emotional states of others and less understanding of the sources of others' emotions.

Other factors believed to promote empathic responses include a secure early attachment to parents, encouragement to see similarities between oneself and others, and discouragement of excessive competition (Barnett, 1987). Parents who help children to feel secure are not only modeling nurturant, loving behavior that children can later try out with others, but they are likely to be less preoccupied with their own needs and to be more attentive to the needs of others. One of the characteristics associated with abusive individuals is their own need to be loved. When insecure parents or spouses do not get the respect or attention they want from family members, they may become abusive (Walker, 1984).

The role of early parental behavior in the development of empathy is supported further by a study by Koestner, Franz, and Weinberger (1990). The researchers found a group of adults (age 31) who had been subjects in a study of parenting behaviors when they were 5 years old. Children whose fathers were strongly involved in their care and whose mothers tolerated their dependency were most likely to show empathic concern for others as an adult. The authors could not identify what mothers' tolerance for dependency meant behaviorally since the original study did not provide a definition. However, it is likely to signify high levels of maternal-child interaction and acceptance of the child's expressed needs. These characteristics, coupled with high paternal involvement, suggest a home atmosphere that may be nurturant and satisfying to the child. Adult empathy was also predicted, albeit less strongly, by their mother's attempts to curb their child's aggression and by their mother's satisfaction with her maternal role.

Interaction between Biological and Social Determinants

The study of empathy provides a good example of both biological and social determinants of aggression. Furthermore, it provides an example of how the two classes of causation might interact to produce nonempathic and aggressive individuals. Several routes to an interaction effect have been suggested (Plomin, DeFries, & Loehlin, 1977; Rushton et al., 1986; Scarr & McCartney, 1983). Researchers have termed the first route *passive*. Children may inherit genes from their parents that not only limit empathic responding, but promote aggression. Then, because the parents are likely to behave in a nonempathic and aggressive manner, the environment presented to the child will reinforce the child's genetic endowment. Other children, of course, inherit characteristics and are exposed to an environment that promotes empathy.

A second approach is termed *evocative*. A child who enters the world with aggressive tendencies is likely to stimulate matching responses from others (Dodge, 1986), whereas a child who is kind and appears to empathize with those around him or her will elicit empathy. Thus, again the initial predispositions will be reinforced.

The third approach is termed *active* in acknowledgment that people show initiative in creating environments. However, because they are likely to choose activities that correspond to initial proclivities, an empathic child or adult may select as friends people who will respond well to empathic displays (Rushton et al., 1986). A child who is nonaggressive is unlikely to feel comfortable among people who behave aggressively and will select an environment to complement his or her personality.

These models provide a template through which to understand the development of empathic and nonempathic behavior and to understand how biology and environment might interact to exaggerate one's predilections. However, mismatches between the environment and biology do occur, which would be expected to moderate the degree of empathy shown. And let us not forget that forces outside the family affect behavior as well and may modify the child's biological predispositions. Many people who display violence in the family were not born to aggressive parents, nor did they grow up in an aggressive home environment.

Alcohol and Drug Use

As you have seen, empathic behavior is a function of both social and biological determinants and thus further demonstrates the multifaceted nature of the roots of aggression. This lesson will be repeated in this section on alcohol and drug use.

Relationship to Violence

Alcohol and drug use have been implicated in a variety of violent crimes, including assault and homicide (cf. Frieze & Browne, 1989). The National Research Council (Reiss & Roth, 1993) suggests that as many as half of recent violent crimes were preceded by the use of drugs or alcohol and that users of illegal drugs are disproportionately represented among those who commit violent crimes.

The same relationship between alcohol and drug use and violence has been observed in families. Hotaling and Sugarman (1986) report that in seven of the nine studies that investigated this phenomenon, men who assault their partners were more likely to abuse alcohol, compared to nonassaultive men. Furthermore, abusive men who have alcohol or drug problems are violent more frequently and often more severely than abusive men without such problems (Frieze & Browne, 1989; Walker, 1984).

Alcohol abuse has also been observed among child-abusing parents (cf. Zigler & Hall, 1989), but the correlation is not as strong as in cases of spousal assault. It is much more likely that alcohol-abusing parents will neglect their children or inflict psychological harm than physical harm, and there is some evidence that alcoholic parents, while quite willing to harm their partners, refrain from disciplining their children (cf. Pagelow, 1984). In contrast, moderate or heavy use of cocaine among women is associated with child abuse and neglect and with the women's participation in violent activities outside the home (Inciardi, Lockwood, & Pottieger, 1993).

Biochemical Determinants

What might account for the association between alcohol and violence in the home? Alcohol is a depressant both cognitively and physiologically. Its effects depend upon gender, the time since eating, general health, and experience with drinking (Jung, 1994). Women, for example, tend to have higher amounts of body fat than men and, therefore, will show higher concentrations of alcohol in the body after drinking the same amount as men. Although the exact reaction to alcohol then is difficult to predict, laboratory tests (Taylor & Gammon, 1975) have shown that low amounts of alcohol (e.g., .5 ounces/40 pounds of body weight) may inhibit aggression towards another person, but that high amounts of alcohol (e.g., 1.5 ounces/ 40 pounds of body weight) promote aggressive behavior.

Alcohol disrupts the passage of chemicals among the neurons in our central nervous system (Jung, 1994). In small doses it may just dull one's reaction to external events and reduce anxiety, but at higher doses alcohol may bring out negative moods. Serotonin, for example, is a neurotransmitter that helps to regulate moods; serotonin levels are lower among heavy drinkers and, incidentally, among people who engage in violent or impulsive behaviors (Jung, 1994). Dopamine, another neurotransmitter that helps us to experience pleasure, increases initially with alcohol use, but then declines. When the alcohol has worn off, there is commonly a rebound effect as well, wherein the drinker feels uncomfortable, anxious, and, in extreme cases, may experience hallucinations (Jung, 1994).

Alcohol impairs judgment and may lead individuals to misinterpret cues given by others (Hull & Bond, 1986). It has also been suggested that alcohol acting on the central nervous system disinhibits normal restraints against acting in antisocial or socially undesirable ways. While under the influence of alcohol people may be encouraged to act upon hostile impulses or angry reactions to those around them.

The relationship between violence and drugs other than alcohol varies according to the dosage and the nature of the drug (Reiss & Roth, 1993). Moderate dosages of marijuana and opiates reduce aggression in humans and other animals. But withdrawal from opiates heightens aggression, and chronic use of opiates, marijuana, and amphetamines affects the central nervous system, causing increased paranoia and hostility and decreasing effective social interactions (Reiss & Roth, 1993).

Social Determinants

The link between drug and alcohol use and aggression varies across studies and across individuals within studies, suggesting that we should also look for social determinants of the consequences of using alcohol and other drugs. For example, Steele and Southwick (1985) suggest that alcohol may disinhibit behaviors that are typically strongly suppressed and about which individuals may feel strong conflict. They cite the example of a juvenile delinquent who is taunted by peers to throw a brick through a school window. In this situation the juvenile is under strong conflict: Should he or she respond to peers or to his or her own conscience? Under the influence of alcohol the juvenile may be less likely to consider the severe consequences that might result from throwing the brick and the brick will be thrown. When faced with a less conflicted decision, the juvenile's behavior may not be affected by alcohol consumption. Steele and Southwick (1985) reexamined evidence from 34 studies of the effects of alcohol on social behavior and found, consistent with their prediction, that in high conflict situations people who had been drinking behaved more extremely than those who were sober. Also, alcohol produced this strong effect in high conflict situations, not in low ones. Thus, the researchers concluded that less conflictual behaviors do not require the disinhibitory effects of alcohol consumption.

Other researchers suggest that alcohol and drug use may not always be a direct cause of violence, and that instead some other factor may cause both the substance abuse and the violence. Substance abuse, for example, may result from social or environmental instability (Burgess & Draper, 1989). People who undergo severe economic or personal hardships may turn to alcohol or other drugs and they may also take out their frustrations on family members.

Leonard and Blane (1992) tested whether personality characteristics of alcohol abusers might moderate their violence. Surveying a sample of young married or cohabiting men, they examined the relationships among the men's alcohol use, violence towards a partner, and such characteristics as hostility, self-consciousness, and satisfaction with their relationship. The researchers found that aggression towards a partner was greater among men who reported a greater number of symptoms of alcohol abuse (e.g., blackouts, sneaking drinks, hangovers). However, personality characteristics moderated this relationship; the correspondence between alcohol dependency and violence was lower among men low in hostility and especially low among those who also reported satisfying marriages.

The inconsistent reactions, especially to the use of alcohol, have fueled another hypothesis: some people may drink or use drugs to provide themselves with a justification for violence (Hull & Bond, 1986). Marlatt and Rohsenow (1980) summarize research showing that, regardless of the alcohol content of a drink, people who think they consumed alcohol are more aggressive when provoked than those who think they consumed a nonalcoholic drink.

The idea that people may use alcohol as an excuse to perform socially undesirable or even illegal activities is consistent with the fact that reactions to alcohol are so varied. MacAndrew and Edgerton (1969) provide cross-cultural evidence that, while in some societies excessive drinking leads to frivolity, in others people drink deliberately before engaging in violent acts. "Relative to our comportment when sober, we may, for instance, become boisterous or solemn, depressed or euphoric, repugnantly gregarious or totally withdrawn, vicious or saintly . . ." (MacAndrew & Edgerton, 1969, p. 14). Reactions to alcohol also vary by gender. Women do not exhibit the same violent tendencies as men after ingesting alcohol (Reiss & Roth, 1993), even though their lower weight and higher body fat content might predict more extreme reactions. While endocrinological differences may underlie the varied reactions, differences in expectations about how women are supposed to behave are more likely to account for this phenomenon (Jung, 1994). Accordingly then, the cross-cultural and gender evidence strongly contradicts the disinhibition explanation for the relationship between alcohol and violence. Instead, the reaction to alcohol appears to be socially and culturally prescribed.

Another important point is that reactions to alcohol or drugs vary within the individual as well. Any given assailant does not always aggress when drunk, nor always refrain from aggressing when sober (cf. Frieze & Browne, 1989). A study by Roy (1977) also can be interpreted as support for this position. Roy found that the overwhelming majority of women who called a hotline for help with a violent husband reported that their husbands had problems with alcohol or drug abuse. Severely alcoholic or drug-abusing husbands beat their wives whether they were intoxicated or sober. In contrast, 80 percent of abusive husbands who could be characterized as "occasional drinkers" beat their wives only when they are drinking.

One final note: research on drugs or alcohol and aggression almost invariably uses cross-sectional methodology and thus leaves us to ponder the causal relationship between the two. We often do not know whether drug or alcohol use preceded or was concurrent with violent behavior (or victimization) or whether perpetrators get high or intoxicated following their involvement in such activities. Animal studies show that among those that had previously shown aggressive tendencies, ingestion of alcohol increased the rate of aggression; in contrast, ingestion of alcohol had no effect among those that had not been aggressive previously (Reiss & Roth, 1993). Furthermore, studies on humans show that childhood aggressiveness is a strong predictor of both alcohol use and violence as an adult (Reiss & Roth, 1993). Therefore, we cannot always characterize alcohol or drugs as the cause of violence.

Alcohol or Drug Use by the Victim

Expectations about the disinhibiting effects of alcohol may even affect victims of violence (cf. Frieze & Browne, 1989). As noted previously, battered partners often accept the "alcohol excuse," which permits them to avoid the recognition that their spouse is truly a violent person. Such excuses also give them hope that, if the drinking ceases, the violence will cease as well.

Alcohol use among victims has also been noted in the family violence literature. While Hotaling and Sugarman's (1986) review noted that only one out of six studies reported greater alcohol use

TABLE 8.1 Attributions of Responsibility for Wife Abuse

Condition	Percentage of Blame Attributed to:			
	Man	Woman	Situation	Chance
Man drunk				
Yes	49.46	21.21	21.07	8.26
No	52.88	22.73	15.89	8.51
Woman drunk				
Yes	46.41	25.35	20.47	7.77
No	55.11	18.95	17.05	8.90

Source: Adapted from Richardson, D. C., & Campbell, J. L. (1980). Alcohol and wife abuse: The effects of alcohol on attributions of blame for wife abuse. *Personality and Social Psychology Bulletin, 6,* p. 54. Copyright 1980, Sage Publications. Used with permission.

among the partners of abusive men, other people have found fairly high rates of drinking among victims (e.g., Walker, 1984).

Victims who drink are held more responsible for their victimization than those who are sober (e.g., Dent & Arias, 1990). Richardson and Campbell (1980) asked college students to read a description of a "typical incident of wife abuse" and to assign blame for the event to the husband, wife, situation, or chance (see Table 8.1). When the abusive husband was drunk, blame was significantly more likely to be assigned to the "situation." When the victim was drunk, she received significantly more blame and her husband received significantly less blame.

A couple of explanations have been given to account for this phenomenon (Dent & Arias, 1990). First, since victims of spouse assault are usually women and drunkenness among women is seen as less socially desirable than among men, an intoxicated female victim may present an unattractive picture to many people. Second, given that people look for explanations of violence and try to assure themselves that it will not happen to them, they may settle upon any available clue. Knowing that people who have been drinking often act in obnoxious ways may lead individuals to assume that this victim did likewise. Thus, they may imagine that the intoxicated victim provoked the partner's violence.

Concluding Remarks

This chapter shows examples of how both biological and social explanations can be used to understand violence in the family. We learned that the relationship between empathy and violence has been studied from sociobiological, genetic, physiological, social learning, and attachment perspectives. Similarly, the role of alcohol and other drugs in violent behavior has a rich history of empirical research from a variety of viewpoints. The way to conceptualize all of these viewpoints is nicely illustrated by the following statement by Burgess & Draper (1989). After reviewing theories of family violence, they noted that

> . . . they are not simple competitors in a theoretical contest. They, instead, may be viewed as potential collaborators that have directed our attention to different correlates, aspects, and manifestations of family violence. (p. 68)

Now that we have explored the factors that promote aggression within the family, let us turn our attention to efforts to handle family violence and to prevent it. In the next chapter we will examine legal and social service responses to violence. In the final chapter we will study efforts to prevent violence and efforts to intervene after violence has occurred.

Legal and Social Service Interventions in Cases of Family Violence

CHAPTER OBJECTIVES

Moving from Tolerance to Intolerance of Family Violence
The Growth of Mandatory Arrest Policies
Theory and Evidence about the Effect of Arrest
Victim Involvement with the Arrest
Prosecution of Family Violence Cases
Victim and Witness Accuracy
Variations in Interview Techniques

Confidence in the Testimony of Witnesses and Victims
Expert Testimony
Professionals' Failure to Report
Ambiguity of the Evidence
Victim Denial
Biased Processing of Evidence
Belief That Reporting is Wrong
Benefits of Reporting
Compassion versus Punishment
Concluding Remarks

If privacy has any physical locale in modern society, it is in the home, properly renowned as a haven in the heartless world. If privacy has any social focus, it is in the family, within a set of intimate relationships that can flourish only when sufficiently protected from public scrutiny. But privacy can metastasize into a Hobbesian arena where the strong prey on the weak, and the weak prey on those who are weaker still. Life's greatest moments occur behind closed doors. So, too, do some of modern life's most outrageous exploitations. (Zimring, 1989, pp. 547–548)

The quotation above aptly describes the dilemma facing a society plagued by family violence. As violence in the home becomes more and more a subject of public discussion and media attention, lay-people, psychologists, and other professionals must contemplate just how much and when violence within the family should be subject to public scrutiny and judgment.

Public response to recent cases of family violence includes indifference to the event, compassion for the victim and perpetrator, and efforts to punish the violator (Gelles & Straus, 1988). In this chapter we will consider the advantages and disadvantages of different types of public response. We will focus specifically on the criminalization of family violence and the roles of social service professionals. Does it help to arrest people who assault family members, or is more harm done in the long run? What factors impede the prosecution of cases of family violence? Why do professionals such as psychologists, physicians, and the clergy hesitate to refer cases for legal action? We will address these questions and discuss whether we have now gone too far in making family violence a matter of legal, and therefore public, concern. Although we have begun to identify the issues that must be considered in this complex debate, the questions raised have no ready answers.

Moving from Tolerance to Intolerance of Family Violence

On June 10, 1983, a man named Charles Thurman went to a home in Torrington, Connecticut, where his son and his wife, Tracy, had been living (Gombossy, 1985). Since October of 1982, when Charles physically attacked her, Tracy had called the police on numerous occasions and complained about his threats to kill her. On this day Tracy again called the police and then went outside to reason with her husband and try to prevent another attack. When a police officer arrived, he heard a "woman's screams" and saw Charles holding a bloody jackknife. Then the officer saw him drop the knife and kick Tracy in the head. After this, police arrested him. Tracy Thurman, who is now partially paralyzed, sued the city of Torrington and its police officers for failing to provide her with equal protection of the law, which is guaranteed by the Fourteenth Amendment to the U.S. Constitution. She claimed that the police would have treated her differently had her assailant not been her husband. Tracy Thurman won her suit and was awarded $2.3 million. Her son was also awarded money for the emotional suffering he had experienced. Tracy Thurman's case served as the impetus for a law in Connecticut and other states that requires police officers to arrest offenders when there is reasonable evidence of family violence.

In most jurisdictions police may arrest alleged offenders when there is evidence of a felony, a serious injury, or a weapon present. When police believe that a misdemeanor charge is appropriate, police may arrest only when the offender commits the crime in the presence of the officer and when the victim agrees to be responsible for the arrest by signing the complaint (Goolkasian, 1986). Tracy Thurman's suit followed class action suits filed by victims, mostly battered wives, in New York City, Cleveland, and Oakland. These suits asserted that police officers rarely arrest family violators and that, accordingly, familial victims are not protected to the same extent as stranger victims (Gelles & Straus, 1988). A longitudinal study of the Connecticut criminal justice system (Herzberger & Channels, 1991) found similarly that alleged violent offenders who were related to their victims were required to post substantially less bail ($15,650 less) upon their arrest than alleged offenders not related to victims, thereby reducing one of the impediments of a release from pretrial detention.

Some experts, however, find no overwhelming evidence that police protect family victims less than other victims of assault. Elliott (1989) cites studies that show either no reduction in arrest for family offenses, or differences in arrest rates that are attributable not to the relationship between offender and victim, but to the presence or absence of legitimate arrest criteria. Police officers are more likely to arrest people when evidence of serious injury or a weapon is present or when the victim requests that an arrest be made (Buzawa & Austin, 1992/1993); such evidence and the victim's request may be more likely in nonfamily offenses.

Regardless of whether differential treatment of family members occurred in a few or many instances, cases such as Tracy Thurman's and increased media attention to family violence have influenced public policy. Since the early 1980s public officials have become less tolerant of family violence and more committed to public rather than private solutions to the problem. The 1984 U.S. Attorney General's Task Force on Family Violence report, for example, included fifty-eight references to the involvement of the police or other criminal justice officials in cases of family violence (cf. Zimring, 1989). All fifty states have now passed laws that require professionals such as psychologists, social workers, medical personnel, day care workers, teachers, and sometimes clergy to report all suspected cases of family violence to public agencies, and the laws prescribe substantial legal penalties (usually at least a misdemeanor charge) for failure to report (Maney, 1988). Even if psychologists or social workers feel that they may be able to counsel the family and control the violent person in a relatively private fashion, the law no longer permits this.

However, the transition from tolerance and privacy to public and official judgment has not been smooth and has provoked much controversy along the way. Let us look at some of the more persistent problems.

The Growth of Mandatory Arrest Policies

About the same time that Tracy Thurman's story was being publicized widely, an experiment was conducted with the cooperation of the Minneapolis Police Department (Sherman & Berk, 1984) that was equally, if not more, influential among professionals. Prior to this experiment most police around the country were trained to mediate disputes when called to the home during or after domestic violence. Police would often talk to both parties and ensure that a calm atmosphere prevailed before they left the home. Sometimes police officers would require the offending partner to leave the home for a number of hours and, of course, police had the right to arrest the offender should the evidence warrant such an action.

Sherman and Berk's (1984) study revolutionized the handling of domestic violence cases. Police officers in Minneapolis, when called to a domestic violence dispute, consulted a randomly generated list to determine how misdemeanor or "moderate" cases of violence should be handled. Thus, depending upon random assignment, police officers were required to mediate the dispute and advise the parties, to order the perpetrator to leave the home for eight hours, or to arrest the perpetrator. The researchers largely eliminated police discretion and were able to assess the consequences of each type of intervention. They followed the families for six months, interviewing the victims to determine whether violence had recurred and checking police records for further arrests. Both indices revealed that arrest was substantially more effective in reducing recidivism than the other interventions. For example, official records show that only 10 percent of the suspects who were arrested repeated their violence, whereas 19 percent of those advised and 24 percent of those who were ordered out of the home did so.

This study has been criticized for a number of reasons (e.g., Elliott, 1989). Officers knew what intervention was required when they determined whether a case was eligible for inclusion in the study (e.g., whether evidence pointed to a misdemeanor charge as opposed to a felony for which arrest was mandatory). Thus, officers' discomfort with the assigned intervention may have influenced their judgments about the eligibility of some cases. Also, only those police officers who volunteered participated in the study. These officers may differ from nonvolunteering officers in ways that would affect the results of more widespread arrest policies in Minneapolis and in other cities.

Yet, despite the criticisms and despite Sherman and Berk's (1984) advice against mandatory arrest policies, the Minneapolis findings encouraged police departments across the country to change the way that they handle cases of domestic violence (Goolkasian, 1986). By 1991 fifteen states had created laws that required mandatory arrest (Sherman, Smith, Schmidt, & Rogan, 1992) and many others encouraged officers to do so. Thus, police officers in many locales lost the power to use their own discretion in cases of family violence. The impact has been enormous, increasing the rates of arrest as much as twenty times those of the pre-mandatory arrest period (e.g., Jaffe, Wolfe, Telford, & Austin, 1986). In stark contrast to some periods of history when abuse of family members received less official attention, now family violence is supposed to receive special protection in the eyes of the criminal justice community.

Theory and Evidence about the Effect of Arrest

Why might arresting the offender produce less future violence? Arrest is believed to produce *general deterrence* (Blumstein, Cohen, & Nagin, 1978); that is, arrest is a sign to society at large that the behavior in question will not be tolerated. While the amount of potential crime that is deterred may vary depending upon such factors as the nature of the crime and the size of the city in which the arrested parties live (Blumstein et al., 1978; Brown, 1978), the accumulated research suggests that arrest is an effective general deterrent to crime.

Arrest also conveys a message to the victim. When a family member is arrested, victims, perhaps for the first time, may feel as though someone cares about their plight and they may develop the courage to leave the abusive relationship or to seek further help. Furthermore, should the abuse continue following an arrest, victims may recognize that the violence is deep-rooted and thereby give up hope for a change in the relationship.

Arrest is also theorized to have a *specific deterrent* effect, reducing recidivism in the punished individual, as was shown in the study by Sherman and Berk (1984). Some theorists, however, propose that with certain individuals arrest may not deter violence and, in fact, might enhance its likelihood. Sherman and his colleagues (Sherman et al., 1992; Sherman, 1992) summarize these arguments. They suggest that we need to distinguish between *formal* and *informal* constraints upon behavior, with the possibility of being arrested considered a formal constraint. Informal controls upon behavior are derived from social sanctions, such as the influence of arrest upon one's marriage, employment, or social standing. The threat of legal action, they suggest, may act as a deterrent only among people with strong informal social networks that would be imperiled by public notification of the violence. These people will, upon arrest, feel shame and will be chastened by the experience. However, in accordance with a ''labeling'' perspective, the authors suggest that too much shame and too little social interdependence can be hurtful to the arrested person. Once labeled as ''deviant'' and rejected by mainstream society, arrested offenders may seek social recognition among other deviants (Becker, 1964). In this case, offenders will be likely to commit further violent crime.

Another problem with arrest is that the violent offender may discover that the penalty for domestic violence is small. Most offenders spend little, if any, time in prison (Goolkasian, 1986). For this reason the possibility of arrest may be more likely to dissuade only those who have not yet committed assault and who thus possess little knowledge of the weak consequences.

Given the varied arguments on both sides of this issue, Sherman, Berk, and other researchers (Berk, Campbell, Klap, & Western, 1992; Sherman et al., 1992; Pate & Hamilton, 1992) designed new experimental investigations of the effect of arrest on domestic violence. They gained cooperation with police departments in several locations (Milwaukee, Omaha, Colorado Springs, and Dade County, Florida) to test for the generalizability of their earlier findings and to determine whether the characteristics of the population contribute to varying effects of arrest. In particular, they hypothesized that arrest among employed and married individuals would deter future violence, while arrest among unemployed and unmarried individuals would not.

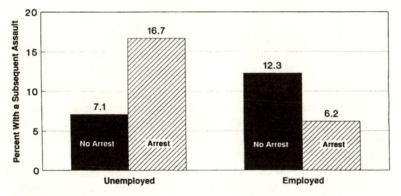

FIGURE 9.1
Percent of suspects with a subsequent assault by employment status and
arrest status

Source: Pate, A. M., & Hamilton, E. E. (1992). Formal and informal deterrents to
domestic violence: The Dade County spouse assault experiment. *American Sociological
Review, 57,* p. 695. Copyright 1992, American Sociological Association. Reprinted by
permission.

To varying degrees, the results of the new experiments supported
the proposal that informal ties are important determinants of the effect
of arrest (Sherman, 1992). Among those who would suffer informal
social sanctions due to arrest, arrest acted as a deterrent. Among those
with a low stake in conformity to social norms (e.g., marriage, employment), arrest acted as a boon to future violence. An example of
the results from Dade County are shown in Figure 9.1 (Pate & Hamilton, 1992).

Berk and his colleagues (Berk et al., 1992) caution against assuming that the results support any particular model of the effect of
arrest. The studies present no evidence, for example, that arrested
offenders change their self-concept in the manner suggested by labeling theory. Nor can we know for sure that the married or employed
people in these studies were strongly concerned about informal sanctions. Marriage and employment were merely "indicators" of social
control; social control itself was not measured.

But the results are certainly provocative. As Sherman et al.
(1992) state:

> The effectiveness of legal sanctions rests on a foundation of informal
> control. If formal sanctions deter only those with a stake in
> conformity, it makes little sense to increase formal sanctions for
> suspects whose stakes are low. If exercise can only strengthen a

well-fed body, more exercise would be a foolish prescription for a starving body. . . . For domestic violence offenses, the findings raise troubling policy implications. A policy of arresting employed persons but not unemployed persons would punish employment. A policy of not arresting at all may erode the *general* deterrent effect of arrest on potential spouse abusers. (p. 688)

Many questions remain to be answered before social science can truly inform the national debate over this legal dilemma. For example, we know little about the *long-term effects* of arrest or non-arrest on domestic violence (Elliott, 1989). Some findings suggest that arrest decreases the threat of violence in the short-term, but may enhance the threat after the initial shock of arrest has dissipated (Schmidt & Sherman, 1993). And what aspects of the arrest procedure influence the alleged offender? Is it the humiliation of being taken from one's home by the police? Is it spending a little bit of time in jail? Since arrest rarely leads to prosecution, we also need information about the lessons learned by offenders whose cases are subsequently dismissed.

Carmody and Williams (1987) provide further evidence that the threat of possible arrest may be a relatively weak sanction. They surveyed a national sample of adult men living with a female partner, gathering their judgments about whether they were likely to experience certain sanctions if they hit their partner and the seriousness of those perceived sanctions. The researchers asked men whether their partner would retaliate and would leave or seek a divorce, and whether they would be arrested and would suffer disapproval from friends and other relatives. The men believed that retaliation, arrest, and divorce or separation were quite unlikely consequences of hitting their partner. Should they happen, however, the men regarded all but retaliation to be serious events. The men did expect to suffer disapproval and loss of respect, and these were seen as serious too.

Carmody and Williams (1987) also distinguished between men who admitted to assaulting their partner within the last year and those who did not. Few differences were found. While assaultive men believed that their partners were significantly more likely to retaliate than nonassaultive men, neither group viewed this as a serious concern. But nonassaultive men believed that they would suffer more serious social condemnation.

These results led Carmody and Williams (1987) to be pessimistic about the current role of sanctions in deterring assault against women in this country. At most, the expectation of disapproval from friends or relatives might deter male assault; the possibility of other sanctions was not taken seriously. Carmody and Williams suggest, however, that the study points to possible interventions other than criminal action. Using educational campaigns to stress the shame and disapproval experienced by violators might tap into men's existing concerns and thus might be effective in reducing violence against women.

Victim Involvement with the Arrest

Another recent change in police procedures is the decreased use of victim complaints as a criterion for arrest. The Attorney General's Task Force on Family Violence (1984) urged that police officers not require victims to sign complaints and that instead police officers list themselves as the complainant. This shift in policy recognizes the conundrum of the victim. Those who fear retribution from arrested perpetrators can feel less responsible for the perpetrators' plight. Furthermore, the policy communicates that it is not the victim's decision whether an arrest is warranted; rather, it is the right and obligation of the state to protect its citizens, even when citizens do not ask for protection. Of course, victims who do not cooperate with the state in the arrest and subsequent efforts to prosecute make it harder to penalize the perpetrator.

These changes may not relieve all impediments to the arrest of familial perpetrators, however. Police officers are less likely to make an arrest when called to the scene of domestic violence by the victim than by a third party (Berk & Loseke, 1980–81). Berk and Loseke suggest that a victim who is prevented from calling the police either by the assailant or because of injury may be perceived to be especially harmed, while a victim who can call for help may be perceived to be relatively unscathed by the conflict. Also, conflicts that come to the attention of a third party, such as a neighbor who calls the police, may be seen as more troublesome to the community. This reasoning is supported by the findings of Buzawa and Austin (1992/1993). Their research with Detroit police found that when bystanders were present, even when the bystander was a child, an assailant was more likely to be arrested (see Table 9.1). Once again, when the violence takes place in private, it is more likely to be regarded as a private affair.

Prosecution of Family Violence Cases

Prosecution of family violence cases is rarely successful. Some people suggest that this is for the same reasons that prosecution of nonfamily assault often fails (Elliott, 1989). Evidence presented by uninvolved witnesses dramatically enhances the likelihood of prosecution and conviction; yet often no outside, credible witness to the assault is available. In addition, the victim may not cooperate fully

TABLE 9.1 Percentage of Arrests by Presence or Absence of Bystanders

Offender Arrested	Bystander/Witnesses Present		Children Present	
	Yes (N)	No (N)	Yes (N)	No (N)
Yes	49 (24)	22 (21)	42 (28)	22 (19)
No	51 (25)	79 (83)	58 (39)	78 (66)

Source: Adapted from Buzawa, E. S., & Austin, T. (1992/1993). Determining police response to domestic violence victims: The role of victim preference. *American Behavioral Scientist, 36,* pp. 614, 615. Copyright 1992/93, American Behavioral Scientist. Reprinted by permission.

due to worry that prosecution will destroy their relationship with the offender, will lead to financial hardship for themselves and other family members, and will further anger and provoke the offender. Without a cooperative witness, prosecutors are often dependent solely upon evidence collected by the police at the time of the alleged offense. Even when cooperative witnesses exist, prosecutors may have difficulty convincing a judge or jury about the veracity and the importance of the complaint. Let us examine some of these impediments.

Victim and Witness Accuracy

Research over many years has examined the conditions under which witnesses and victims of crime provide accurate and inaccurate accounts of the event. For example, we know that people are more accurate when they testify about familiar and recent events and people become less accurate when subjected to suggestive questioning. One well-known study of this phenomenon demonstrated the power of suggestive language. Asking viewers of a film how fast the cars were going when they ''smashed'' (or ''collided'' or ''bumped'') into each other produced a higher estimate than by asking how fast they were going when they ''hit'' (or ''contacted'') each other (Loftus & Palmer, 1974; see Table 9.2). Furthermore, in a second experiment witnesses were asked whether they saw broken glass. People who were questioned about the speed of the cars using the ''smashed'' wording were more likely to report seeing glass than people who were questioned using ''hit'' or who were not questioned about speed. No glass was depicted in the film.

TABLE 9.2 Speed Estimates for the Verbs Used in Experiment I

Verb	Mean Speed Estimate
Smashed	40.8
Collided	39.3
Bumped	38.1
Hit	34.0
Contacted	31.8

Source: Loftus, E. F., & Palmer, J. C. (1974). Reconstruction of automobile destruction: An example of the interaction between language and memory. *Journal of Verbal Learning and Verbal Behavior, 13,* p. 586. Copyright 1974, Academic Press. Reprinted by permission.

Special circumstances prevail in cases of family violence. The identity of family members is rarely in doubt, and the witness or victim often can describe a series of events involving the offender and victim, rather than the short, one-time occurrence that characterizes many instances of nonfamily assault. But for prosecution to be successful the witness or victim must describe accurately the event upon which prosecution is based. When questioned repeatedly, especially when suggestive questioning has been used, accuracy can suffer (Hall, Loftus, & Tousignant, 1984).

Legal professionals and psychologists have been especially concerned about the accuracy and truthfulness of child witnesses to family violence. Under some circumstances children have more difficulty than do adults in discriminating real versus imagined occurrences (Johnson & Foley, 1984), but at least some studies show that from quite a young age children are as accurate as adults when they are familiar with the people or events they recall (Johnson & Foley, 1984; Loftus & Davies, 1984). Furthermore, although children do lie when motivated to do so, there is no evidence that children are different in this regard than adults (Ceci & Bruck, 1993).

One of the most controversial lines of investigation has examined whether children are more suggestible. Ceci and Bruck (1993) reviewed studies of this question and found that 83 percent of them showed preschoolers to be more suggestible than older children and adults and, therefore, more likely to provide unbelievable testimony. Ceci and Bruck propose that young children's encoding of information in memory is weaker; older children and adults interpret information as it is encoded and thereby strengthen their memory for the event and their resistance to suggestion. Younger children also may be more likely to regard adults as credible sources of information and, therefore, they may incorporate new information they hear about during questioning. Ceci and Bruck (1993) propose that, for these reasons, the repeated questioning of child witnesses by a variety of interviewers may especially detract from their accuracy.

One intriguing series of studies on this topic, however, did not find a major problem with suggestibility and accuracy among young children (Goodman, Rudy, Bottoms, & Aman, 1990). The first study compared memory for an observed, neutral event versus one in which the individual participated. A neutral event was used because the researchers investigated whether they could through suggestion elicit false testimony about sexual abuse in an otherwise innocuous context. Four- and seven-year-old children were taken in pairs to a dilapidated trailer where a male confederate played games with one of the children, while the other watched. The confederate and participant child, among other activities, touched each other's knees while playing Simon Says, and the child was lifted onto a table and photographed.

Almost two weeks later the children were questioned about what happened in the trailer. Leading, incorrect questions were asked about the identity of the confederate (''He had a beard and a mustache, right?'') and about activities that might prompt an allegation of sexual abuse (''He took your clothes off, didn't he?''). Older children spontaneously recalled more correct information than did younger children and were more correct in response to questions about the events. In response to questions about abuse the 7-year-olds were accurate 93 percent of the time and 4-year-olds were accurate 83 percent of the time. Table 9.3 provides the number of correct and incorrect answers to each question. Errors are listed according to whether the child made a ''commission'' error (saying something occurred when it did not), an ''omission'' error (neglecting to report that something occurred when it did), or said ''I don't know'' in response to the question. The authors report that most of the errors were made by only a few children, one of whom was confused throughout the interview and another who reported that she liked to pretend. Omission errors were more prevalent than commission errors.

Participant children were more resistant to suggestion about nonabuse questions than children who merely witnessed the events (94 percent accuracy for participants, 79 percent for observers). But almost all members of both groups resisted any suggestion that abusive treatment had occurred (91 and 92 percent, respectively).

TABLE 9.3 Number of Children Who Provided a Correct Response, a Commission Error (CO), an Omission Error (OM), or a "Don't Know" (DK) in Response to Abuse Questions

	4-Year-Olds				7-Year-Olds			
	Correct	CO	OM	DK	Correct	CO	OM	DK
He took your clothes off, didn't he?	18	0	0	0	18	0	0	0
He took the other girl's (boy's) clothes off, didn't he?	18	0	0	0	18	0	0	0
How many times did he spank you?	17	1	0	0	18	0	0	0
How many times did he spank the other girl (boy)?	17	1	0	0	18	0	0	0
The person in the trailer didn't touch you, did he?	10	1	6	1	13	1	2	2
The person in the trailer didn't touch the other girl (boy), did he?	10	2	4	2	13	0	2	3
Did he kiss you?	17	1	0	0	18	0	0	0
Did he kiss the other girl (boy)?	16	2	0	0	18	0	0	0
Did he put anything in your mouth?	18	0	0	0	18	0	0	0
Did he put anything in the other girl's (boy's) mouth?	17	1	0	0	18	0	0	0
Did he take a picture of you?	13	2	2	1	18	0	0	0
Did he take a picture of the other girl (boy)?	18	0	0	0	17	0	1	0
Did you touch him?	10	2	5	1	5	0	4	0
Did the other girl (boy) touch him?	11	0	5	2	9	0	7	2

Source: Goodman, G. S., Rudy, L., Bottoms, B. L., & Aman, C. (1990). Children's concerns and memory: Issues of ecological validity in the study of children's eyewitness testimony. In R. Fivush & J. A. Hudson (Eds.), *Knowing and remembering in young children* (pp. 249–284). Cambridge: Cambridge University Press, p. 263. © Cambridge University Press, 1990. Reprinted with the permission of Cambridge University Press.

In another study Goodman et al. (1990) unobtrusively observed 3- to 6-year old children who received inoculations during a physical and rated the degree of stress each child exhibited. Some were relatively calm about the event; others were greatly distressed, crying and yelling for help. Generally, stress level correlated positively with children's enhanced recall of the event upon being interviewed a few days or a week later. Not only did stressed children recall more information, but they were less suggestible.

Often in child abuse prosecutions children are interviewed long after the event. Thus, Goodman et al. (1990) decided to interview the same children a year later to discern whether they would recall the event as vividly and, again, to see if a report of ''abusive'' actions could be elicited. Children showed substantial losses in their memory for the events, but all children correctly answered ''no'' when questioned whether the nurse hit them or kissed them.

These studies are important because they directly test matters of interest to criminal prosecution of child abuse. The studies suggest that even young children can provide accurate answers to questions, and, contrary to what many people think, most children actively resist the suggestion that abuse occurred when it did not. This type of investigation should increase our confidence in children's reports of traumatic events (but see the discussion in Box 9.1 about adults' repressed memories of childhood abuse).

Perhaps, as Goodman et al. (1990) suggest, our impression that adults and children have such poor memory and are quite suggestible stems from the fact that most research tests memory for trivial matters. Many of the studies, such as the study by Loftus and Palmer (1974), present filmed events or tell stories about innocuous incidents that do not involve the research participants. Goodman et al. (1990) believe that memory for events and resistance to suggestion is particularly strong when people are questioned about important events that have meaning to them. This makes a good deal of sense. Try to recall what you ate at each meal during the last three days. Unless you have just broken a fast, you will probably find this a difficult and uninteresting task. Now recall what you did on your last birthday or on the last major holiday. You should perform much better on the latter task.

Variations in Interview Techniques

Other research has studied how various interview styles affect a person's accuracy and memory for events. Saywitz, Geiselman, and Bornstein (1992), for example, have explored the benefits of the *cognitive* interviewing techniques. The cognitive interview comprised

BOX 9.1

You have probably read in the newspaper about cases of repressed memory of abuse that occurred during childhood. In these cases a person, who went many years without awareness of being abused, will discover or remember one or more such incidents. Elizabeth Loftus (1993), a psychologist who has done significant research on topics related to eyewitness and expert testimony, has reviewed many cases of repressed memory and concludes that we need to be extremely careful about assuming that the discovered memories are authentic.

Examples of repressed memory include the case of the father who was convicted of murdering his daughter's childhood friend (Loftus, 1993). His conviction was based upon the daughter's newly revived memories of the incident that allegedly transpired twenty years earlier. Another case involves a former Miss America who repressed memory for her childhood sexual molestation until she was 24. Not all cases of repressed memory end up in the courts, but it can be lucrative for the victim. Plaintiffs who sued relatives for abuse after recovering their memories for the incident have won as much as $5 million.

Some researchers claim that repressed memory for sexual abuse is common. Briere and Conte (1993), for example, found that 59 percent of a clinical sample experienced amnesia for the abuse they suffered. Loftus, however, doubts this statistic. She points to various pressures to imagine that the incidents took place. She notes that therapists may create "memories" of abuse in their clients through suggestion, and she cites examples of therapists telling clients that their symptoms resemble those of people who have been abused and then prodding the clients to contemplate whether this happened to them. Some therapists even interpret clients' dreams as evidence of repressed memory for abuse.

Loftus is careful to note that we cannot know yet which cases of repressed memory are accurate. Even if most cases are somehow found to be invalid, it is possible that some cases are real. But she worries that therapists, overzealously probing for hidden cases of abuse, will elicit false accusations through the power of suggestion, and thus will bring tragedy into the lives of many innocent families.

three phases: rapport-building, elicitation of a complete narrative account, and then specific questions designed to clarify and expand upon the narrative. The interviewer might ask about the smells experienced during the event or how the scene might look from the perspective of others in the room, or might ask the interviewee to recall the events in backward order.

Third- and sixth-graders witnessed two staged events; one included a disagreement over the use of a slide projector and the other revolved around a man in a waiting room. Then the children received a "practice" interview, conducted by trained college students, and a "target" interview, conducted by professional detectives. The practice interview, following one of the staged events, was designed either just to build rapport between the interviewer and interviewee *or* to enhance memory through cognitive techniques. The target interview used cognitive techniques or more standard, less structured procedures.

While the accuracy of the information recalled did not vary much across conditions (at least 85 percent accuracy), children recalled more items of information when they received the cognitive interview, especially when they were able to practice on this technique as well. Specific aspects of the cognitive techniques were also explored. The backward-order procedure elicited new information about half the time and asking the interviewee to assume a different perspective elicited new information 75 percent of the time.

The researchers employed many interviewers for this study and found wide variation in the effectiveness of each (National Institute of Justice Research in Brief, 1992). Some interviewers were characterized as "ambivalent" because they appeared to be bored with the task. Their interviews took less than ten minutes, less than half the average interview time, and elicited the least amount of information. "Condescending" interviewers asked the most questions, but did so in a way that conveyed their lack of confidence in the respondent's answers. They gathered more information than ambivalent interviewers, but more of the information was inaccurate. "Positive" interviewers appeared to be interested in the interviewee and encouraged the respondent to expand upon initial answers. They, as you might imagine, elicited the most information and the most accurate information.

The Saywitz et al. (1992) study suggests that interview style and content critically influence the information gathered. Since interviewing occurs at all phases of prosecution (initial investigation, testimony during court proceedings), officials must be well trained in interview techniques and understand the implications of using one form of questioning versus another.

Even when memories are full and accurate, however, respondents may not want to disclose information to the investigator. As we have discussed previously, fear, loyalty, or even affection for the perpetrator may make family members less forthcoming, and perpetrators themselves may not want to disclose information that could lead to formal sanctions. Sudman and Bradburn (1982) summarize techniques for enhancing disclosure of threatening information. For example, they emphasize the importance of making respondents feel comfortable by using familiar words when asking about sensitive topics. Asking people how often they "hit" or "belt" someone in an average month is likely to produce a higher response rate than asking how often they "assault" or "abuse" another.

Another technique for enhancing disclosure is the use of *loaded questions,* an example of which is the familiar, "When did you stop beating your wife" (Sudman & Bradburn, 1982). Loaded questions often assume that the respondent was involved in the undesirable behavior and, therefore, they are risky to use. However, they make admitting one's participation in the activity much easier. Another way of eliciting a more truthful response is to embed the undesirable behavior of interest in a list of more and less threatening behaviors. An interviewer might, according to this strategy, ask a wife who was thought to have been beaten by her husband's fists whether her husband ever shot her, stabbed her, threw her down stairs, and so on. Then, after disclaiming victimization by these more horrid methods, the woman may feel less threatened about responding in the affirmative to the question about being beaten.

Confidence in the Testimony of Witnesses and Victims

All the accuracy and detailed information a person can muster may not matter if listeners do not believe the account. Loftus and Goodman's (1985) review of the literature on witness credibility suggests a variety of ways in which witnesses destroy others' trust in their story. They report evidence that witnesses who speak in standard English as opposed to jargon or who have no discernable accent are believed more than other speakers. Those who exhibit such weak and non-confident speech characteristics as hedging (e.g., "I think . . .") or hesitation are also less credible. A confident, strong voice convinces listeners that the speaker is telling the truth and remembers the events accurately.

Unfortunately, there is little or no association between being confident about one's testimony and being accurate (Wells & Murray, 1984). People who are sure they remember details correctly generally are no more accurate about the details than those who are unsure. To compound this problem, women and children display speech characteristics that often make them appear less certain (Goodman, Golding, & Haith, 1984; Tannen, 1990). Thus, they often are perceived to be less credible witnesses. For example, children sometimes react strangely in a formal courtroom situation, especially when they are forced to confront the alleged offender about whom they are testifying. This reaction is likely to be misunderstood by observers (see Box 9.2).

In addition to being misled by a confident witness, people misjudge accounts because they have trouble discerning the differences between a lie and the truth and between accurate and inaccurate memory for events. They also allow stereotypes and misinformation to affect their judgments. In one study (Goodman, Bottoms, Herscovici, & Shaver, 1989) mock jurors believed that older children presented more accurate and more truthful accounts of their visit to a nurse for an inoculation. In reality the jurors could not identify the children who provided accurate accounts.

Even professionals are confused about when to believe witnesses. Leippe, Brigham, Cousins, and Romanczyk (1989) report that prosecutors have more faith in the testimony of an eyewitness to a crime than do attorneys for the defense. Prosecutors believe that both children and adults generally give accurate accounts of crimes that they have witnessed (over 80 percent of the time); defense attorneys, in contrast, believe that adults give accurate testimony only 67 percent of the time and children younger than age 10 do so only 46 percent of the time.

Once in a while an alleged victim of assault retracts testimony given earlier. In a study of attorney reactions to children's retracted accounts of sexual abuse, Leippe et al. (1989) found that, as predicted, defense attorneys and prosecutors see different reasons for the retraction. As Table 9.4 shows, defense attorneys are more likely to believe that the previous testimony was false; they are also less likely to believe that the child was pressured to retract evidence by a family member.

Differences in beliefs about the accuracy and truthfulness of witnesses lead to substantial differences in their credibility in the eyes of jurors, judges, and attorneys. Someone who is perceived to lack confidence or the ability to remember accurately may not have an

BOX 9.2

Pynoos and Eth (1984) describe the unfortunate case of 4-year-old "Julie," who witnessed her father kill her mother:

> . . . (A)t the time of the divorce, Julie's father had publicly threatened to kill his ex-wife. . . . Although the father lacked an alibi for the night of the crime, there was no physical evidence linking him to the homicide. During our initial interview with Julie, weeks after the murder, . . . she consistently placed her father at the scene, described significant portions of the central action, and recounted her father's efforts to clean up prior to leaving. . . .
>
> Only after the district attorney saw Julie stabbing a pillow, crying, "Daddy pushed mommy down," did he become convinced that the father indeed was the murderer. . . .
>
> On the morning of the trial, Julie played freely outside the courtroom and chatted spontaneously with her relatives and us. However, on the stand she could not qualify as a witness. . . . No effort was made to put the little girl at ease. The judge did not introduce himself beforehand; he refused to use his chambers, and excluded her closest family members. . . .
>
> Julie was not prepared for the sight of her father, whom she had not seen in over six months, dressed in prison garb. On her way to the stand, she walked over and gave him a big hug. . . . Once seated, she placed both hands over her mouth. The district attorney began the examination by showing her a coloring book; she shrugged silently, and the judge looked annoyed. The district attorney then asked her if she was a girl or a boy, and she fidgeted shyly. The judge interrupted by stating, "It doesn't appear to the court that she can qualify." He then abruptly dismissed her. Without her testimony, the father was acquitted and Julie was returned to his care. (pp. 100–101)

Cases such as this one convince many legal and psychological professionals to vary the court proceedings to fit the characteristics of the child witness or victim (e.g., Goodman et al., 1992). Some advocates urge that children be allowed to testify in a more relaxed setting than a courtroom and that the judge not wear a robe. They also urge that children's initial testimony be taped for later presentation in court, so that the child need not appear in court or be forced to face the offender. Of course, these suggestions are often protested by defense attorneys because they potentially violate their client's right to a fair and impartial hearing.

TABLE 9.4 Reasons for Retraction of Testimony: Percentages of Attorneys Reporting Each Is "Often" or "Very Often" a Reason Why a Child Reports Sexual Abuse and Later Retracts the Statement

	Defense Attorneys (%)	Prosecuting Attorneys (%)
Pressure from parent or family member	65	82***
Embarrassment about the incident(s)	45	31*
Feeling responsible for, or guilty about, the incident	34	43
Fear of retaliation or harm	29	45
Fear of being on the witness stand	26	16
Knowledge that the previous testimony was false	25	2**

Note: *Prosecutor and defense attorney percent distributions differ by a chi-square test at $p<.05$; **at $p<.01$; ***at $p<.001$.

Source: Leippe, M. R., Brigham, J. C., Cousins, C., & Romanczyk, A. (1989). The opinions and practices of criminal attorneys regarding child eyewitnesses: A survey. In S. J. Ceci, D. F. Ross, & M. P. Toglia (Eds.), *Perspectives on children's testimony.* New York: Springer-Verlag, p. 113. Copyright 1989 by Springer-Verlag. Reprinted by permission.

opportunity to present evidence about a witnessed account or, given the opportunity, may have his or her testimony summarily dismissed by the listener. Yet, given that our assessment of accuracy is so poor, one wonders how often justice is well served by human judgment.

Expert Testimony

Research findings such as these suggest that jurors, attorneys, and perhaps judges, need general information about eyewitness testimony and about the behavior of victims of family violence before they can make informed decisions. More and more, judges, who are responsible for deciding whether an expert may provide such background information for the jury, are deciding that the information is needed.

Expert testimony is permissible when it goes beyond knowledge held by the average juror and is critical to decisions that need to be made about the case. Firearms specialists testify about the workings of guns precisely because most jurors and judges lack this knowledge base. For similar reasons, medical personnel testify about the causes and consequences of injuries, and psychologists and psychiatrists testify about mental states at the time of the alleged crime. Often now experts testify about the problems inherent in eyewitness testimony and the lack of correspondence between someone's perceived confidence and the accuracy of the testimony.

An interesting example of the use of experts emerges during prosecution of women who have retaliated against their abusive husbands. For years advocates for battered women have argued that expert testimony is needed to explain why and under what circumstances battered women fight back and seriously injure or even kill their abuser (e.g., Greene, Raitz, & Lindblad, 1989). Experts can be used to explain why the woman may have fought back instead of leaving the abuser, calling the police, or taking other action that would get her out of the abusive situation (see Box 9.3).

However, not all judges permit expert testimony, claiming that jurors already understand the abusive situation and that, accordingly, testimony by an expert is superfluous. Studies of lay knowledge about battered women suggest that this may be partially correct (Greene et al., 1989). Modern jurors have learned enough about family violence to recognize that abused women are often anxious and depressed, that they feel helpless to prevent the violence even by leaving the home, and that they worry that their husbands will kill them if they leave or seek help. However, the same study (Greene et al., 1989) showed that jurors are less well-informed about women's tendency to blame themselves for the abuse and their susceptibility to their husbands' persuasion attempts. Jurors also did not know that abused women sometimes provoke violence when they see tension building in an effort to forestall a more serious attack.

Research such as this demonstrates that expert testimony may be valuable. Jurors not exposed to expert testimony may not be able to evaluate evidence about a case from an informed perspective. They may find it difficult to imagine what a life of constant fear is like, may overestimate the victim's ability to seek help from outsiders, and may overestimate the amount of help available to abused family members. Experts also promote skepticism on the part of jurors, which allows the jurors to discount factors, such as a witness's confidence, that are irrelevant to the case and to weigh more appropriately information that is relevant (Borgida, Gresham, Kovera, & Regan, 1992).

The use of expert witnesses remains controversial, however, with some claiming that psychologists who serve as experts are intervening

BOX 9.3

In her book, *When Battered Women Kill,* Angela Browne (1987) presents the legal and psychological arguments that support a plea of self-defense by women who murder their assaultive partners. She reports that the characteristics of women who murder do not differ in meaningful ways from those who do not murder, but that the partner's behavior is different.

> Men in the homicide group used drugs more frequently than did men in the comparison group, and they become intoxicated much more often. They were also more frequently given to threats and assaultive behavior: Significantly more men in the homicide group threatened to kill someone other than themselves; more of them abused a child or children, as well as their women partners; and their abuse of their mates was more frequent, more injurious, and more likely to include sexual assault. (pp. 181–182)

Through interviews with women who murdered their assailants, Browne found that, just like other abuse victims, the women learned over time to minimize the threat to themselves by adapting their behavior, responding to the abuser with concern, and attempting to reason with him. But the violence became harsher and the abuser seemed less and less concerned with the consequences of the violence. If the women left home, they were brought back.

> This lack of safe alternatives for the women, combined with the men's threats of retaliation if they left . . . . , convinced most of these women that they could not escape their partners and survive. . . . Most of the women began to live with almost an expectation of death.
>
> The women's perception of entrapment in a desperate situation led to increasingly extreme degrees of adaptation, as they shifted the range of what they could endure to incorporate the

**BOX 9.3
(Continued)**

attacks they were experiencing. Yet, eventually, the violence escalated beyond the point to which the women could adapt. . . . (A) formerly passive woman would suddenly take action in her own defense or in the defense of a child. (pp. 182–183)

Browne argues that the circumstances described above render a plea of self-defense reasonable. Use of force in self-defense is justifiable when a person believes that he or she is in danger of bodily harm and will avoid the harm through the use of force. People who act in self-defense need not have acted immediately after the attack, but can defend oneself hours after the event if a reasonable belief exists that the risk is still present (*People v. Garcia,* Cr. No. 4259, Superior Court, Monterey County, California, 1977). In contrast to violence outside the home, during which victims are expected to attempt to retreat before defending themselves, in the home people are allowed to respond to force with reasonable force (*People v. McGrandy,* 156 N.W.2d 48, 9 Mich, App. 187, 1967). Furthermore, while "reasonable force" in most circumstances is defined as force equal to that used by the assailant, a concept that is based upon fighting between two men of roughly equal size and strength, this definition does not work in most conflicts between men and women. Case law has clarified that differences between men's and women's potential to harm may render understandable a woman's use of a lethal weapon in self-defense (*State v. Wanrow,* 88 Wash, 2d 221, 559 P.2d 548, 1977). Finally, the person who murders in self-defense need only demonstrate that the perception of danger was reasonable, even if it is inaccurate (*Wyoming v. Austin,* No. 7828 Natrona Co. D.C., 1979). Thus, if a husband threatens to murder his wife with a knife and she shoots him as he returns from a trip to the kitchen, her perception that she was about to be stabbed may seem legitimate, even when no knife is found on her husband's body.

in matters that should be under the strict purview of the jury panel (Pachella, 1988). Others (cf. Berliner, 1988) worry that, given inconsistencies in the research literature on many topics, experts hired by both sides will contradict each other and further confuse the jury.

Professionals' Failure to Report

One of the most common impediments to legal intervention is the failure of professionals to report cases of abuse that come to their attention. The problem is present in cases of spousal or elderly assault, but is especially apparent in cases of child abuse, which professionals in all states are required to report. Estimates range from fourteen to fifty-two incidents of unreported child sexual abuse for each incident that is reported (Maney, 1988). One nationwide study compared cases of child maltreatment that were reported to a local child protective services (CPS) agency to statistics drawn from surveys of professional agencies (e.g., schools, hospitals, day care, police) in the same community (National Center on Child Abuse and Neglect, 1988). The proportion of reported cases ranged from 16 percent (reported by day care centers) to 66 percent (hospitals). By far the most cases appear to become known to schools, and schools report a small proportion of cases that come to their attention (24 percent). The report estimates that from 1980 to 1986, reports of abuse increased from 33 percent of known cases overall to 40 percent.

Ambiguity of the Evidence

Some of the failure to report may be due to uncertainty about whether the characteristics of particular cases warrant the attention of legal authorities. An example of the ambiguities is presented by Morris, Johnson, and Clasen (1985). When shown a picture of a young boy who allegedly had fallen off his tricycle and hit his head, some physicians decided quickly to report the case ("The last time I saw a child like this with a story like this, he ended up dead"), while others were not so sure ("If this were one of my patients, and they came in with that story, I'd probably believe them"; Morris et al., 1985, p. 195). Even protective service employees, whose job is to decide whether a suspected case of abuse warrants more investigation, have trouble deciding what constitutes child maltreatment (e.g., Nagi, 1977). Thus, when professionals are told that they must report "suspected" cases of abuse, they may have trouble deciding the criteria that should arouse suspicion.

But there is also evidence that professionals may not want to be suspicious or do not take the time to question clients in a way that would allay or heighten their suspicions. More than half of the primary-care physicians interviewed by Sugg and Inui (1992) admitted that their fear of offending patients kept them from asking critical questions that might have led to disclosures about abuse. One news report of a physician's failure to intervene (Spencer-Molloy, 1992) cites an example of a physician writing in the medical chart, "Patient was struck by glass." As another medical specialist said, "Well, how did that glass get in the air?"

Physicians may not be trained to think of such questions and, given their discomfort about discovering family violence, may not even want to. However, a recent report of the Council on Scientific Affairs (Browne, 1992) recommended to the American Medical Association that it encourage physicians to incorporate routine screening for family violence into office visits by patients and to be alert for injuries that correspond to those often seen among abuse patients. Evidence of former injuries, bruises independent of the presenting symptoms, and injuries to the central part of the body (chest, abdomen) may distinguish abuse from accident victims (Browne, 1992).

Another suggestion is to question patients directly about violence in the home. Richard Jones, who in 1992 served as President of the American College of Obstetricians and Gynecologists noted his surprise about the incidence of violence:

> "When I saw a woman with black and blue marks in my office, I used to ask her how she got them. This gave her the obvious opportunity to say 'I'm clumsy,' " . . . About 2 years ago, Jones began to ask directly, "Have you been hit or harmed any time in the past year?" "Are you in any danger?" or "Is someone doing this to you?"
> . . . "Whereas, in the past, I would confront a case of battering a few times a year, now I was confronting these cases two or three times a week.
> "I had viewed myself as a reasonably perceptive, reasonably kind and caring physician—and I had missed all this." (Randall, 1992, p. 3131)

Victim Denial

Another problem that faces professionals occurs when the victim fails to verify the suspicions of the professional, or at first admits to being abused, but then retracts the admission. Just as a retraction or denial poses a dilemma for attorneys, other professionals are unsure about its meaning. Attias and Goodwin (1984) found that only one-half of the psychiatrists surveyed and two-thirds of other professionals (psychologists, pediatricians) would report a case following the child's retraction of an incest complaint. Chang, Oglesby, Wallace, Goldstein, and Hexter (1976) found that only half of the professionals they surveyed recommended a follow-up physical examination after a retracted sexual abuse claim, but *all of the professionals recommended a psychological examination of the alleged victim.*

Biased Processing of Evidence

In Chapter 2 we discussed how judgments about the seriousness of violence in families varied according to the characteristics of the victim and perpetrator. Professionals share the same biased judgment processes as laypeople when faced with a case of abuse (Herzberger, 1988). Just as laypeople categorize others on the basis of gender, race, and socioeconomic status (Fiske & Taylor, 1983), professionals allow such factors to influence their decisions too. Thus, professionals' failure to report sometimes stems from stereotypes about likely perpetrators and likely victims. Hampton and Newberger (1985), for example, found that hospital personnel underreport abuse cases in which the perpetrator is white or high in socioeconomic status. O'Toole, Turbett, and Nalepka (1983) report that some professionals explicitly use demographic factors as clues to abuse; one doctor in their study noted, "I always look at race first. That's an important indicator."

Let me give you a personal example of this bias among health care workers. Ironically, one day as I was working on a paper for an American Bar Association conference on professional biases in the reporting of child abuse (Herzberger, 1985), my 3-year-old ran into a doorknob in his room, the impact of which broke two of his teeth and swelled his face to twice its normal size. Just three months earlier I had rushed the same child to the same dentist after he had fallen against the corner of a chair and knocked a tooth loose. Now, I realized with trepidation, I should be facing a suspicious dentist. To make matters worse on this second occasion, when the dentist asked my child how this happened, my child cried and reported that he did not know! But, true to what we would expect from the literature, the dentist must have assumed that a white, middle-class, educated woman like me could not have inflicted this on her child. He repaired my child's teeth and, without further questioning, sent us on our way.

An editorial in the *Journal of the American Medical Association* (*JAMA*) recently called for physicians to support adult victims of partner violence, but to refrain from acting in a manner that runs contrary to the victim's wishes. Drawing a distinction between child abuse and spouse abuse, Flitcraft (1992) urged that physicians help women to find shelter from violence *if they want the help,* but not to violate patient autonomy. Flitcraft believes that women must make decisions for themselves and feel empowered enough to gain control over their own lives. A physician who reports the abuse to protective services or investigates the abuse over the protests of the victim shows little respect for the patient.

Belief That Reporting is Wrong

Not all of the non-reporting stems from ambiguity of the evidence or personal bias. Some professionals do not believe that reporting makes a difference, and others believe that more harm than good comes from this practice (e.g., Zellman, 1990). Physicians and social service professionals who work with the elderly, for example, worry that an intervention in a case of abuse will merely exacerbate the problem (Pierce & Trotta, 1986). Calling in the police may enhance the tension between the elderly person and his or her caretaker. Also, removing the elderly victim to a nursing home against his or her will may stimulate further physical deterioration and end up with the elderly person feeling worse than before.

Psychologists and the clergy believe that professional ethics or religious dogma that call for confidentiality between client and professional cannot be nullified by statutory obligations (cf. Wells, 1988). Professionals believe that the benefits derived from clients or penitents feeling free to disclose any kind of information and to seek help in their own way outweigh the benefits that potentially might derive from professional reporting (see Box 9.4). After all, if clients know that professionals will disclose their confidences, why would clients make disclosures?

Psychologists, the clergy, and physicians often feel that they are in a better position to monitor the problem and intervene with the violent person than overworked public servants with no history of interaction with or commitment to the individual (Conte, 1988; Wells, 1988; Zellman, 1990). They claim that public agencies charged with the responsibility for receiving family violence complaints are mostly interested in learning the truth or falsity of a report, not in understanding what the incident means to the victim or in ensuring that the victim is helped. Professionals see their role as counselor to the perpetrator or victim and, as long as they believe that proper treatment is being administered and the victim is safe, they often believe that they are fulfilling their obligations best by not reporting the case to the authorities.

Many of the reports of family violence are not substantiated by a child protection worker or a police officer due to lack of sufficient evidence or a finding that the injuries or danger involved is not enough to warrant public attention. In these circumstances, the cases are dropped. One study (National Center on Child Abuse and Neglect, 1988), for example, found that 53 percent of the cases of child abuse reported to CPS agencies were substantiated. Professionals who report unsubstantiated cases then wonder what led to the dismissal and think twice about troubling over reports on subsequent occasions. Conte, Fogarty, and Collins (1991) surveyed professional counselors on how they divide their work week. The researchers found that the work involved in gathering evidence about the allegations took 12 percent of the average work week and that time spent in preparing testimony should the cases go to court amounted to 6 percent of the average work week. Of all cases, only 41 percent of the offenders were actually charged, and 18 percent were penalized with a jail term.

Many people may wonder whether the trauma to the victim or witnesses caused by the drawn-out process of prosecution is worth the effort, especially given the low success rate of prosecution. Most of the research on the trauma of prosecution has concentrated on child victims or witnesses. From the arrival of police officers following an incident through the trial, children suffer through numerous stressful events. Child witnesses to an assault or murder of a family member are usually separated from other members of the family for questioning and often will be prohibited from contact with the alleged offender until the resolution of the case (Pynoos & Eth, 1984). Furthermore, older children are aware that the information they provide to investigators will influence the outcome of the proceedings. Pynoos and Eth (1984) recount one case in which two adolescents were asked to discuss their observations during their mother's murder.

> (W)e interviewed two teenagers from a divorced family who had resided with different parents and who colored their accounts accordingly. The boy neglected to mention having seen his father load the gun, whereas his sister's account included this fact but omitted her mother's defiant taunt, "Okay, show what a big man you are. Shoot." (p. 99)

The children in such cases are likely to feel guilt over implicating family members or failing to be completely loyal to other family members and may fear retribution should the offender be released (Berliner & Barbieri, 1984).

A recent study (Goodman, Taub, Jones, England, Port, Rudy, & Prado, 1992), however, suggests that the detrimental effects of testifying are short-lived and that once the case is resolved, regardless of the verdict, children who testify show the same adjustment as those who do not testify. Children who do not testify may suffer ill-effects too. For example, children report feeling sad when they do not have an opportunity to "come to the aid of their slain relative" (Pynoos & Eth, 1984, p. 101), and may become distressed if they feel that through their failure to testify the offender was acquitted (Goodman et al., 1992).

Benefits of Reporting

Above we noted that some emotional benefits may be derived by the victim or a witness from contributing to the prosecution of a violent offender. Other benefits may also ensue from reporting cases. Besharov (1991) claims that nationwide child abuse deaths have been cut in half or even by two-thirds as a result of mandated reporting laws. Professionals make mistakes about their ability to control violence through counseling or lectures to the perpetrator, and they do not always have access to full information about the violence. Reporting the event increases the likelihood that more people are involved in overseeing the working of the family. Thus, reporting may provide better service to some families and decrease future violence.

Reporting also communicates to the perpetrator and the victim that society has the right to be interested in the well-being of family members and that family matters are sometimes subject to the control of the state. It is unknown whether reporting serves as a general deterrent for the population as a whole. But some professionals believe that, at the very least, victims may learn from hearing about other cases that society no longer tolerates abusive treatment and they may get the courage to try to end their abusive relationship.

Compassion versus Punishment

As this chapter suggests, there is considerable ambivalence about involving the legal system in cases of violence. Although some people call for more punitive control efforts, others argue that the intervention effort should head in the other direction. They believe that, when attention is directed to controlling and penalizing the perpetrator, too often the effort fails and neither the perpetrator's nor the victim's needs are met.

Newberger (1987) strongly argues for a compassionate, social welfare approach to family violence, asserting that efforts to prosecute offenders will mainly "provide excellent political opportunities for district attorneys" and "work for lawyers" (p. 115). To Newberger, prosecution serves as a "smokescreen" that isolates a few offenders, but hides the real causes of abuse and often punishes the victim. In an interview with *Law Enforcement News,* Sherman echoes this perspective. Citing his findings on the effects of arrest (Sherman et al., 1992), Sherman worries that "criminal law can backfire and cause more crime" (Clark, 1993, p. 1).

Others believe, however, that until as much money is funneled into domestic violence treatment and prevention programs as is now funneled into the criminal justice system, calls for noncriminalized, social means of handling cases of domestic violence may be unproductive, if not dangerous. "Properly funded, an effective treatment system for family violence would be capable of identifying all the victims in need of services, quickly and effectively intervening to protect victims, and providing support for families under stress" (Gelles & Straus, 1988, pp. 190–191). Yet, at present:

> . . . (N)ine out of ten women and children who die have already come to public attention before their deaths. We know many of the victims who need services, and yet we have not organized ourselves in such a way as to help. (Gelles & Straus, 1988, p. 189)

Family violence is a complex problem that calls for complex solutions. So far, neither compassionate treatment strategies nor control efforts have eradicated this public health concern. And much more research is needed on each approach to this problem.

Concluding Remarks

In this chapter we have studied numerous factors that impede formal efforts to intervene in cases of family violence. Not only do a small percentage of cases come to the attention of authorities, but once they receive attention there is no guarantee that a judicious resolution will prevail. Certainly there are false allegations of abuse, but most evidence suggests that these are rare. However, sorting false from veridical allegations is not easy for human beings who are misled by superficial clues and who possess no template for accurate decision-making.

Experts differ on the appropriate intervention once a case comes to the attention of social or legal professionals. While some call for more punitive measures, others suggest that punishment is inappropriate and possibly more harmful than doing nothing. Some experts would rather see professionals offer compassionate treatment to all members of the involved family, including the perpetrator. As we have seen, it is unlikely that one intervention will work for all people, and more research is needed on individual differences in response to punitive versus compassionate treatment.

10

The Prevention and Treatment of Family Violence

CHAPTER OBJECTIVES

Prevention
  Education and Support to
    Potential Perpetrators
  Education and Empowerment of
    Potential Victims
  Changes in the Law
  Changes in the Media Portrayal
    of Violence
  Multifaceted Prevention Efforts
Treatment Programs
  Determinants of Behavior
    Change
  Therapeutic Interventions with
    Offenders

  Self-Help Groups
  Intervention with Victims of
    Partner Abuse
  Intervention with Victims of
    Child Abuse
  Intervention with Victims of
    Elderly Abuse
  Intervention in Cases of Sibling
    Violence
  Individual Reactions to
    Intervention
Concluding Remarks

From reading this book and through exposure to other information, you probably have many ideas about changes needed to reduce family violence. And you should know enough about perpetrators, their family situation, and the surrounding culture to suggest changes that might prevent or treat violent behavior. This chapter provides a brief overview of other peoples' ideas and the programs that have been developed to deal with this major social problem. We will start with prevention efforts.

Prevention

At the heart of most research on family violence is an effort to understand this phenomenon and then to eliminate it. Researchers believe that if we understand the immediate and long-term causes of assault within the family, we can devise programs that prevent family members from assaulting one another.

Prevention efforts are based upon a variety of views of the primary causes and effective solutions to the problem. People who believe that violence is caused by the personality or behavioral tendencies of individuals will seek largely individual interventions. Consequently, they will try to identify people who, by virtue of their characteristics, may become aggressive and then will devise interventions for these individuals. Others believe that violence is largely caused by stressful societal conditions and that, given exposure to the same circumstances, many of us would succumb to violence. Those who share this philosophy often will seek societal changes or will work to alleviate the social ills that undercut positive interpersonal relations. Of course, many theorists and prevention experts fall between these two extremes, believing that a combination of individual proclivities and environmental circumstances produces violence. The models by Belsky and Vondra (1989) and by Kaufman and Zigler (1989) presented in Chapter 4 outline this perspective.

The range of perspectives about the causes of family violence can be seen in the range of solutions sought. Let us take a look at a few representative prevention programs and study their rationale, their intended consequences, and the inevitable drawbacks.

Education and Support to Potential Perpetrators

A variety of education and support programs have been developed to prevent abuse. One example of such a program is aimed at potential child abusers. You have probably heard the comment that more education is required to secure a driver's license than to parent a child. In fact, no education is required for the latter. Ironically, many pregnant women undergo six weeks or more of training to prepare for the birth process. They learn breathing and relaxation techniques and pain control methods, and even what to pack for the hospital visit. But they learn nothing about what to do with the child once the delivery is complete. Often, hospitals require that expectant fathers accompany their partners to prenatal classes before being allowed in the delivery room for the blessed event. What happens after the father leaves the delivery room, though, is not the concern of the hospital.

Therefore, it should not be surprising that so many people enter parenthood lacking knowledge that might help them in understanding and reacting supportively to a child's misbehavior or an infant's cries. Parents do not necessarily know anything about effective discipline techniques or socialization practices that might help them in promoting a positive family environment and healthy child development.

Combine this lack of knowledge with economic or other personal stresses, a childhood or adolescent environment that fosters the learning of violence, and aggressive biological proclivities, and the potential for child abuse increases substantially. For this reason, many child abuse prevention efforts have been directed at parents—especially first-time parents.

Parent education efforts have come a long way from the time when Klaus and Kennell (1976) urged hospitals to arrange for parents to have extended time with their infant immediately after delivery to aid in parent-infant bonding during the "critical" hours immediately after birth. They believed that hospitals that separated the infant and parents following the delivery risked creating an unhealthy rift in the parent-child relationship. While subsequent studies (cf. Olds and Henderson, 1989) have disputed the notion of a set period in which parent-child bonding occurs (as adoptive parents could have told us all along), Klaus and Kennell's work alerted us to the importance of the early postpartum period and the principle of providing a supportive environment for the development of parent-child relations.

The introduction of a new child into the family is stressful for many parents. Olds and Henderson (1989) developed a prevention program designed to support parents through this stressful period. They believe that, by virtue of youth, poverty, and single-parent status, some people are at risk of developing a host of problems, one of which may be abusive behavior towards a child. But, aware of the problems of falsely labeling someone as a potential abuser, the researchers accepted any applicants to their parenting program who were expecting their first child. Olds and Henderson randomly assigned applicants to groups that differed in the amount of service provided to the parent. The control group received no services or received free transportation to physical exams and health screening for their babies. One experimental group ("NV pregnancy") received visits from a nurse about every two weeks during the pregnancy and another experimental group ("NV infancy") received visits throughout the pregnancy and during the first two years after the child's birth. The nurse visitors talked to parents about fetal and infant development, encouraged family members and friends to support the mother and to become involved in the care of the child, and urged mothers to use health and other support services as needed.

The pattern of results showed that the supportive services provided by the nurse visitor, especially when the visits continued throughout infancy, prevented incidents of child abuse and neglect measured throughout the first two years after the birth (see Table 10.1). The intervention was particularly effective with mothers who experienced the triple threat of being young, poor, and unmarried. Among this group of mothers, 4 percent of those who received nursing care throughout the child's infancy abused their child, in contrast to 19 percent of the control group. Parents who received nurse visitors also demonstrated decreased levels of maternal-child conflict and child scolding, better maternal handling of the child's cries, and were more likely to provide children with age-appropriate play materials. Thus, the nurses influenced a large set of behaviors that fed into an emotionally healthy home atmosphere.

Programs such as the one offered by Olds and his colleagues (Olds & Henderson, 1989) have demonstrated substantial benefits to involved families. The intensive contacts over a substantial period of time, either delivered by paraprofessionals or trained clinicians, have been shown to enhance maternal responsivity to children's needs and to improve the child's physical care, as well as to reduce the parent's use of welfare services and improve their job training (cf. Daro, 1988).

This kind of intervention, as you might imagine, is expensive. However, as Olds and Henderson (1989) note, a substantial proportion of the cost is offset by decreased costs of foster-home placement, hospital care, and child-protection worker time avoided whenever we prevent abuse. Furthermore, given that abused children are over-represented among juvenile delinquents and adult violent offenders (Widom, 1989a), avoidance of abuse offsets the costs associated with the arrest, trial, and incarceration of future offenders.

Educational and support programs could also be developed to prevent spouse abuse or abuse of the elderly. How many people take courses to prepare for the conflicts that inevitably arise during marriage? Especially in a society where divorce and single parenthood are so prevalent, we cannot assume that all couples are exposed

TABLE 10.1 Mean Treatment Differences for Child Abuse and Neglect: Adjusted for Husband/Boyfriend Support

Treatment Group	Sample								
	Whole	Nonrisk	Nonpoor	Married	Older (≥19 Years)	Poor	Unmarried	Teenager (<19 Years)	Poor Unmarried Teenagers
Comparison	0.10	0.05	0.08	0.10	0.05	0.12	0.10	0.15	0.19
NV pregnancy	0.08	0.00	0.00	0.09	0.10	0.17	0.08	0.07	0.18
NV infancy	0.05	0.00	0.04	0.04	0.06	0.07	0.06	0.05*	0.04*

Note: * $p < .10$ for test of Comparison vs. NV infancy means

Source: Adapted from Olds, D. L., & Henderson, C. R., Jr. (1989). The prevention of maltreatment. In D. Cicchetti & V. Carlson (Eds.), *Child maltreatment: Theory and research on the causes and consequences of child abuse and neglect* (p. 744). Cambridge: Cambridge University Press. Copyright © Cambridge University Press 1989. Reprinted with permission of Cambridge University Press.

throughout their childhood to positive models of conflict management and spousal interaction. Therefore, courses could be designed to introduce different modes of interaction.

To the extent that elderly abuse is fostered by the stress of taking care of an aged person, programs that support caretakers also are useful (Wolf & Pillemer, 1989). Options include providing respite care during the day or over a weekend, both of which can be done at the elderly person's home or in an institution.

Some educational programs have been directed at children and are specifically focused upon violence prevention. Programs for adolescents, which are offered largely through school systems, teach about the risks inherent in the use of violence, encourage alternative strategies for settling conflicts, and discourage the use of drugs and alcohol that so often leads to violence (Reiss & Roth, 1993). However, the evidence of program effectiveness is slight, especially as measured by changes in behavior rather than increased knowledge. Substance abuse prevention programs have shown success in delaying the onset of drug or alcohol use, but the long-term effectiveness of this type of educational effort has not been examined (Reiss & Roth, 1993).

One program known to be highly successful was begun in Norway in the 1980's (Olweus, 1992). This largely school-based program was aimed at cutting the incidence of bullying among children. Because bullying is known to be a precursor of adult criminality and alcoholism, the program had potential long-term benefits. Program components included a strong message to children and their parents that bullying would not be tolerated and then quick intervention in incidents that did occur. Getting students, teachers, and parents to share responsibility for changing the school culture was a primary goal of the project. The program not only succeeded in reducing the degree of bullying in school and outside of school time, but there was an improvement in attitudes toward school and truancy.

Reiss and Roth (1993) suggest that interventions designed to prevent violence may be most effective when initiated with preschoolers or, at the latest, during the elementary school years. Aggression is a stable trait, evident by early childhood and remaining consistent throughout development (Olweus, 1979). You will recall the suggestion in Chapter 8 that children who display early aggression may narrow their exposure to nonaggressive environments and instead create an environment where aggression is further inculcated (Rushton et al., 1986). The earlier an intervention is started, then, the more likely it is that the factors that exacerbate a propensity to violence can be thwarted.

Education and Empowerment of Potential Victims

Similar to programs that educate adults and children in an effort to forestall their abusive behavior, many programs have been established to educate potential victims and to forestall their involvement in violent situations. Many programs have concentrated on the prevention of child sexual abuse, but we can glean lessons from these about how the programs might be used to prevent physical maltreatment. Daro (1988) notes that the curricula of all programs have certain common elements. They instruct the child about the differences between good and bad touching, teach children that they have the right to control what happens to their body, and discuss the importance of disclosing bad touching to someone who can help. Children are also taught assertiveness and self-defense skills to defend themselves against sexual abuse.

There is little evidence, however, about the general effectiveness of these programs (Daro, 1988). Very few studies have included control groups that would enable the researchers to test differences in the attitudes or behaviors of children who had participated or had not participated in the program. While older children understand and retain at least some of the material presented, studies that include comparison groups suggest that the information added by education programs is slight (Reppucci & Haugaard, 1989). Children in the comparison groups already know much of what is taught in the programs. And the long-term results of program participation are unknown (Daro, 1988; Reppucci & Haugaard, 1989). We do not know the extent to which participants apply their new knowledge in their own lives, and there is no evidence that children who have received this education have prevented sexual abuse more than those who have not.

Furthermore, the potential negative effects of this type of intervention have not been well documented (Daro, 1988; Reppucci & Haugaard, 1989). The proliferation of sexual abuse education programs, for example, may have limited the willingness of teachers or other adults to be appropriately affectionate with children. We hear often now about day care or nursery school teachers who worry about hugging children or holding them on their laps for fear of being falsely accused of abuse. The programs also may have increased children's fear of innocent family members. Clearly, more research should be done on this common means of preventing abuse.

Material in earlier chapters provides hints about other programs that might be useful to prevent victimization. For example, prevention programs could be designed around the known deficits in problem-solving skills displayed by victims of violence (Launius & Jensen, 1987). Educational campaigns might teach children or young adults to devise effective solutions to problem situations and then to carry them out. Assertiveness training programs, focused upon teaching children how to stand up for their rights and to feel comfortable about doing so, might accomplish similar ends. Also, programs should be in place to convince us that, as a frequent bumper sticker admonishes, "people are not for hitting." A byproduct of this campaign may be that fewer potential victims will see such treatment as deserved.

Changes in the Law

Some experts argue that preventive intervention at the level of the individual or the family or even the school is inefficient and unproductive in the long run. At some point nurses, teachers, and other support services will be removed and the family must cope on its own. More importantly, early prevention efforts eventually must compete with messages of violence in the surrounding neighborhood and a society that views aggression as a common tool for problem-solving and punishment.

For this reason some people advocate large-scale attempts to eliminate the potential for violence and interventions at the level of society, rather than directed at any individual, family, or neighborhood. Enacting rules that require arrest for spouse abuse, for example, communicates that maltreatment of a spouse will not be tolerated by society. Legislation banning corporal punishment in the schools is cited as a step in the direction of outlawing corporal punishment altogether and inculcating the value that "people are not for hitting" (Pagelow, 1984). In 1979 Sweden, which banned corporal punishment in schools in 1952, banned corporal punishment by parents (cf. Gelles & Straus, 1988). Even though no legal remedy exists for violation of the law, it is widely followed. As a recent public radio report noted (Gediman, 1994), to most children in Sweden spanking is in the "realm of fantasy" and parents automatically take time to talk out problems with children, rather than hitting them.

As we saw in the preceding chapter, laws forbidding violence against a spouse or a child may provide an incentive to forestall violent tendencies or just serve as a reminder to society at large that the welfare of family members is a state concern. The passage of laws may prevent violence because they imply social consensus about an issue, and maintaining an opinion or behavior contrary to this consensus is difficult, especially if high-status individuals (e.g., elected officials) appear to agree with the new law (e.g., Colombotos, 1969).

Changes in the Media Portrayal of Violence

Another route to large-scale prevention attempts is through decreasing the amount of violence that is purveyed through the media, whether it be on news programs or fictional entertainment. As noted earlier, media portrayal of violence promotes aggression because it introduces information about novel, aggressive behaviors, provides attractive role models of aggression, and desensitizes people to the consequences of aggression (Liebert, Sprafkin, & Davidson, 1982). Heavy viewers of television also express a greater fear of real world violence and develop greater mistrust and alienation (Gerbner, Morgan, & Signorielli, 1994). This outlook may lead people to behave in a manner that will provoke aggression from others.

Various groups, such as the American Medical Association, Parent-Teacher Associations and a number of government agencies, have asked television producers to reduce the amount of violence in programs (Gerbner et al., 1994; Liebert et al., 1982). Yet, one day's viewing of children's and adult's programming reveals that violent content is still widespread (see Box 10.1).

Because television programming may not change any time soon, some people advocate attempting to get parents to monitor children's viewing and to explain to children the consequences of televised aggression (e.g., Singer & Singer, 1986). In one study (Huesmann, Eron, Klein, Brice, & Fischer, 1983) researchers trained first- and third-graders to recognize that television shows did not portray the behaviors of people in "real life" problem-solving situations and that camera techniques and special effects created the illusions shown on TV. Children in a control group received no instruction about television's unrealistic nature. When measured several months after the completion of the training program, experimental-group children were regarded by their peers as significantly less aggressive than the control-group children. Experimental-group children also displayed less aggression after continuing to watch violent programs. This powerful study demonstrates that teaching children a new perspective through which to view television violence may mitigate the harmful effects of television viewing.

Another potential route to reducing the harmful effects of television programming is through the courts. Aggressive pornography,

BOX 10.1

A report by the Center for Media and Public Affairs (Lichter & Amundson, 1992) graphically illustrates the prevalence of violence on television. The Center analyzed eighteen hours of programming offered by network and cable stations on a fairly typical day. Box Table 10.A below shows the number of scenes in which various forms of violence were depicted.

Box Table 10.A

Types of Violence Overall	Number of Scenes
Serious assaults*	389
Gunplay	362
Isolated punches	273
Pushing/dragging	272
Menacing threat with weapon	226
Athletic violence	134
Slaps	128
Deliberate property destruction	95
Simple assaults	73
All other types	28
TOTAL	1,980

*Excluding the use of guns.

Source: Adapted from Lichter, S. R., & Amundson, D. (1992). *A day of television violence* (pp. 15–16). Center for Media and Public Affairs, Washington, DC. Reprinted by permission.

for example, is known to increase the risk of violence and sexual attacks against women (Malamuth & Donnerstein, 1982) and, consequently, some people want a ban on such materials. However, because an outright ban may be impossible due to First Amendment rights (cf. Donnerstein, Linz, & Penrod, 1987), some people ingenuously have lobbied instead for litigation under *product liability* codes. Manufacturers are liable for harm caused by the products they make and for "misuse" of their products under certain circumstances, even when only a small proportion of people are harmed in this manner. For example, a young girl sued the National Broadcasting Company for negligently producing and distributing a "product"

BOX 10.1
(Continued)

As other studies have shown, violence was most prominent during hours when children are likely to be watching (165.7 acts per hour from 6 A.M. to 9 A.M. and 203.0 acts per hour from 2 P.M. to 5 P.M., in contrast to 58.8 acts per hour from 9 A.M. to 2 P.M.). Perhaps most alarming were the findings that approximately half of the violent scenes showed no evidence of physical harm to the victim and 83 percent contained no message about the wrongfulness or acceptability of violence. Only 12 percent of the violent acts were accompanied by a judgment that the violence was criminal or wrong.

Gerbner and his colleagues (1994) have been tracking violence on television since 1973. While their definition of violence produces substantially fewer counts of violence per hour than produced by Lichter and Amundson (1992), their findings are nonetheless startling. For example, a review of prime-time dramatic programs in 1992 and 1993 revealed that 65 percent of the programs contained violent acts (an average of 2.9 per hour) and 46 percent of the major characters were involved in violent acts. The same analysis of Saturday morning children's programs revealed that 90 percent of the programs contained violent acts (an average of 17.9 per hour) and 81 percent of major characters were involved in violence.

(i.e., film) that stimulated other juveniles to attack her violently (Liebert et al., 1982). While this particular suit failed, litigation of this type may cause the media to reassess the content of their programming and eliminate material that is shown to cause the most potential harm. In fact, the second time NBC showed this film, it did so late at night and after substantial editing (Liebert et al., 1982).

While television producers seem to believe that violent programming is what the public wants now, their attention to the "bottom line" will lead them to switch programming should the public give notice that it wants different things.

Multifaceted Prevention Efforts

Governmental prohibition of parental or spousal violence, reduction in the violence portrayed in the media, and adult or child education may not be sufficient to stop family violence altogether. As you have seen throughout this book, violence is often linked to stressful life conditions, circumstances which are exacerbated by inequities in the economic and social structure of our society (Burgess, 1994; Gelles & Straus, 1988). A straightforward illustration of this phenomenon is the disproportionate involvement of poor people in violent acts both inside and outside the family (Reiss & Roth, 1993). Major social and economic programs, which currently have only as a secondary goal the prevention of violence, may be needed before we stem the rate of family violence in this society. Similarly, programs designed to decrease the rate of alcohol or drug use will not only help the individual user, but may reduce the incidence of family violence.

Treatment Programs

Treatment programs established for violent assailants can be thought of as *secondary prevention* efforts. They are designed to prevent the recurrence of violent behaviors and to make family members healthy again.

Some treatment programs are directed specifically at the perpetrator of violence and others are directed at the entire family. As you might imagine, there is significant controversy about involving victims or other family members in the treatment process (O'Leary, 1993; Saunders & Azar, 1989). Some experts (e.g., Neidig & Friedman, 1984) believe that family dynamics, and not just offender characteristics, lead to abusive behavior and that accordingly, changes in the offender need to be reinforced by changes in the behavior of other family members. From this perspective, even though it is still the responsibility of the batterer to curb violence, battering is seen as a ''relationship'' problem to which both parties contribute. Others, however, view treatment directed at family members as ''blaming the victim'' and as counterproductive. Treatment of the family may absolve the offender of full responsibility for the assault and thus may undermine the offender's willingness to change. Joint treatment of victim and offender also may make the victim hesitant to disclose information for fear of angering the offender even more.

Because the explicit goal of the intervention in child abuse cases is keeping the child within the biological family (e.g., Gelles & Straus, 1988), there is usually less interest in placing blame than there is in ensuring a healthy family unit. Thus, treatment of the family is often a prominent feature of interventions designed for dealing with child abuse. It also is believed that any gains experienced by the child victim from the therapeutic process will be voided if the family is not also treated (Saunders & Azar, 1989).

Treatment specialists are much less concerned about family disruption in the case of adult-to-adult violence. Thus, while some programs are designed for intervention with couples (e.g., Neidig & Friedman, 1984), others are directed at only changing the behavior of the offender or aiding the victim (e.g., Jennings, 1987).

Determinants of Behavior Change

Few good evaluation studies have been done on programs designed to change violent behavior in families (Saunders & Azar, 1989) and we know little about which program components operate successfully and which do not. While we may think that violent behavior is different from other behaviors that are inappropriate or maladaptive, in fact efforts to change aggressive behaviors may bear some resemblance to other focused interventions. Thus, through comparison with other behavior change programs, we might glean some thoughts about the components of an appropriate intervention program.

Zimbardo and Leippe (1991) note that people do all kinds of things that they know are generally unhealthy or unsafe, but they do so because they are difficult to eliminate and they may be enjoyable, and thereby deemed as worth the risk. Similarly, most people who engage in violent behavior towards a family member are well aware that it is inappropriate and they would like to stop, but they often lack the means to stop without help. Furthermore, violence may be reinforcing, providing a feeling of power over another person and producing compliance with their desires and demands.

What do we know about behavior change methods, then, that might lead to a reduction in violence? First, we need to clarify for violent people the benefits of nonviolence, as well as the potential hazards of violent action. Successful smoking cessation programs, for example, concentrate on the positive consequences of not smoking to provide an incentive for the deprivation that program members will feel when they first stop smoking (Zimbardo & Leippe, 1991). From this perspective, teaching the violent person to imagine the benefits of a calm, happy home in which the recently nonviolent person receives increased love and respect from his or her family may start the process of change.

Tversky and Kahneman (1986), however, suggest a different message. They believe that messages *framed* in terms of what might be lost through continued maladaptive behavior are more effective than messages about what would be gained through change. In studies of decisions about medical treatment and about financial prospects, they find that people will take more risks to retain what they have than to improve their current situation. Tversky and Kahneman's (1986) advice coincides with the conclusions of Bowker (1983), discussed in Chapter 3. Over half of the women surveyed by Bowker believed that their partners ceased violent activities when it became apparent that the woman would seek a divorce or involve the police. Action designed to raise the "cost" of battering dissuaded the batterer from violent behavior (Bowker, 1983). Thus, positive messages about gains may need to be bolstered by a fear-provoking message about potential loss.

Second, behavior change programs must tailor the message to each audience. Just as advertisers vary their sales pitch according to their intended targets (Zimbardo & Leippe, 1991), programs designed to reduce violence must do this as well. Some people, for example, deny that they are an "abuser" (e.g., a father might state "I'm not an abuser; I just slap him around once in a while—not all the time") and thereby avoid messages that they deem are only valid for "real abusers." Effective messages might avoid socially undesirable labels, but describe behaviors that particular groups of people need to eliminate (e.g., "If you feel the need to hit your spouse or child, here is a program that can help you").

Third, programs need to provide ways for people to change their behavior and convince themselves that change is indeed possible. As Zimbardo and Leippe (1991) report, some smokers keep the habit going until they observe several others quit and are convinced that they can do it too.

When developing behavior change programs, it is important to recognize that people adapt to change in stages. Prochaska, DiClemente, and Norcross (1992) have identified five stages that individuals go through in the process of changing addictive behaviors, such as smoking or alcoholism: precontemplation, contemplation, preparation, action, and maintenance. Most addicted individuals pass through these stages in a spiral pattern, in which they relapse to earlier stages one or more times. At each stage the individual completes tasks necessary to prepare for the next stage (see Tables 10.2 and 10.3).

Thinking about the process of change in stages helps the individuals desirous of change and the facilitators of change to fit the treatment to the individual's current needs. Prochaska and his colleagues

Process	Definitions: Interventions
Consciousness raising	Increasing information about self and problem: observations, confrontations, interpretations, bibliotherapy
Self-reevaluation	Assessing how one feels and thinks about oneself with respect to a problem: value clarification, imagery, corrective emotional experience
Self-liberation	Choosing and commitment to act or belief in ability to change: decision-making therapy, New Year's resolutions, logotherapy techniques, commitment enhancing techniques
Counterconditioning	Substituting alternatives for problem behaviors: relaxation, desensitization, assertion, positive self-statements
Stimulus control	Avoiding or countering stimuli that elicit problem behaviors: restructuring one's environment (e.g., removing alcohol or fattening foods), avoiding high risk cues, fading techniques
Reinforcement management	Rewarding one's self or being rewarded by others for making changes: contingency contracts, overt and covert reinforcement, self-reward
Helping relationships	Being open and trusting about problems with someone who cares: therapeutic alliance, social support, self-help groups
Dramatic relief	Experiencing and expressing feelings about one's problems and solutions: psychodrama, grieving losses, role playing
Environmental reevaluation	Assessing how one's problem affects physical environment: empathy training, documentaries
Social liberation	Increasing alternatives for nonproblem behaviors available in society: advocating for rights of repressed, empowering, policy interventions

Source: Prochaska, J. O., DiClemente, C. C., & Norcross, J. C. (1992). In search of how people change: Applications to addictive behaviors. *American Psychologist, 47,* p. 1108. Copyright 1992 by the American Psychological Association. Reprinted by permission.

TABLE 10.3 Stages of Change in Which Particular Processes of Change Are Emphasized

Precon-templation	Contemplation	Preparation	Action	Maintenance
Consciousness raising				
Dramatic relief				
Environmental reevaluation				
	Self-reevaluation			
		Self-liberation		
			Reinforcement management	
			Helping relationships	
			Counterconditioning	
			Stimulus control	

Source: Prochaska, J. O., DiClemente, C. C., & Norcross, J. C. (1992). In search of how people change: Applications to addictive behaviors. *American Psychologist, 47,* p. 1109. Copyright 1992 by the American Psychological Association. Reprinted by permission.

(Prochaska et al., 1992) suggest that behavior change programs that present material or activities that are not matched with the individual's stage will most likely fail. Consider, for example, a smoker who abruptly decides to throw out the cigarettes and quit. Most smokers who attempt to change their behavior in this way lack the contemplative basis and the awareness of the problem that reinforces their decision, and they quickly give up when change becomes difficult. Thus, Prochaska et al. (1992) emphasize that change ''depends on doing the right things (processes) at the right time (stages)'' (p. 1110).

Now we will take a look at some of the types of programs available to change violent behavior.

Therapeutic Interventions with Offenders

A variety of therapeutic or counseling interventions have been developed for abusive offenders. Most interventions include a number of approaches that can be characterized as cognitive or behavioral in orientation (Deffenbacher, 1988; Novaco, 1975, 1986). For example, the programs train people in relaxation techniques. As the person begins to feel angry or provoked, he or she is taught to take deep breaths and to relax muscle groups. Behaviors related to relaxation are incompatible with those related to violent behavior. Therefore, relaxation is thought to block anxious or aggressive reactions. These programs also teach new ways to think during anger-provoking situations. Novaco (1975) teaches program participants to remind themselves to distinguish between times when anger is legitimate and when it is not, and to think well of themselves when they engage in cooperative actions or become relaxed during an encounter.

We learned earlier that batterers often are nonassertive and lack knowledge of alternative ways to resolve disputes (Maiuro et al., 1986). Thus, some programs train people in interpersonal communication and problem-solving skills. Often these programs also promote *cognitive restructuring*. This means that program participants are taught new ways to view relationships between men and women or between parent and child (see Box 10.2).

One example of a comprehensive child abuse treatment program is Project 12-Ways (Lutzker & Rice, 1987), which enrolls families identified as having abused or neglected their children or who are at high risk for doing so. It goes beyond the typical cognitive and behavioral methods by supplementing services that meet the family's social and economic needs. The program might oversee the family's healthcare, provide referrals to alcohol treatment, and even teach skills for finding jobs. Families that had participated in Project 12-Ways were followed for five years after program completion and compared to a similar group of control-group families. Although the program did produce less recidivism, the difference between treated and untreated families narrowed over the follow-up period. Twelve percent of Project 12-Ways families recidivated within a year after program completion, compared to 26 percent of control families. But five years after the program ended 35 percent of the treated families recidivated, compared to 41 percent of control families. This finding reinforces the importance of conducting long-term assessments of intervention programs and of providing continuous follow-up support for families at risk of further violence.

Pharmacological therapy also has been used successfully with aggressive individuals (Cloninger, 1987). Cloninger notes that the prescribed treatment, however, depends upon the type of aggressive person being seen. For example, aggressive people who are impulsive and who seek novelty and risk can be treated with catecholamine agonists (e.g., imipramine). Aggressive individuals

BOX 10.2

A recent *New York Times Magazine* article (Hoffman, Feb. 16, 1992) demonstrates some of the problems of trying to produce change among battering men. The article describes a multifaceted program in Duluth, Minnesota, called Domestic Abuse Intervention Project (D.A.I.P.).

> Six glum faces, 12 crossed arms—nobody thinks they did anything wrong, so why do they have to be here? Ty Schroyer, a D.A.I.P. group leader, assumes an expression of determined cheeriness as he greets this week's recruits, all ordered by the court to the batterer's program. Some ground rules:
>
> "We don't call women 'the old lady,' 'the wife,' 'that slut,' . . ." The list quickly becomes unprintable.
>
> "So what should we call her—'it'?" says a man who calls himself Dave, as the others snicker.
>
> "How about her name?" snaps Schroyer, who himself was arrested nearly a decade ago for pounding his wife's head against a sidewalk. (pp. 27, 64)

Hoffman reports that 250 programs in the United States are trying to change batterers' treatment of women. The programs vary in philosophy and in length of treatment, with programs as long as one year or as short as twelve weeks.

> Edward W. Gondolf, a Pittsburgh sociologist . . . , says, "We're making a dent with garden-variety batterers"—first-time or sporadic offenders—"but there's another cadre, the most lethal, who are still out of our reach. . . ."

who exhibit strong anger, resentment, and suspicion are treated successfully with tranquilizers such as lithium.

Self-Help Groups

Another strategy common to many intervention programs is to direct abusers into groups where members help each other and themselves to change. Jennings (1987), who has studied battering men's self-help groups, has identified a common list of tasks on which

BOX 10.2
(Continued)

He cautions women not to be taken in when their partners enter counseling. "Counseling is the American way to heal a problem," he says. "She'll think, 'If he's trying, I should support him,' while he's thinking, 'I'll go to the program until I get what I want—my wife back.' But his being in counseling may increase the danger for her because she has got her guard down." (p. 64)

Along with traditional counseling, Duluth's twenty-six-week batterers' program offers counseling aimed simultaneously at getting men to take responsibility for their abuse and to see the social and cultural factors that promote maltreatment of women.

Bill, 30, admits that he once believed "you were allowed to hit a woman if you were married—the license was for possession. . . ." (p. 64)

Because the group leaders have also assaulted their partners, they are able to see through the rationalizations offered by new recruits:

Schroyer and the other group leaders stress that when the violence does erupt, contrary to a batterer's favorite excuse, he has not lost control. "You chose the time, the place, the reason, how much force you'd use," Schroyer tells them. "She didn't."

But convincing men that they are better off without that control is perhaps the most challenging impediment to treatment. One night a batterer huffily asked, "Why should men want to change when we got it all already?" (pp. 64–65).

members work: developing new problem-solving and interpersonal skills, learning tolerance and flexibility, providing mutual support and understanding, and enhancing each man's ability to feel empathy. Since group members have been violent themselves, they can readily confront abusers who are providing excuses for the abuse. Furthermore, the group serves as a subculture for a new way to view masculinity and male-female and adult-child relations, which is an example of Prochaska et al.'s (1992) "stimulus control." As one former batterer said,

I was able to remember everybody's face in the group, remember why I was going there, and if I couldn't handle something with my wife, I'd get the hell out of the room. . . . I am trying to make my life as I want it to be by showing my wife that she is my equal. I haven't accomplished that yet, I'm working on it. (Gondolf & Hanneken, 1987, p. 186)

Sometimes the groups are led by professional counselors who act as facilitators during discussions and model appropriate forms of expressing anger and assertiveness. Thus, the function of helping members is shared by the leaders and the members. The groups developed by Sonkin, Martin, and Walker (1985) are led by two counselors who can provide needed feedback to each other about the group process and can together make decisions about a group member's progress or potential for future violence. Sonkin et al. also require telephone checks with the group member's partner to determine whether techniques for anger control discussed in the group meetings are being implemented at home. After the members have made a commitment to nonviolence and have accepted responsibility for their abusive behavior, often group leaders recommend counseling for the couple, while the member continues to attend group meetings.

One of the most renowned self-help organizations is Parents Anonymous (PA), which was founded by two abusive parents and a volunteer professional, and since has spread nationwide (Saunders & Azar, 1989). Unlike Alcoholics Anonymous (AA), PA meetings are usually attended by a professional counselor who guides and supports the work of the group leader and provides information to group members. Similar to AA, however, the meetings are designed so that members provide emotional support for other group members and educate themselves about nonviolent child rearing techniques. Also, new members usually receive the phone number of another member whom they may call during a crisis at home. Longer-term members of the group may serve as role models for newer members, which might enhance the senior members' self-esteem and sense of effectiveness. In addition, newer members may benefit from seeing that others just like them have risen above their problem behaviors. While these groups are often seen as a treatment option, some members join to prevent the violence that they worry may result from parenting difficulties they are experiencing.

Evaluation studies of the effectiveness of self-help groups are rare and most are methodologically unsophisticated (cf. Gondolf, 1987; Saunders & Azar, 1989). Group members often receive other therapeutic interventions in addition to the self-help group, or were sent to the self-help group through a court order following arrest. Therefore, separating the effects of one treatment versus another, or even the effect of treatment versus arrest, may be impossible.

Also, it is not enough to compare membership in a treatment group to nonmembership. We need to study which people most likely will benefit from self-help and which will not. One study of male batterers (Chen, Bersani, Myers, & Denton, 1989) found that decreased recidivism was evident only among those group members who attended at least 75 percent of the group meetings. Those who attended fewer meetings subsequently manifested rates of violence comparable to men who were not referred to the program. These results are consistent with findings from other research that the amount of effort expended on behalf of a program corresponds to the degree of commitment to behavior change (Axsom & Cooper, 1985). Furthermore, choosing to attend self-help programs, as opposed to being required to attend, would be expected to enhance personal commitment to the new behaviors (Mendonca & Brehm, 1983). If perpetrators see themselves as having a choice about changing their violent behaviors and they view themselves as expending great effort to have learned new ways of relating to family members, the programs will be more effective.

Intervention with Victims of Partner Abuse

Most of the victims of spouse abuse who come to the attention of social services are women. Even though some research suggests that women are as likely as men to assault spouses, the women are more likely to be in danger from the abuse and to suffer greater physical harm (e.g., Bograd, 1990; Browne & Williams, 1989). Furthermore, male victims are more likely than female victims to hide their victimization or to respond to it by becoming violent toward others (Janoff-Bulman & Frieze, 1987; McNeely & Mann, 1990). Women, in contrast, are more likely to isolate themselves socially (Walker, 1984).

When women do seek help, they are offered a variety of services from psychological to employment counseling. These services are generally aimed at enhancing the alternatives for women currently in abusive relationships and ensuring that women understand that they do have alternatives (cf. Saunders & Azar, 1989).

Since battered women tend to be unassertive (Launius & Jensen, 1987), many experts on battered women encourage the provision of assertiveness training courses. Others, however, suggest that battered women may display unassertive behaviors in their relationship with the violent offender in an adaptive effort to avoid further attacks (O'Leary, Curley, Rosenbaum, & Clarke, 1985). If programs train battered women to stand up for their rights in their relationship, according to this perspective, they may be contributing to further victimization. The irony, however, is that appeasement of a perpetrator also leads to further violence because giving in and behaving submissively reinforces the partner's use of power (Reiss & Schulterbrandt, 1990). Thus, assertiveness training, combined with other means of controlling exposure to violence, may be necessary.

Remember that Bowker's study (1983) showed that in half of the cases in which partners desisted from abuse, women believed that their appeal to outside support effectuated the change. If assertiveness training encourages women to seek the help they deserve, and simultaneously to convince the batterer that they intend to stand up for their rights, such training may produce desirable change.

Shelters for victims of violence may aid women in turning their lives around in this way. Shelters provide a temporary place to live, enable the victim to escape from immediate harm, and enable them to make a decision about returning home or leaving the abusive relationship. Shelters often offer services such as personal, employment, and financial counseling and referral to social agencies. While the effectiveness of shelters has not been fully investigated, proponents suggest that going to a shelter convinces the batterer that the woman is serious about ending the violence. However, in line with the reasoning above, some argue that a victim's trip to a shelter may just anger the batterer and, should the victim return home, she will do so at her peril.

Acknowledging these opposing hypotheses, Berk, Newton, and Berk (1986) suggested that a shelter stay may reduce the likelihood of violence only when the batterer interprets a visit to a shelter as evidence of the likelihood of losing the partner. When the victim has sought other ways to stop the violence (e.g., calling the police), the batterer may be influenced to desist. Their hypothesis was supported in a study conducted with battered women in California. While a shelter stay, by itself, did not significantly decrease the amount of violence experienced in the next six weeks, one that was preceded by other recent attempts to seek help substantially reduced the rate of violence experienced after the stay.

This study reinforces the notion that, when the victim convinces the batterer that she is "back in control of her life," violence may not bring the same benefits to the batterer and instead now may be seen as likely to produce major losses. The study also reminds us that desistance from violence among batterers occurs not overnight, but may be best characterized by the stage model (Prochaska et al., 1992). A partner's earlier attempts to secure help may have started the batterer on the road to contemplating a change, and her visit to a shelter may have reinforced the need for change and moved him into the "action" stage where behavior change occurs.

Battered women also may benefit from participating in victim support groups (Tutty, Bidgood, & Rothery, 1993). A 10–12 week program offered in Waterloo, Canada, for example, found significant improvement immediately following the program and also six months later in the women's self-esteem and stress levels, as well as a reduction in the abuse suffered. No control group was monitored; therefore, we do not know the extent to which the changes observed were a function of group participation. But the results are consistent with the notion that women who seek help will feel better about themselves and will communicate to their partners that they are serious about stopping the abusive treatment.

Support for victims of partner abuse may also forestall violence against the perpetrator. You will recall Browne and Williams's (1989) research, which demonstrated that the proportion of women who murdered their husbands or partners was substantially connected to the availability of support services for the women.

Intervention with Victims of Child Abuse

What interventions exist for child victims of violence? They sometimes are removed from their homes and placed in foster care, often because it is legally simpler to remove the child than the offending parent (Saunders & Azar, 1989). This practice is lauded by some professionals because it provides protection for the victim and motivates the abuser to change in order to have the child returned. Other professionals, however, believe that removal of a child may further traumatize the victim and destroy the family unit. Little evidence is available to resolve these claims (Saunders & Azar, 1989).

But whether the child secures treatment in the home or while in foster care, most professionals agree that abused children are likely to need some form of therapy. As we discussed earlier in this book, abuse itself may not account for the psychological maladjustment seen in children; instead abuse is probably best regarded as one symptom of a variety of ills manifest in the abusive family relationship (Wolfe, Wekerle, & McGee, 1992). For this reason, treatment for abused children is usually accompanied by treatment for the child's parents.

The child's developmental level at the time of the abuse will mediate the consequences of the disordered family life, as well as the focus for intervention efforts (Shirk, 1988). For example, an infant whose main developmental tasks are to develop trust in and attachment to others will be affected differently than will an older child who has already passed through these developmental milestones. Age differences will affect how the abuse is experienced and interpreted by the child and how the child expresses the effects of abuse (Shirk, 1988).

Nevertheless, a review of the literature on the consequences of abuse suggests common components needed for intervention programs with abused children (Shirk, 1988; Wolfe et al., 1992). Abused children need interventions that will enhance their social and emotional development and their competence in social interactions with peers. They need to develop more social sensitivity that will permit them to distinguish among the emotions experienced by others, to take another's perspective, and to respond appropriately to other's nonaggression (Dodge, 1986). Abused children especially need to strengthen their self-control, learn to manage anger effectively, and to reduce their tendency to misbehave (Reid et al., 1981; Trickett & Kuczynski, 1986).

Many programs focus on social skill remediation and include group therapy where children may interact with their peers (Daro, 1988). Younger children may be placed in therapeutic day care, which provides peer interaction and intense contact between the abused child and a supportive teacher. The programs also commonly include treatment for both parent and child to improve the pattern of parent-child interactions. Daro's (1988) review of these programs suggests that they are generally successful in remediating the developmental problems experienced by abused children. However, the success rate is lessened when parents do not make similar progress in changing their behaviors and their interaction with the child.

Intervention with Victims of Elderly Abuse

As noted throughout this book, intervention with elderly victims of abuse is particularly difficult because of their desire for privacy and their lessened involvement in social networks that would spot the abuse (Wolf & Pillemer, 1989). Perpetrators in cases of elderly abuse tend to be mentally ill and dependent in some way upon their victim (Wolf & Pillemer, 1989). This dependency and the resistance on the part of both victim and perpetrator to allow intervention stymie attempts to help the victim. Often only following a change of residence for either the perpetrator or victim will the situation improve.

Once cases do come to the attention of medical or social service agencies, the abuse tends to be handled through *case management,* where social workers or other professionals oversee a range of services needed by a particular victim and his or her family. Three model intervention projects followed by Wolf and Pillemer (1989) had several goals for remediation: to provide health, counseling, and other social services to the victim and family members and to mediate conflicts between the victim and the perpetrator.

Intervention in Cases of Sibling Violence

As you might imagine, given society's acceptance of sibling fights, except in cases of severe violence, few intervention programs for sibling abuse exist. Patterson's (1984) research, however, shows that often families with one coercive child have patterns of interaction that are dysfunctional and should be remedied (see also Loeber & Tengs, 1986). One coercive sibling stimulates coercion in others, and even in the parents. Patterson (1984) recommends teaching parents in such families to use *time out* when their child engages in inappropriate behavior towards a sibling or parent. Time out disrupts the escalation of violence and the chain of aggressive interactions so evident in sibling violence (Loeber & Tengs, 1986; Patterson, 1984). This discipline technique also teaches a nonaggressive conflict resolution strategy.

Individual Reactions to Intervention

Those who devise behavior change programs recognize that all violent offenders should not be lumped into one category (Fagan, 1989). Blumstein, Farrington, and Moitra (1985) suggest that there are at least three types of criminal offenders. The first group, the *innocents,* stop after a few criminal acts. *Desisters* have a period of criminal activity, but then stop, sometimes with no evident outside intervention. The third group, the *persisters,* demonstrate lengthy and frequent involvement in criminal activity. While this trichotomy was established to characterize and understand criminal behavior in general, it might be applied usefully to family violence offenders (cf. Fagan,

1989). Some people will need only a little nudge to get them back on the path of nonviolence; others, as suggested in Box 10.2, will be more recalcitrant. As Fagan (1989) notes, ". . . (I)t is not likely that one arrest or a stint on probation will initiate processes of 'unlearning' to desist from a pattern of battering" (p. 387). Similarly, more than short-term counseling may be needed with people whose battering behavior has been extensive.

It is also wise to assess the generality of aggression and other antisocial tendencies displayed by the offender (cf. Fagan, 1989; Holtzworth-Munroe & Stuart, 1994). At the beginning of this book, we learned that some people confine their abuse to within the family, while others are more generally violent (Holtzworth-Munroe & Stuart, 1994; Hotaling & Straus, 1989; Shields et al., 1988). The violence of family-only offenders may be evoked by a more constrained set of circumstances (e.g., when one's authority within the family structure is questioned) and, therefore, a more focused intervention program may be sufficient to produce a change. More generally violent people may require a multifaceted intervention.

Fagan (1989) reminds us that the process of desistance from family violence goes through several stages and support is needed to sustain the change in behavior throughout this process. Because of the need for support, perpetrators who are well embedded in a subculture that reinforces the violence may need substantially more intervention. They will need to build more contact with a different, nonviolent subculture in order to sustain changes in behavior.

A history of abuse in one's family-of-origin may also characterize people who require more substantial interventions. Shepard (1992) found, in an evaluation of the D.A.I.P. program discussed in Box 10.2, that men who had experienced abuse in childhood were more likely to recidivate within five years following their participation in the program than men who had no such childhood history. This result makes sense; a lifetime of thinking that aggression is one of the options for solving interpersonal dilemmas may be difficult to counter.

Shepard (1992) also found that dependency upon alcohol or drugs was a predictor of recidivism, even when the batterers had received evaluation and treatment for their problem. Remember, abuse is rarely explained by one factor. We cannot turn to any particular stressor or to a single event in one's childhood and say that this is *the* cause of abuse. Instead, we know that abusers tend to have multiple risk factors present in their lives. Shepard's results remind us that they will also be present in the lives of those who are provided with treatment and are on the road to change. Therefore, treatment programs that address the varied needs of the perpetrator may be more successful.

Concluding Remarks

This chapter provides only a short overview of the types of programs that are available to prevent violence from occurring or to intervene in families after its onset. Some programs involve professional therapists, but others offer the support and help of volunteers. Prevention efforts have been directed at children and adults and have involved attempts to intervene at the level of the individual and society.

Most people would agree that it is better to prevent abuse than to clean up in its aftermath. Even if a treatment program restores an individual's mental and physical health, prevention efforts could have eliminated the suffering that was endured.

Economic arguments also bolster the plea for prevention rather than treatment. For example, in her book, *Confronting Child Abuse,* Daro compares the costs of various prevention and treatment efforts and then contrasts these to the costs incurred from growing up in a violent family. Abused children may suffer from physical injuries and health problems, intellectual impairments, and emotional disturbance. Furthermore, they may become delinquent and have problems in school. These are only the relatively short-term consequences of abuse. Daro points out that the costs over a longer period of special education programs, juvenile or adult court costs, therapy, and loss of potential income must be tabulated as well. Then we must consider the costs incurred if the victim of the violence becomes violent in his or her adult family relationships. Finally, we must recognize that even successful treatment programs are not effective with all victims. So, some of the money spent on interventions with victims of abuse will be wasted. Daro (1988) concludes:

> Given the high cost of treatment services and their limited promise for remediating the consequences of maltreatment, prevention efforts appear to be a more efficient alternative. Approximately $1.3 billion would purchase two years of weekly parenting education and supervised parent-child interactions for *all* adolescent mothers. By way of contrast, this amount would be insufficient to cover even one year of lay therapy for all families reported to CPS last year for maltreatment. Supporting families through the birth of their first child carries the potential for a significant reduction in the health care and

therapeutic service costs associated with maltreatment, savings that would most certainly cover the costs of such prevention efforts.
(p. 198)

Daro (1988) further reminds us that reducing the incidence of maltreatment will not occur through isolated prevention efforts. Just as abuse is not caused by a single factor, a coordinated system of services, directed at individual, familial, and societal levels, may be needed to eliminate problems as complex as family maltreatment.

Prevention services, however, may do more harm than good if they stigmatize innocent people. As Daro (1988) notes, even when services are offered to volunteers, some potential recipients may not feel free to refuse to participate, especially when the service is offered by governmental agencies from whom they receive other forms of aid (e.g., welfare office). When prevention programs are built into existing service delivery systems, however, and offered to all people who are served by the system, not only is the risk of stigmatization lessened, but the costs are reduced. Programs built into the curriculum offered to all students in the public schools or incorporated into routine visits to health agencies are efficient and relatively non-intrusive ways of preventing abuse—that is, if they are effective. Prevention programs, as well as their treatment counterparts, must be evaluated for their success.

Daro's (1988) arguments about prevention of child abuse can be replicated when we examine other forms of family violence. The disruption of lives due to partner battering may be just as harmful to the individual families involved and as costly to society.

While efforts to eliminate violence in families may appear to be overwhelmingly difficult, the human and economic costs of failure to try are even greater. Yet, our nation devotes woefully few resources to solving the problems of violence. The National Research Council (Reiss & Roth, 1993) recently documented that in 1989 federal expenditures for research into solutions to violence amounted to $31 per year of "potential life lost" due to a violent death. This figure compares unfavorably to the expenditures devoted to research on other life-threatening causes; $794, $697, and $441 were spent on research on cancer, AIDs, and heart, lung, or blood disease, respectively.

The National Research Council, understanding the biological and social roots of violence, recommended that research funds be devoted to

> the biological and psychosocial development of individuals' potentials
> for violent behavior, with special attention to preventing brain damage

associated with low birthweight and childhood head trauma, cognitive-behavioral techniques for preventing aggressive and violent behavior and inculcating prosocial behavior, and the learning of attitudes that discourage violent sexual behavior. (Reiss & Roth, 1993)

While the National Research Council spoke about violence in general, efforts directed at reducing the incidence of violence in the home will benefit from knowledge about the causes of violence outside the home.

REFERENCES

Abramson, L. Y., Metalsky, G. I., & Alloy, L. B. (1988). The hopelessness theory of depression: Does the research test the theory? In L. A. Abramson (Ed.), *Social cognition and clinical psychology: A synthesis* (pp. 33–65). New York: Guilford Press.

Abramson, L. Y., Seligman, M. E. P., & Teasdale, J. D. (1978). Learned helplessness in humans: Critique and reformulation. *Journal of Abnormal Psychology, 87,* 49–74.

Ainsworth, M. D. S. (1980). Attachment and child abuse. In G. Gerbner, C. J. Ross, & E. Zigler (Eds.), *Child abuse: An agenda for action* (pp. 35–47). New York: Oxford University Press.

Ajzen, I., & Fishbein, M. (1980). *Understanding attitudes and predicting social behavior.* Englewood Cliffs, NJ: Prentice-Hall.

Albee, G. W. (1980). Primary prevention and social problems. In G. Gerbner, C. J. Ross, & E. Zigler (Eds.), *Child abuse: An agenda for action* (pp. 106–117). New York: Oxford University Press.

Alloy, L. B., & Abramson, L. Y. (1982). Learned helplessness, depression, and the illusion of control. *Journal of Personality and Social Psychology, 42,* 1114–1126.

Allport, G. W. (1985). The historical background of social psychology. In G. Lindzey & E. Aronson (Eds.), *Handbook of social psychology* (Vol. I) pp. 1–46. New York: Random House.

American Humane Association. (1987). *Highlights of official child neglect and abuse reporting, 1985.* Denver: American Humane Association.

Arias, I., & Beach, S. R. H. (1987). Validity of self-reports of marital violence. *Journal of Family Violence, 2,* 139–149.

Arias, I., & Johnson, P. (1989). Evaluations of physical aggression among intimate dyads. *Journal of Interpersonal Violence, 4,* 298–307.

Attias, R., & Goodwin, J. (1984, September). *Knowledge and management strategies in incest cases: A survey of physicians, psychologists and family counselors.* Paper presented at the Fifth International Congress on Child Abuse and Neglect, Montreal, Canada.

Attorney General's Task Force on Family Violence (1984, September). *Final report* (Publication No. 027-000-01197-7). Washington, DC: U.S. Department of Justice.

Axsom, D., & Cooper, J. (1985). Cognitive dissonance and behavior change in psychotherapy. *Journal of Experimental Social Psychology, 21,* 149–160.

Ball-Rokeach, S. J. (1973). Values and violence: A test of the subculture of violence thesis. *American Sociological Review, 38,* 736–749.

Bandura, A. (1973). *Aggression: A social learning analysis.* Englewood Cliffs, NJ: Prentice-Hall.

Bandura, A. (1986). *Social foundations of thought and action: A social cognitive theory.* Englewood Cliffs, NJ: Prentice-Hall.

Bank, S. P., & Kahn, M. D. (1982). *The sibling bond.* New York: Basic Books.

Barahal, R. M., Waterman, J., & Martin, H. P. (1981). The social cognitive development of abused children. *Journal of Consulting and Clinical Psychology, 49,* 508–516.

Barnett, M. A. (1987). Empathy and related responses in children. In N. Eisenberg & J. Strayer (Eds.), *Empathy and its development* (pp. 146–162). Cambridge: Cambridge University Press.

Barnett, M. A., Feierstein, M. D., Jaet, B. P., Saunders, L. C., Quackenbush, S. W., & Sinisi, C. S. (1992). The effect of knowing a rape victim on reactions to other victims. *Journal of Interpersonal Violence, 7,* 44–56.

Barnett, M. A., Tetreault, P. A., & Masbad, I. (1987). Empathy with a rape victim: The role of similarity of experience. *Violence and Victims, 2,* 255–262.

Baumrind, D. (1971). Current patterns of parental authority. *Developmental Psychology Monographs, 4,* 1–63.

Bebber, C. C. (1994). Increases in U.S. violent crime during the 1980s following four American military actions. *Journal of Interpersonal Violence, 9,* 109–116.

Becker, H. S. (1964). *The other side: Perspectives on deviance.* New York: Free Press.

Becker, W. C., & Krug, R. S. (1965). The Parent Attitude Research Instrument: A research review. *Child Development, 36,* 329–365.

Belsky, J. (1980). Child maltreatment: An ecological integration. *American Psychologist, 35,* 320–335.

Belsky, J. (1984). The determinants of parenting: A process model. *Child Development, 55,* 83–96.

Belsky, J., & Vondra, J. (1989). Lessons from child abuse: The determinants of parenting. In D. Cicchetti & V. Carlson (Eds.), *Child maltreatment: Theory and research on the causes and consequences of child abuse and neglect* (pp. 153–202). Cambridge: Cambridge University Press.

Bem, D. J. (1972). Self-perception theory. In L. Berkowitz (Ed.), *Advances in experimental social psychology* (Vol. 6, pp. 1–62). New York: Academic Press.

Bem, S. L. (1993). *The lenses of gender: Transforming the debate on sexual inequality.* New Haven: Yale University Press.

Berk, R. A., Campbell, A., Klap, R., & Western, B. (1992). The deterrent effect of arrest in incidents of domestic violence: A Bayesian analysis of four field experiments. *American Sociological Review, 57,* 698–708.

Berk, S. F., & Loseke, D. R. (1980–81). Handling family violence: Situational determinants of police arrest in domestic disturbances. *Law and Society Review, 15,* 318–346.

Berk, R. A., Newton, P. J., & Berk, S. F. (1986). What a difference a day makes: An empirical study of the impact of shelters for battered women. *Journal of Marriage and the Family, 48,* 481–490.

Berliner, L. (1988). Expert evidence and eyewitness testimony. *Journal of Interpersonal Violence, 3,* 108–110.

Berliner, L., & Barbieri, M. K. (1984). The testimony of the child victim of sexual assault. *Journal of Social Issues, 40,* 125–137.

Besharov, D. J. (1991). Reducing unfounded reports. *Journal of Interpersonal Violence, 6,* 112–115.

Biglan, A., Lewin, L., & Hops, H. (1990). A contextual approach to the problem of aversive practices in families. In G. R. Patterson (Ed.), *Depression and aggression in family interaction* (pp. 103–129). Hillsdale, NJ: L. Erlbaum.

Blackman, J. (1989). *Intimate violence.* New York: Columbia University Press.

Blanchard, D. C., & Blanchard, R. J. (1986). Punishment and aggression: A critical reexamination. In R. J. Blanchard and D. C. Blanchard (Eds.), *Advances in the study of aggression* (Vol. 2), pp. 121–164. Orlando: Academic Press.

Bleier, R. (1984). *Science and gender: A critique of biology and its theories on women.* New York: Pergamon.

Blumenthal, M. D., Chadiha, L. B., Cole, G. A., & Jayaratne, T. E. (1975). *More about justifying violence: Methodological studies of attitudes and behavior.* Ann Arbor: University of Michigan Press.

Blumstein, A., Cohen, J., & Nagin, D. (1978). *Deterrence and incapacitation: Estimating the effects of criminal sanctions on crime rates.* Washington, DC: National Academy of Sciences.

Blumstein, A., Farrington, D. P., & Moitra, S. (1985). Delinquency careers: Innocents, desisters, and persisters. In M. Tonry & N. Morris (Eds.), *Crime and justice: An annual review of research* (Vol. 6), pp. 187–219. Chicago: University of Chicago Press.

Bograd, M. (1990). Why we need gender to understand human violence. *Journal of Interpersonal Violence, 5,* 132–135.

Boldizar, J. P., Perry, D. G., & Perry, L. C. (1989). Outcome values and aggression. *Child Development, 60,* 571–579.

Booth, A., & Dabbs, J. M., Jr. (1993). Testosterone and men's marriages. *Social Forces, 72,* 463–477.

Borgia, G. (1980). Human aggression as a biological adaptation. In J. S. Lockard (Ed.), *The evolution of human social behavior* (pp. 165–191). New York: Elsevier.

Borgida, E., Gresham, A. W., Kovera, M. B., & Regan, P. C. (1992). Children as witnesses in court: The influence of expert psychological testimony. In A. W. Burgess (Ed.), *Child trauma: Issues and research* (pp. 131–165). New York: Garland.

Bowker, L. H. (1983). *Beating wife-beating*. Lexington, MA: Lexington Books.

Bowlby, J. (1969). *Attachment and loss* (Vol. 1), London: Hogarth.

Bradbury, T. N., & Fincham, F. D. (1990). Attributions in marriage: Review and Critique. *Psychological Bulletin, 107,* 3–33.

Briere, J., & Conte, J. (1993). Self-reported amnesia for abuse in adults molested as children. *Journal of Traumatic Stress, 6,* 21–31.

Brown, D. W. (1978). Arrest rates and crime rates: When does a tipping effect occur? *Social Forces, 57,* 671–682.

Browne, A. (1987). *When battered women kill.* New York: Free Press.

Browne, A. (1992, June 17). Violence against women: Relevance for medical practitioners. Report of the Council on Scientific Affairs. *JAMA, 267,* 3184–3189.

Browne, A., & Flewelling, R. (1986, November). Women as victims or perpetrators of homicide. Paper presented at the Annual Meeting of the American Society of Criminology, Atlanta.

Browne, A., & Williams, K. R. (1989). Exploring the effect of resource availability and the likelihood of female-perpetrated homicides. *Law & Society Review, 23,* 75–94.

Browne, A., & Williams, K. R. (1993). Gender, intimacy, and lethal violence: Trends from 1976–1987. *Gender & Society, 7,* 78–98.

Bryant, B. K. (1989). The child's perspective of sibling caretaking and its relevance to understanding social-emotional functioning and development. In P. G. Zukow (Ed.), *Sibling interaction across cultures: Theoretical and methodological issues* (pp. 143–163). New York: Springer-Verlag.

Bugental, D. B., Mantyla, S. M., & Lewis, J. (1989). Parental attributions as moderators of affective communication to children at risk for physical abuse. In D. Cicchetti & V. Carlson (Eds.), *Child maltreatment: Theory and research on the causes and consequences of child abuse and neglect* (pp. 254–279). Cambridge: Cambridge University Press.

Buhrmester, D., & Furman, W. (1990). Perceptions of sibling relationships during middle childhood and adolescence. *Child Development, 61,* 1387–1398.

Burgdorf, K. (1980). *Recognition and reporting of child maltreatment: Findings from the National Study of the Incidence and Severity of Child Abuse and Neglect.* Washington, DC: National Center on Child Abuse and Neglect.

Burgess, R. L. (1994). The family in a changing world: A prolegomenon to an evolutionary analysis. *Human Nature, 5,* 203–221.

Burgess, R. L., & Draper, P. (1989). The explanation of family violence: The role of biological, behavioral, and cultural selection. In L. Ohlin & M. Tonry (Eds.), *Family violence* (pp. 59–116). Chicago: University of Chicago Press.

Burgess, R. L., & Garbarino, J. (1983). Doing what comes naturally? An evolutionary perspective on child abuse. In D. Finkelhor, R. J. Gelles, G. T. Hotaling, & M. A. Straus (Eds.), *The dark side of families: Current family violence research* (pp. 88–101). Beverly Hills: Sage.

Burt, M. R. (1980). Cultural myths and supports for rape. *Journal of Personality and Social Psychology, 38,* 217–230.

Buss, D. M., & Schmitt, D. P. (1993). Sexual strategies theory: An evolutionary perspective on human mating. *Psychological Review, 100,* 204–232.

Buzawa, E. S., & Austin, T. (1992/1993). Determining police response to domestic violence victims: The role of victim preference. *American Behavioral Scientist, 36,* 610–623.

Caesar, P. L. (1988). Exposure to violence in the families-of-origin among wife abusers and maritally nonviolent men. *Violence and Victims, 3,* 49–63.

Carmody, D. C., & Williams, K. R. (1987). Wife assault and perceptions of sanctions. *Violence and Victims, 2,* 25–38.

Caspi, A., & Elder, G. H., Jr. (1988). Emergent family patterns: The intergenerational construction of problem behaviour and relationships. In R. A. Hinde & J. Stevenson-Hinde (Eds.), *Relationships within families: Mutual influences* (pp. 218–240). Oxford: Clarendon.

Caspi, A., Elder, G. H., Jr., & Bem, D. J. (1987). Moving against the world: Life-course patterns of explosive children. *Developmental Psychology, 23,* 308–313.

Ceci, S. J., & Bruck, M. (1993). Suggestibility of the child witness: A historical review and synthesis. *Psychological Bulletin, 113,* 403–439.

Celano, M. P. (1992). A developmental model of victims' internal attributions of responsibility for sexual abuse. *Journal of Interpersonal Violence, 7,* 57–69.

Chang, A., Oglesby, A., Wallace, H., Goldstein, H., & Hexter, A. (1976). Child abuse and neglect: Physicians' knowledge, attitudes and experiences. *American Journal of Public Health, 66,* 1199–1201.

Chen, H., Bersani, C., Myers, S. C., & Denton, R. (1989). Evaluating the effectiveness of a court sponsored abuser treatment program. *Journal of Family Violence, 4,* 309–322.

Cialdini, R. B., Kenrick, D. T., & Hoerig, J. H. (1976). Victim derogation in the Lerner paradigm: Just world or just justification? *Journal of Personality and Social Psychology, 33,* 719–724.

Clark, J. R. (1993, April 30). Where to now on domestic violence? Studies offer mixed policy guidance. *Law Enforcement News, 19,* pp. 1, 17.

Clarke, A. E., & Ruble, D. N. (1978). Young adolescents' beliefs concerning menstruation. *Child Development, 49,* 231–234.

Clarke-Stewart, K. A. (1973). Interactions between mothers and their young children: Characteristics and consequences. *Monographs of the Society for Research in Child Development, 38* (6–7, Serial No. 153).

Cloninger, C. R. (1987). Pharmacological approaches to the treatment of antisocial behavior. In S. A. Mednick, T. E. Moffitt, & S. A. Stack (Eds.), *The causes of crime: New biological approaches* (pp. 329–349). Cambridge: Cambridge University Press.

Cloninger, C. R., & Gottesman, I. I. (1987). Genetic and environmental factors in antisocial behavior disorders. In S. A. Mednick, T. E. Moffitt, & S. A. Stack (Eds.), *The causes of crime: New biological approaches* (pp. 92–109). Cambridge: Cambridge University Press.

Coates, D., Wortman, C. B., & Abbey, A. (1979). Reactions to victims. In I. H. Frieze, D. Bar-Tal, & J. S. Carroll (Eds.), *New approaches to social problems* (pp. 21–52). San Francisco: Jossey-Bass.

Coleman, D. H., & Straus, M. A. (1986). Marital power, conflict, and violence in a nationally representative sample of American couples. *Violence and Victims, 1,* 141–157.

Coller, S. A., & Resick, P. A. (1987). Women's attributions of responsibility for date rape: The influence of empathy and sex-role stereotyping. *Violence and Victims, 2,* 115–125.

Colombotos, J. (1969). Physicians and medicare: A before-after study of the effects of legislation on attitudes. *American Sociological Review, 34,* 318–334.

Conger, R. D., McCarty, J. A., Yang, R. K., Lahey, B. B., & Kropp, J. P. (1984). Perception of child, childrearing values, and emotional distress as mediating links between environmental stressors and observed maternal behavior. *Child Development, 55,* 2234–2247.

Conte, J. R. (1988). Structural reconciliation of therapeutic and criminal justice cultures. In A. Maney & S. Wells (Eds.), *Professional responsibilities in protecting children: A public health approach to child sexual abuse* (pp. 139–149). New York: Praeger.

Conte, J. R., Fogarty, L., & Collins, M. E. (1991). National survey of professional practice in child sexual abuse. *Journal of Family Violence, 6,* 149–166.

Coopersmith, S. (1967). *The antecedents of self-esteem.* San Francisco: W. H. Freeman.

Crittenden, P. M., & DiLalla, D. L. (1988). Compulsive compliance: The development of an inhibitory coping strategy in infancy. *Journal of Abnormal Child Psychology, 16,* 585–599.

Crowne, D. P., & Marlowe, D. (1964). *The approval motive: Studies in evaluative dependence.* New York: Wiley.

Dabbs, J. M., Jr. (1992). Testosterone measurements in social and clinical psychology. *Journal of Social and Clinical Psychology, 11,* 302–321.

Daro, D. (1988). *Confronting child abuse: Research for effective program design.* New York: Free Press.

Davis, M. H. (1994). *Empathy: A social psychological approach.* Dubuque, IA: Brown & Benchmark.

Dawkins, R. (1976). *The selfish gene.* New York: Oxford University Press.

Deffenbacher, J. L. (1988). Cognitive-relaxation and social skills treatments of anger: A year later. *Journal of Counseling Psychology, 35,* 234–236.

Dent, D. Z., & Arias, I. (1990). Effects of alcohol, gender, and role of spouses on attributions and evaluations of marital violence scenarios. *Violence and Victims, 5,* 185–193.

DiLalla, L. F., & Gottesman, I. I. (1991). Biological and genetic contributors to violence—Widom's untold tale. *Psychological Bulletin, 109,* 125–129.

Dix, T. (1991). The affective organization of parenting: Adaptive and maladaptive processes. *Psychological Bulletin, 110,* 3–25.

Dix, T. H., & Grusec, J. E. (1985). Parent attribution processes in the socialization of children. In I. E. Sigel (Ed.), *Parental belief systems: The psychological consequences for children* (pp. 201–233). Hillsdale, NJ: L. Erlbaum.

Dobash, R. E., & Dobash, R. P. (1979). *Violence against wives.* New York: Free Press.

Dodge, K. A. (1986). Social information-processing variables in the development of aggression and altruism in children. In C. Zahn-Waxler, E. M. Cummings, & R. Ianotti (Eds.), *Altruism and aggression: Biological and social origins* (pp. 280–302). Cambridge: Cambridge University Press.

Dodge, K. A., Bates, J. E., & Pettit, G. S. (1990). Mechanisms in the cycle of violence. *Science, 250,* 1678–1683.

Donnerstein, E., Linz, D., & Penrod, S. (1987). *The question of pornography: Research findings and policy implications.* New York: Free Press.

Dunn, J. (1992). Siblings and development. *Current Directions in Psychological Science, 1,* 6–9.

Dweck, C. S. (1975). The role of expectations and attributions in the alleviation of learned helplessness. *Journal of Personality and Social Psychology, 31,* 674–685.

Easterbrooks, M. A., & Emde, R. N. (1988). Marital and parent-child relationships: The role of affect in the family system. In R. A. Hinde & J. Stevenson-Hinde (Eds.), *Relationships within families: Mutual influences* (pp. 83–139). Oxford: Clarendon.

Edelson, J. L., Eisikovits, Z. C., Guttmann, E., & Sela-Amit, M. (1991). Cognitive and interpersonal factors in woman abuse. *Journal of Family Violence, 6,* 167–182.

Egeland, B., Jacobvitz, D., & Papatola, K. (1987). Intergenerational continuity of abuse. In R. J. Gelles and J. B. Lancaster (Eds.), *Child abuse and neglect: Biosocial dimensions* (pp. 255–276). New York: Adline de Gruyter.

Egeland, B., Jacobvitz, D., & Sroufe, L. A. (1988). Breaking the cycle of abuse. *Child Development, 59,* 1080–1088.

Ehrenkranz, J., Bliss, E., & Sheard, M. H. (1974). Plasma testosterone: Correlation with aggressive behavior and social dominance in man. *Psychosomatic Medicine, 36,* 469–475.

Elder Abuse (An Examination of a Hidden Problem). (1981). *A report (with additional views) by the Select Committee on Aging, U.S. House of Representatives* (Comm. Pub. No. 97-277). Washington, DC: U.S. Government Printing Office.

Elder, G. H., Jr., Caspi, A., & Downey, G. (1986). Problem behavior and family relationships: Life course and intergenerational themes. In A. Sorenson, F. Weinert, and L. Sherrod (Eds.), *Human development: Interdisciplinary perspectives* (pp. 293–340). Hillsdale, NJ: Erlbaum.

Elder, G. H., Jr., Nguyen, T. V., and Caspi, A. (1985). Linking family hardship to children's lives. *Child Development, 56,* 361–375.

Elliott, D. S. (1989). Criminal justice procedures in family violence cases. In L. Ohlin & M. Tonry (Eds.), *Family violence* (pp. 427–480). Chicago: University of Chicago Press.

Erickson, M. F., Egeland, B., & Pianta, R. (1989). The effects of maltreatment on the development of young children. In D. Cicchetti & V. Carlson (Eds.), *Child maltreatment: Theory and research on the causes and consequences of child abuse and neglect* (pp. 647–684). Cambridge: Cambridge University Press.

Ervin-Tripp, S. (1989). Sisters and brothers. In P. G. Zukow (Ed.), *Sibling interaction across cultures: Theoretical and methodological issues* (pp. 184–195). New York: Springer-Verlag.

Fagan, J. (1989). Cessation of family violence: Deterrence and dissuasion. In L. Ohlin & M. Tonry (Eds.), *Family violence* (pp. 377–425). Chicago: University of Chicago Press.

Fagan, J., & Wexler, S. (1987). Crime at home and in the streets: The relationship between family and stranger violence. *Violence and Victims, 2,* 5–23.

Fazio, R. H. (1986). How do attitudes guide behavior? In R. M. Sorrentino & E. T. Higgins (Eds.), *Handbook of motivation and cognition: Foundations of social behavior* (pp. 204–243). New York: Guilford.

Feingold, A. (1992). Gender differences in mate selection preferences: A test of the parental investment model. *Psychological Bulletin, 112,* 125–139.

Felson, R. B. (1983). Aggression and violence between siblings. *Social Psychology Quarterly, 46,* 271–285.

Ferguson, T. J., & Rule, B. G. (1988). Children's evaluations of retaliatory aggression. *Child Development, 59,* 961–968.

Feshbach, N. D. (1989). The construct of empathy and the phenomenon of physical maltreatment of children. In D. Cicchetti & V. Carlson (Eds.), *Child maltreatment: Theory and research on the causes and consequences of child abuse and neglect* (pp. 349–373). Cambridge: Cambridge University Press.

Finkelhor, D. (1984). *Child sexual abuse: New theory and research.* New York: Free Press.

Fishbein, M., & Ajzen, I. (1975). *Belief, attitude, intention, and behavior: An introduction to theory and research.* Reading, MA: Addison-Wesley.

Fiske, S. T., & Taylor, S. E. (1983). *Social cognition.* Reading, MA: Addison-Wesley.

Fiske, S. T., & Taylor, S. E. (1991). *Social Cognition.* New York: McGraw Hill.

Flanzraich, M., & Dunsavage, I. (1977, November–December). Role reversal in abused/neglected families: Implications for child welfare workers. *Children Today,* pp. 13–15, 36.

Flitcraft, A. H. (1992). Violence, values, and gender. *JAMA, 267,* 3194–3195.

Floody, O. R. (1983). Hormones and aggression in female mammals. In B. B. Svare (Ed.), *Hormones and aggressive behavior* (pp. 39–89). New York: Plenum.

Freud, S. (1948). *Beyond the pleasure principle.* London: Hogarth Press.

Friedrich, W., and Boriskin, J. (1976). The role of the child in abuse: A review of the literature. *American Journal of Orthopsychiatry, 46,* 580–590.

Friedrich, W. N., & Einbender, A. J. (1983). The abused child: A psychological review. *Journal of Clinical Child Psychology, 12,* 244–256.

Frieze, I. H. (1979). Perceptions of battered wives. In I. H. Frieze, D. Bar-Tal, & J. S. Carroll (Eds.), *New approaches to social problems: Applications of attribution theory* (pp. 79–108). San Francisco: Jossey-Bass.

Frieze, I. H., (1987). The female victim: Rape, wife battering, and incest. In G. R. VandenBos & B. K. Bryant (Eds.), *Cataclysms, crises, and catastrophes: Psychology in action* (pp. 109–145). Washington, DC: American Psychological Association.

Frieze, I. H., & Browne, A. (1989). Violence in marriage. In L. Ohlin & M. Tonry (Eds.), *Family violence* (pp. 163–218). Chicago: University of Chicago Press.

Frieze, I. H., & McHugh, M. C. (1992). Power and influence strategies in violent and nonviolent marriages. *Psychology of Women Quarterly, 16,* 449–465.

Frodi, A. (1981). Contribution of infant characteristics to child abuse. *American Journal of Mental Deficiency, 85,* 341–349.

Frodi, A. M., & Lamb, M. E. (1980). Child abusers' responses to infant smiles and cries. *Child Development, 51,* 238–241.

Frodi, A. M., Lamb, M. E., Leavitt, L. A., Donovan, W. L., Neff, C., & Sherry, D. (1978). Fathers' and mothers' responses to the faces and cries of normal and premature infants. *Developmental Psychology, 14,* 490–498.

Furman, W., & Buhrmester, D. (1985). Children's perceptions of the qualities of sibling relationships. *Child Development, 56,* 448–461.

Gandelman, R. (1983). Hormones and infanticide. In B. B. Svare (Ed.), *Hormones and aggressive behavior* (pp. 105–118). New York: Plenum.

Garbarino, J. (1976a). A preliminary study of some ecological correlates of child abuse: The impact of socioeconomic stress on mothers. *Child Development, 47,* 178–185.

Garbarino, J. (1988). Ethical obstacles to professional reporting of child maltreatment. In A. Maney & S. Wells (Eds.), *Professional responsibilities in protecting children: A public health approach to child sexual abuse* (pp. 45–53). New York: Praeger.

Garbarino, J. (1989a). Troubled youth, troubled families: The dynamics of adolescent maltreatment. In D. Cicchetti & V. Carlson (Eds.), *Child maltreatment: Theory and research on the causes and consequences of child abuse and neglect* (pp. 647–684). Cambridge: Cambridge University Press.

Garbarino, J. (1989b). The incidence and prevalence of child maltreatment. In L. Ohlin & M. Tonry (Eds.), *Family violence* (pp. 219–261). Chicago: University of Chicago Press.

Garbarino, J., Guttmann, E., & Seeley, J. W. (1987). *The psychologically battered child.* San Francisco: Jossey-Bass.

Garbarino, M. S. (1976b). *Native American heritage.* Boston: Little, Brown.

Gediman, D. (Producer) (1994, April). *Breaking the cycle.* Radio broadcast. Louisville, KY: Milestone Productions.

Geen, R. G., & Quanty, M. B. (1977). The catharsis of aggression: An evaluation of a hypothesis. In L. Berkowitz (Ed.), *Advances in experimental social psychology* (Vol. 10), pp. 1–37. New York: Academic Press.

Gelles, R. J. (1974). *The violent home.* Beverly Hills: Sage.

Gelles, R. (1976). Abused wives: Why do they stay? *Journal of Marriage and the Family, 38,* 659–668.

Gelles, R. (1979). *Family violence.* Beverly Hills: Sage.

Gelles, R. J. (1983). An exchange/social control theory. In Finkelhor, D., Gelles, R. J., Hotaling, G. T., & Straus, M. A. (Eds.), *The dark side of families: Current family violence research* (pp. 151–165). Beverly Hills: Sage.

Gelles, R. J. (1988). Violence and pregnancy: Are pregnant women at greater risk of abuse? *Journal of Marriage and the Family, 50,* 841–847.

Gelles, R. J. (1990). Methodological issues in the study of family violence. In G. R. Patterson (Ed.), *Depression and aggression in family interaction* (pp. 49–74). Hillsdale, NJ: Lawrence Erlbaum.

Gelles, R. J., & Cornell, C. P. (1985). *Intimate violence in families.* Beverly Hills: Sage.

Gelles, R. J., & Straus, M. A. (1988). *Intimate violence.* New York: Simon & Schuster.

Gerbner, G., Morgan, M., & Signorielli, N. (1994). *Television violence profile: The turning point. From research to action.* Philadelphia: University of Pennsylvania, Annenberg School of Communication.

Gil, D. G. (1970). *Violence against children: Physical child abuse in the United States.* Cambridge, MA: Harvard University Press.

Giovannoni, J. M., & Becerra, R. M. (1979). *Defining child abuse.* New York: Free Press.

Goldsmith, H. H., & Gottesman, I. I. (1981). Origins of variation in behavioral style: A longitudinal study of temperament in young twins. *Child Development, 52,* 91–103.

Goldsmith, T. H. (1991). *The biological roots of human nature: Forging links between evolution and behavior.* New York: Oxford University Press.

Gombossy, G. (1985, June 26). Woman wins $2.3 million in suit against Torrington police. *The Hartford Courant,* pp. A1, A6.

Gondolf, E. W. (1987). Evaluating programs for men who batter: Problems and prospects. *Journal of Family Violence, 2,* 95–108.

Gondolf, E. W., & Hanneken, J. (1987). The gender warrior: Reformed batterers on abuse, treatment, and change. *Journal of Family Violence, 2,* 177–191.

Goodman, G. S., Bottoms, B. L., Herscovici, B. B., & Shaver, P. (1989). Determinants of the child victim's perceived credibility. In S. J. Ceci, D. F. Ross, & M. P. Toglia (Eds.), *Perspectives on children's testimony* (pp. 1–22). New York: Springer-Verlag.

Goodman, G. S., Golding, J. M., & Haith, M. M. (1984). Jurors' reactions to child witnesses. *Journal of Social Issues, 40,* 139–156.

Goodman, G. S., Rudy, L., Bottoms, B. L., & Aman, C. (1990). Children's concerns and memory: Issues of ecological validity in the study of children's eyewitness testimony. In R. Fivush & J. A. Hudson (Eds.), *Knowing and remembering in young children* (pp. 249–284). Cambridge: Cambridge University Press.

Goodman, G. S., Taub, E. P., Jones, D. P. H., England, P., Port, L. K., Rudy, L., & Prado, L. (1992). Testifying in criminal court. *Monographs of the Society for Research in Child Development, 57,* 1–141.

Goodwin, M. P., & Roscoe, B. (1990). Sibling violence and agonistic interactions among middle adolescents. *Adolescence, 25,* 451–467.

Goolkasian, G. A. (1986). *Confronting domestic violence: A guide for criminal justice agencies.* Washington, DC: National Institute of Justice.

Gottman, J. M. (1979). *Marital interaction: Experimental investigations.* New York: Academic Press.

Gray, E., & Cosgrove, J. (1985). Ethnocentric perception of childrearing practices in protective services. *Child Abuse and Neglect, 9,* 389–396.

Green, A. H. (1978). Self-destructive behavior in battered children. *American Journal of Psychiatry, 135,* 579–582.

Greenblat, C. S. (1985). ''Don't hit your wife . . . unless . . . '': Preliminary findings on normative support for the use of physical force by husbands. *Victimology, 10,* 221–241.

Greene, E., Raitz, A., & Lindblad, J. (1989). Jurors' knowledge of battered women. *Journal of Family Violence, 4,* 105–125.

Groth-Marnat, G. (1990). *Handbook of psychological assessment* (2nd ed.). New York: John Wiley and Sons.

Grusec, J., and Dix, T. (1986). The socialization of prosocial behavior: Theory and reality. In C. Zahn-Waxler, E. M. Cummings, & R. Ianotti (Eds.), *Altruism and aggression: Biological and social origins* (pp. 218–237). Cambridge: Cambridge University Press.

Grych, J. H., & Fincham, F. D. (1992). Interventions for children of divorce: Toward greater integration of research and action. *Psychological Bulletin, 111,* 434–454.

Hackett, G., McKillop, P., & Wang, D. (1988, Dec. 12). A tale of abuse. *Newsweek, 112,* 56–61.

Hall, D. F., Loftus, E. F., & Tousignant, J. P. (1984). Postevent information and changes in recollection for a natural event. In G. L. Wells & E. F. Loftus (Eds.), *Eyewitness testimony: Psychological perspectives* (pp. 124–141). Cambridge: Cambridge University Press.

Hampton, R. L., & Gelles, R. J. (1989). Is violence in black families increasing? A comparison of 1975 and 1985 national survey rates. *Journal of Marriage and the Family, 51,* 969–980.

Hampton, R. L., & Newberger, E. (1985). Child abuse incidence and reporting by hospitals: Significance of severity, class, and race. *American Journal of Public Health, 75,* 56–60.

Hansen, D. J., Pallotta, G. M., Tishelman, A. C., Conaway, L. P., & MacMillan, V. M. (1989). Parental problem-solving skills and child behavior problems: A comparison of physically abusive, neglectful, clinic, and community families. *Journal of Family Violence, 4,* 353–368.

Hartman, C. R., & Burgess, A. W. (1989). Sexual abuse of children: Causes and consequences. In D. Cicchetti & V. Carlson (Eds.), *Child maltreatment: Theory and research on the causes and consequences of child abuse and neglect* (pp. 95–128). Cambridge: Cambridge University Press.

Hartup, W. W., & Laursen, B. (1993). Conflict and context in peer relations. In C. Hart (Ed.), *Children on playgrounds: Research perspectives and applications* (pp. 44–84). Ithaca, NY: State University of New York Press.

Hastings, J. (1963) (Ed.) *Dictionary of the Bible.* New York: Macmillan.

Heath, L., Kruttschnitt, C., & Ward, D. (1986). Television and violent criminal behavior: Beyond the Bobo doll. *Violence and Victims, 1,* 177–190.

Herrenkohl, E. C., & Herrenkohl, R. C. (1979). A comparison of abused children and their nonabused siblings. *Journal of the American Academy of Child Psychiatry, 18,* 260–269.

Herrenkohl, E. C., Herrenkohl, R. C., & Toedter, L. J. (1983). Perspectives on the intergenerational transmission of abuse. In D. Finkelhor, R. J. Gelles, G. T. Hotaling, and M. A. Straus (Eds.), *The dark side of families: Current family violence research* (pp. 305–316). Beverly Hills: Sage.

Herzberger, S. D., (1983). Social cognition and the transmission of abuse. In D. Finkelhor, R. J. Gelles, G. T. Hotaling, & M. A. Straus (Eds.), *The dark side of families: Current family violence research* (pp. 317–329). Beverly Hills: Sage.

Herzberger, S. D. (1985, November). *Recent research regarding the identification and labeling of abuse.* Paper presented to the National Legal Resource Center for Child Advocacy and Protection, American Bar Association, Washington, DC.

Herzberger, S. D. (1988). Cultural obstacles to the labeling of abuse by professionals. In A. Maney & S. Wells (Eds.), *Professional responsibilities in protecting children: A public health approach to child sexual abuse* (pp. 33–44). New York: Praeger.

Herzberger, S. D. (1990). The cyclical pattern of child abuse: A study of research methodology. *American Behavioral Scientist, 33,* 529–545.

Herzberger, S. D., & Channels, N. L. (1991). Criminal justice processing of violent offenders: The effects of familial relationship to the victim. In D. Knudsen & J. Miller (Eds.), *Abused and battered: Social and legal responses to family violence.* New York: Aldine de Gruyter.

Herzberger, S. D., & Hall, J. A. (1993a). Children's evaluations of retaliatory aggression against siblings and friends. *Journal of Interpersonal Violence, 8,* 77–93.

Herzberger, S. D., & Hall, J. A. (1993b). Consequences of retaliatory aggression against siblings and peers: Urban minority children's expectations. *Child Development, 64,* 1773–1785.

Herzberger, S. D., Potts, D. A., & Dillon, M. (1981). Abusive and nonabusive treatment from the child's perspective. *Journal of Consulting and Clinical Psychology, 49,* 81–90.

Herzberger, S. D., & Tennen, H. (1982, August). *The social definition of abuse.* Paper presented at the American Psychological Association Convention, Washington, DC.

Herzberger, S. D., & Tennen, H. (1985a). The effect of self-relevance on moderate and severe disciplinary encounters. *Journal of Marriage and the Family, 47,* 311–318.

Herzberger, S. D., & Tennen, H. (1985b). ''Snips and snails and puppy dog tails'': Gender of agent, recipient and observer as determinants of perceptions of discipline. *Sex Roles, 12,* 853–865.

Hilberman, E., & Munson, K. (1978). Sixty battered women. *Victimology, 2,* 460–471.

Hilton, J. L., & Darley, J. M. (1985). Constructing other persons: A limit on the effect. *Journal of Experimental Social Psychology, 21,* 1–18.

Hinchey, F. S., & Gavelek, J. R. (1982). Empathic responding in children of battered mothers. *Child Abuse and Neglect, 6,* 395–401.

Hoffman, J. (1992, February 16). When men hit women. *The New York Times Magazine,* pp. 22–27, 64, 72.

Hoffman, M. L. (1970). Moral development. In P. H. Mussen (Ed.), *Carmichael's manual of child psychology* (Vol. 2), pp. 261–359. New York: Wiley.

Holden, G. W. (1988). Adults' thinking about a child-rearing problem: Effects of experience, parental status, and gender. *Child Development, 59,* 1623–1632.

Holden, G. W., & Ritchie, K. L. (1991). Linking extreme marital discord, child rearing, and child behavior problems: Evidence from battered women. *Child Development, 62,* 311–327.

Holden, G. W., & Zambarano, R. J. (1992). Passing the rod: Similarities between parents and their young children in orientations toward physical punishment. In I. E. Sigel, A. V. McGillicuddy-DeLisi, & J. J. Goodnow (Eds.), *Parental belief systems: The psychological consequences for children* (2nd ed., pp. 143–172). Hillsdale, NJ: Erlbaum.

Holtzworth-Munroe, A., & Jacobson, N. S. (1985). Causal attributions of married couples: When do they search for causes? What do they conclude when they do? *Journal of Personality and Social Psychology, 48,* 1398–1412.

Holtzworth-Munroe, A., & Stuart, G. L. (1994). Typologies of male batterers: Three subtypes and the differences among them. *Psychological Bulletin, 116,* 476–497.

Hopkins, J., Marcus, M., & Campbell, S. B. (1984). Postpartum depression: A critical review. *Psychological Bulletin, 95,* 498–515.

Horney, J. (1978). Menstrual cycles and criminal responsibility. *Law and Human Behavior, 2,* 25–36.

Hornung, C. A., MuCullough, B. C., & Sugimoto, T. (1981). Status relationships in marriage: Risk factors in spouse abuse. *Journal of Marriage and the Family, 43,* 675–692.

Hotaling, G. T., & Straus, M. A. (1989). Intrafamily violence, and crime and violence outside the family. In L. Ohlin & M. Tonry (Eds.), *Family violence* (pp. 315–375). Chicago: University of Chicago Press.

Hotaling, G. T., & Sugarman, D. B. (1986). An analysis of risk markers in husband to wife violence: The current state of knowledge. *Violence and Victims, 1,* 101–124.

Howe, A. C., Herzberger, S. D., & Tennen, H. (1988). The influence of personal history of abuse and gender on clinicians' judgments of child abuse. *Journal of Family Violence, 3,* 105–119.

Huesmann, L. R., Eron, L. D., Klein, R., Brice, P., & Fischer, P. (1983). Mitigating the imitation of aggressive behaviors by changing children's attitudes about media violence. *Journal of Personality and Social Psychology, 44,* 899–910.

Hull, J. G., & Bond, C. F., Jr. (1986). Social and behavioral consequences of alcohol consumption and expectancy: A meta-analysis. *Psychological Bulletin, 99,* 347–60.

Hunter, R., & Kihlstrom, N. (1979). Breaking the cycle in abusive families. *American Journal of Marriage and the Family, 136,* 1320–1322.

Inciardi, J. A., Lockwood, D., & Pottieger, A. E. (1993). *Women and crack-cocaine.* New York: Macmillan.

Jaffe, P., Wolfe, D. A., Telford, A., & Austin, G. (1986). The impact of police charges in incidents of wife abuse. *Journal of Family Violence, 1,* 37–49.

Jaffe, P. G., Wolfe, D. A., & Wilson, S. K. (1990). *Children of battered women.* Newbury Park, CA: Sage.

Janoff-Bulman, R. (1992). *Shattered assumptions: Towards a new psychology of trauma.* New York: Free Press.

Janoff-Bulman, R. (1979). Characterological versus behavioral self-blame: Inquiries into depression and rape. *Journal of Personality and Social Psychology, 37,* 1798–1809.

Janoff-Bulman, R., & Frieze, I. H. (1987). The role of gender in reactions to criminal victimization. In R. C. Barnett, L. Biener, & G. K. Baruch (Eds.), *Gender and Stress* (pp. 159–184). New York: Free Press.

Janoff-Bulman, R., Timko, C., & Carli, L. L. (1985). Cognitive biases in blaming the victim. *Journal of Experimental Social Psychology, 21,* 161–177.

Jary, M. L., & Stewart, M. A. (1985). Psychiatric disorder in the parents of adopted children with aggressive conduct disorder. *Neuropsychobiology, 13,* 7–11.

Jennings, J. L. (1987). History and issues in the treatment of battering men: A case for unstructured group therapy. *Journal of Family Violence, 2,* 193–213.

Johnson, M. K., & Foley, M. A. (1984). Differentiating fact from fantasy: The reliability of children's memory. *Journal of Social Issues, 40,* 33–50.

Jung, J. (1994). *Under the influence: Alcohol and human behavior.* Pacific Grove, CA: Brooks/Cole.

Kalmuss, D. (1984). The intergenerational transmission of marital aggression. *Journal of Marriage and the Family, 46,* 11–19.

Kantrowitz, B., Quade, V., Fisher, B., Hill, J., & Beachy, L. (1991, April 29). The pregnancy police. *Newsweek, 117,* 52–53.

Katz, A. H. (1981). Self-help and mutual aid: An emerging social movement? *Annual Review of Sociology, 7,* 129–155.

Kaufman, J., & Zigler, E. (1989). The intergenerational transmission of child abuse. In D. Cicchetti & V. Carson (Eds.), *Child maltreatment: Theory and causes and consequences of child abuse and neglect* (pp. 129–150). Cambridge: Cambridge University Press.

Kelder, L. R., McNamara, J. R., Carlson, B., & Lynn, S. J. (1991). Perceptions of physical punishment: The relation to childhood and adolescent experiences. *Journal of Interpersonal Violence, 6,* 432–445.

Klaus, M. H., & Kennell, J. H. (1976). *Maternal-infant bonding.* Saint Louis: C. V. Mosby.

Knudsen, D. D. (1988). Child maltreatment over two decades: Change or continuity. *Violence and Victims, 3,* 129–144.

Koestner, R., Franz, C., & Weinberger, J. (1990). The family origins of empathic concern: A 26-year longitudinal study. *Journal of Personality and Social Psychology, 58,* 709–717.

Korbin, J. E. (1981). *Child abuse and neglect: Cross-cultural perspectives.* Berkeley: University of California.

Korbin, J. E. (1987). Child abuse and neglect: The cultural context. In R. E. Helfer & R. S. Kempe (Eds.), *The battered child* (4th ed., pp. 23–41). Chicago: The University of Chicago Press.

Koski, P. R., & Mangold, W. D. (1988). Gender effects in attitudes about family violence. *Journal of Family Violence, 3,* 225–237.

Kruttschnitt, C., Ward, D., & Sheble, M. A. (1987). Abuse-resistant youth: Some factors that may inhibit violent criminal behavior. *Social Forces, 66,* 501–519.

Lamb, M. E., & Oppenheim, D. (1989). Fatherhood and father-child relationships: Five years of research. In S. H. Cath, A. Gurwitt, & L. Gunsberg (Eds.), *Fathers and their families* (pp. 11–26). Hillsdale, NJ: Analytic Press.

LaPiere, R. T. (1934). Attitudes and actions. *Social Forces, 13,* 230–237.

Larrance, D. T., & Twentyman, C. T. (1983). Maternal attributions and child abuse. *Journal of Abnormal Psychology, 92,* 449–457.

Larzelere, R. E. (1986). Moderate spanking: Model or deterrent of children's aggression in the family. *Journal of Family Violence, 1,* 27–36.

Lau, R. R., & Russell, D. (1980). Attributions in the sports pages. *Journal of Personality and Social Psychology, 39,* 29–38.

Launius, M. H., & Jensen, B. L. (1987). Interpersonal problem-solving skills in battered, counseling, and control women. *Journal of Family Violence, 2,* 151–162.

Launius, M. H., & Lindquist, C. U. (1988). Learned helplessness, external locus of control, and passivity in battered women. *Journal of Interpersonal Violence, 3,* 307–318.

Lavoie, F., Jacob, M., Hardy, J., & Martin, G. (1989). Police attitudes in assigning responsibility for wife abuse. *Journal of Family Violence, 4,* 369–388.

Lawson, A. (1988). *Adultery: An analysis of love and betrayal.* New York: Basic Books.

Leippe, M. R., Brigham, J. C., Cousins, C., & Romanczyk, A. (1989). The opinions and practices of criminal attorneys regarding child eyewitnesses: A survey. In S. J. Ceci, D. F. Ross, & M. P. Toglia (Eds.), *Perspectives on children's testimony* (pp. 100–130). New York: Springer-Verlag.

Leonard, K. E., & Blane, H. T. (1992). Alcohol and marital aggression in a national sample of young men. *Journal of Interpersonal Violence, 7,* 19–30.

Lerner, M. J. (1980). *The belief in a just world: A fundamental delusion.* New York: Plenum.

Levenson, R. W., & Ruef, A. M. (1992). Empathy: A physiological substrate. *Journal of Personality and Social Psychology, 63,* 234–246.

Levinson, D. (1983). Physical punishment of children and wife-beating in cross-cultural perspective. In R. Gelles & C. Cornell (Eds.), *International perspectives on family violence* (pp. 73–77). Lexington, MA: D. C. Heath.

Levinson, D. (1989). *Family violence in cross-cultural perspective.* Newbury Park, CA: Sage.

Lewis, B. Y. (1987). Psychosocial factors related to wife abuse. *Journal of Family Violence, 2,* 1–10.

Lewis, M., and Rosenblum, L. (Eds.) (1974). *The effect of the infant on its caregiver.* New York: Wiley.

Lichter, S. R., & Amundson, D. (1992). *A day of television violence.* Report for the Center for Media and Public Affairs, Washington, DC.

Lidz, C. W., Mulvey, E. P., & Gardner, W. (1993). The accuracy of predictions of violence to others. *JAMA, 269,* 1007–1011.

Liebert, R. M., Sprafkin, J. N., & Davidson, E. S. (1982). *The early window: Effects of television on children and youth.* New York: Pergamon Press.

Linz, D., Donnerstein, E., Bross, M., & Chapin, M. (1986). Mitigating the influence of violence on television and sexual violence in the media. In R. J. Blanchard & D. C. Blanchard (Eds.), *Advances in the study of aggression,* (Vol. 2), pp. 165–194. Orlando: Academic Press.

Livesley, W. J., & Bromley, D. B. (1973). *Person perception in childhood and adolescence.* New York: John Wiley & Sons.

Lloyd, S. A. (1990). Conflict types and strategies in violent marriages. *Journal of Family Violence, 5,* 269–284.

Loeber, R., & Dishion, T. J. (1984). Boys who fight at home and school: Family conditions influencing cross-setting consistency. *Journal of Consulting and Clinical Psychology, 52,* 759–768.

Loeber, R., & Tengs, T. (1986). The analysis of coercive chains between children, mothers, and siblings. *Journal of Family Violence, 1,* 51–70.

Loftus, E. F. (1993). The reality of repressed memories. *American Psychologist, 48,* 518–537.

Loftus, E. F., & Davies, G. M. (1984). Distortions in the memory of children. *Journal of Social Issues, 40,* 51–67.

Loftus, E. F., & Goodman, J. (1985). Questioning witnesses. In S. M. Kassin & L. S. Wrightsman (Eds.), *The psychology of evidence and trial procedure* (pp. 253–279). Beverly Hills: Sage.

Loftus, E. F., & Palmer, J. C. (1974). Reconstruction of automobile destruction: An example of the interaction between language and memory. *Journal of Verbal Learning and Verbal Behavior, 13,* 585–589.

Lore, R. K., & Schultz, L. A. (1993). Control of human aggression: A comparative perspective. *American Psychologist, 48,* 16–25.

Lutzker, J. R., & Rice, J. M. (1987). Using recidivism data to evaluate Project 12-Ways: An ecobehavioral approach to the treatment and prevention of child abuse and neglect. *Journal of Family Violence, 2,* 283–290.

MacAndrew, C., & Edgerton, R. B. (1969). *Drunken comportment: A social explanation.* Chicago: Aldine.

Maccoby, E. E., & Jacklin, C. N. (1980). Sex differences in aggression: A rejoinder and reprise. *Child Development, 51,* 964–980.

Maccoby, E. E., & Jacklin, C. N. (1985). *The psychology of sex differences.* Stanford, CA: Stanford University Press.

Maccoby, E. E., Snow, M. E., & Jacklin, C. N. (1984). Children's dispositions and mother-child interaction at 12 and 18 months: A short-term longitudinal study. *Developmental Psychology, 20,* 459–472.

Macrae, C. N., & Shepherd, J. W. (1989). Sex differences in the perception of rape victims. *Journal of Interpersonal Violence, 4,* 278–288.

Magnusson, D. (1988). Antisocial behavior of boys and autonomic activity/reactivity. In T. E. Moffitt and S. A. Mednick (Eds.), *Biological contributions to crime causation* (pp. 135–146). Dordrecht, Netherlands: Martinus Nijhoff.

Main, M., & George, C. (1985). Responses of abused and disadvantaged toddlers to distress in agemates: A study in the day care setting. *Developmental Psychology, 21,* 407–412.

Maiuro, R. D., Cahn, T. S., & Vitaliano, P. P. (1986). Assertiveness deficits and hostility in domestically violent men. *Violence and Victims, 1,* 279–289.

Malamuth, N. M., & Donnerstein, E. (1982). The effects of aggressive-pornographic mass media stimuli. In L. Berkowitz (Ed.), *Advances in Experimental Social Psychology* (Vol. 15), 103–136. New York: Academic Press.

Malinosky-Rummell, R., & Hansen, D. J. (1993). Long-term consequences of childhood physical abuse. *Psychological Bulletin, 114,* 68–79.

Maney, A. (1988). Professional involvement in public health strategies for the prevention and control of child sexual abuse. In A. Maney & S. Wells (Eds.), *Professional responsibilities in protecting children: A public health approach to child sexual abuse* (pp. 3–22). New York: Praeger.

Mangold, W. D., Jr., & Koski, P. R. (1990). Gender comparisons in the relationship between parental and sibling violence and nonfamily violence. *Journal of Family Violence, 5,* 225–235.

Margolin, G., & Weiss, R. L. (1978). Comparative evaluation of therapeutic components associated with behavioral marital treatments. *Journal of Consulting and Clinical Psychology, 46,* 1476–1486.

Marlatt, G. A., & Rohsenow, D. J. (1980). Cognitive processes in alcohol use: Expectancy and the balanced placebo design. In N. K. Mello (Ed.), *Advances in substance abuse: Behavioral and biological research* (Vol. 1), pp. 159–199. Greenwich, CT: JAI Press.

Mazur, A. (1983). Hormones, aggression, and dominance in humans. In B. B. Svare (Ed.), *Hormones and aggressive behavior* (pp. 563–576). New York: Plenum.

McFarlane, J., Parker, B., Soeken, K., & Bullock, L. (1992). Assessing for abuse during pregnancy: Severity and frequency of injuries and associated entry into prenatal care. *JAMA, 267,* 3176–3178.

McIntire, R. W. (1973). Parenthood training or mandatory birth control: Take your choice. *Psychology Today, 7,* 34, 36, 38–39, 132–133, 143.

McNeely, R. L., & Mann, C. R. (1990). Domestic violence is a human issue. *Journal of Interpersonal Violence, 5,* 129–132.

Mednick, S. A., Gabrielli, W. F., Jr., Hutchings, B. (1984). Genetic influences in criminal convictions: Evidence from an adoption court. *Science, 224,* 891–894.

Mednick, S. A., Gabrielli, W. F., Jr., Hutchings, B. (1987). Genetic factors in the etiology of criminal behavior. In S. A. Mednick, T. E. Moffitt, & S. A. Stack (Eds.), *The causes of crime: New biological approaches* (pp. 74–91). Cambridge: Cambridge University Press.

Mendonca, P. J., & Brehm, S. S. (1983). Effects of choice on behavioral treatment of overweight children. *Journal of Social and Clinical Psychology, 1,* 343–358.

Meyer, C. B., & Taylor, S. E. (1986). Adjustment to rape. *Journal of Personality and Social Psychology, 50,* 1226–1234.

Milgram, S. (1974). *Obedience to authority.* New York: Harper & Row.

Miller, D. I., & Porter, C. A. (1983). Self-blame in victims of violence. *Journal of Social Issues, 39,* 139–152.

Milner, J. S. (1986). *The Child Abuse Potential Inventory: Manual* (2nd ed.). Webster, NC: Psytec Corporation.

Milner, J. S., Robertson, K. R., & Rogers, D. L. (1990). Childhood history of abuse and adult child abuse potential. *Journal of Family Violence, 5,* 15–34.

Minnett, A. M., Vandell, D. L., & Santrock, J. W. (1983). The effects of sibling status on sibling interaction: Influence of birth order, age spacing, sex of child, and sex of sibling. *Child Development, 54,* 1064–1072.

Minuchin, S., & Fishman, H. C. (1981). *Family therapy techniques.* Cambridge, MA: Harvard University Press.

Morris, J. L., Johnson, C. F., & Clasen, M. (1985). To report or not to report: Physicians' attitudes toward discipline and child abuse. *American Journal of Diseases of Children, 139,* 194–197.

Moyer, K. E. (1987). *Violence and aggression.* New York: Paragon House.

Mydans, S. (1993, Nov. 19). Killers as victims: Defending Menendez brothers. *New York Times,* p. A30.

Myers, J. E. B. (1990). Intervention: The best of bad options. *Journal of Interpersonal Violence, 5,* 532–535.

Nachson, I., & Denno, D. (1987). Violent behavior and cerebral hemisphere function. In S. A. Mednick, T. E. Moffitt, & S. A. Stack (Eds.), *The causes of crime: New biological approaches* (pp. 185–217). Cambridge: Cambridge University Press.

Nagi, S. Z. (1977). *Child maltreatment in the United States.* New York: Columbia University Press.

National Center on Child Abuse and Neglect. (1988). *Study findings: Study of National Incidence and Prevalence of Child Abuse and Neglect: 1988.* Washington, DC: Department of Health and Human Services.

National Institute of Justice Research in Brief. (1992, May). *New approach to interviewing children: A test of its effectiveness.* Washington, DC: U.S. Department of Justice.

Neidig, P. H., & Friedman, D. H. (1984). *Spouse abuse: A treatment program for couples.* Champaign, IL: Research Press.

Newberger, C. M., & White, K. M. (1989). Cognitive foundations for parental care. In D. Cicchetti & V. Carlson (Eds.), *Child maltreatment: Theory and research on the causes and consequences of child abuse and neglect* (pp. 302–316). New York: Cambridge University Press.

Newberger, E. H. (1987). Prosecutions: A problematic approach to child abuse. *Journal of Interpersonal Violence, 2,* 112–117.

Newhill, C. E. (1991). Parricide. *Journal of Family Violence, 6,* 375–394.

Novaco, R. W. (1975). *Anger control: The development and evaluation of an experimental treatment.* Lexington, MA: D. C. Heath.

Novaco, R. W. (1986). Anger as a clinical and social problem. In R. J. Blanchard & D. C. Blanchard (Eds.), *Advances in the study of aggression* (Vol. 2) pp. 1–67. Orlando: Academic Press.

Ogbu, J. U. (1981). Origins of human competence: A cultural-ecological perspective. *Child Development, 52,* 413–429.

Olds, D. L., & Henderson, C. R., Jr. (1989). The prevention of maltreatment. In D. Cicchetti & V. Carlson (Eds.), *Child maltreatment: Theory and research on the causes and consequences of child abuse and neglect* (pp. 722–763). Cambridge: Cambridge University Press.

O'Leary, K. D. (1993). Through a psychological lens: Personality traits, personality disorders, and levels of violence. In R. J. Gelles & D. R. Loseke (Eds.), *Current controversies on family violence* (pp. 7–30). Newbury Park, CA: Sage.

O'Leary, K. D., Curley, A., Rosenbaum, A., & Clarke, C. (1985). Assertion training for abused wives: A potentially hazardous treatment. *Journal of Marital and Family Therapy, 11,* 319–322.

Oliver, J. E. (1988). Successive generations of child maltreatment: The children. *British Journal of Psychiatry, 153,* 543–553.

Olweus, D. (1987). Testosterone and adrenaline: Aggressive antisocial behavior in normal adolescent males. In S. A. Mednick, T. E. Moffitt, & S. A. Stack (Eds.), *The causes of crime: New biological approaches* (pp. 263–282). Cambridge: Cambridge University Press.

Olweus, D. (1979). Stability of aggressive reaction patterns in males: A review. *Psychological Bulletin, 86,* 852–875.

Olweus, D. (1992). Bullying among schoolchildren: Interventions and prevention. In R. D. Peters, R. J. McMahon, & V. L. Quinsey (Eds.), *Aggression and violence throughout the life span* (pp. 100–125). Newbury Park, CA: Sage.

O'Toole, R., Turbett, P., Nalepka, C. (1983). Theories, professional knowledge, and diagnosis of child abuse. In D. Finkelhor, R. J. Gelles, G. T. Hotaling, & M. A. Straus (Eds.), *The dark side of families: Current family violence research* (pp. 349–362). Beverly Hills: Sage.

Pachella, R. G. (1988). On the admissibility of psychological testimony in criminal justice proceedings. *Journal of Interpersonal Violence, 3,* 111–114.

Pagelow, M. D. (1984). *Family violence.* New York: Praeger.

Pagelow, M. D. (1989). The incidence and prevalence of criminal abuse of other family members. In L. Ohlin & M. Tonry (Eds.), *Family violence* (pp. 263–313). Chicago: University of Chicago Press.

Parke, R. D., & Slaby, R. G. (1983). The development of aggression. In P. H. Mussen (Ed.), *Handbook of child psychology: Vol. 4, Socialization, personality, and social development* (pp. 547–641). New York: Wiley.

Parlee, M. B. (1987). Media treatment of premenstrual syndrome. In B. E. Ginsburg & B. F. Carter (Eds.), *Premenstrual syndrome: Ethical and legal implications in a biomedical perspective* (pp. 189–205). New York: Plenum.

Pate, A. M., & Hamilton, E. E. (1992). Formal and informal deterrents to domestic violence: The Dade County spouse assault experiment. *American Sociological Review, 57,* 691–697.

Patterson, G. R. (1980). Mothers: The unacknowledged victims. *Monographs of the Society for Research in Child Development, 45*(5, Serial No. 186).

Patterson, G. R. (1984). Siblings: Fellow travelers in coercive family processes. In R. J. Blanchard & D. C. Blanchard (Eds.), *Advances in the study of aggression* (Vol. 1), pp. 173–215. Orlando: Academic Press.

Paulson, M. J., Coombs, R. H., & Landsverk, J. (1990). Youth who physically assault their parents. *Journal of Family Violence, 5,* 121–133.

Pavlov, I. P. (1927/1960). *Conditioned reflexes.* New York: Dover.

Perry, D. G., Perry, L. C., & Weiss, R. J. (1989). Sex differences in the consequences that children anticipate for aggression. *Developmental Psychology, 25,* 312–319.

Perry, D. G., Williard, J. C., & Perry, L. C. (1990). Peers' perceptions of the consequences that victimized children provide aggressors. *Child Development, 61,* 1310–1325.

Petty, R. E., & Cacioppo, J. T. (1981). *Attitudes and persuasion: Classic and contemporary approaches.* Dubuque, IA: Wm. C. Brown.

Phares, V., & Compas, B. E. (1992). The role of fathers in child and adolescent psychopathology: Make room for Daddy. *Psychological Bulletin, 111,* 387–412.

Phillips, D. P. (1983). The impact of mass media violence on U.S. homicides. *American Sociological Review, 48,* 560–568.

Phillips, D. P., & Hensley, J. E. (1984). When violence is rewarded or punished: The impact of mass media stories of homicide. *Journal of Communication, 34,* 101–116.

Piaget, J. (1965). *The moral judgement of the child.* New York: Free Press.

Pierce, R. L., & Trotta, R. (1986). Abused parents: A hidden family problem. *Journal of Family Violence, 1,* 99–110.

Pleck, E. (1989). Criminal approaches to family violence, 1640–1980. In L. Ohlin & M. Tonry (Eds.), *Family violence* (pp. 19–57). Chicago: University of Chicago Press.

Plomin, R., DeFries, J. C., & Loehlin, J. C. (1977). Genotype-environment interaction and correlation in the analysis of human behavior. *Psychological Bulletin, 84,* 309–322.

Plomin, R., DeFries, J. C., & McClearn, G. E. (1990). *Behavioral genetics: A primer.* New York: W. H. Freeman.

Plomin, R., McClearn, G. E., Pedersen, N. L., Nesselroade, J. R., & Bergeman, C. S. (1989). Genetic influence on adults' ratings of their current family environment. *Journal of Marriage and the Family, 51,* 791–803.

Policing vs. Privacy. (1991, May 20). *Newsweek, 117,* pp. 13–14.

Pollock, C., & Steele, B. (1972). A therapeutic approach to the parents. In C. H. Kempe and R. E. Helfer (Eds.), *Helping the battered child and his family* (pp. 3–21). Philadelphia: J. B. Lippincott Co.

Potts, D. A., Herzberger, S. D., & Holland, A. E. (1979, May). *Child abuse: A cross-generational pattern of child rearing?* Paper presented at the Midwestern Psychological Association Convention, Chicago.

Prochaska, J. O., DiClemente, C. C., & Norcross, J. C. (1992). In search of how people change: Applications to addictive behaviors. *American Psychologist, 47,* 1102–1114.

Pruitt, D. L., & Erickson, M. T. (1985). The Child Abuse Potential Inventory: A study of concurrent validity. *Journal of Clinical Psychology, 35,* 426–429.

Pynoos, R. S., & Eth, S. (1984). The child as witness to homicide. *Journal of Social Issues, 40,* 87–108.

Quindlen, A. (1993, Nov. 14). Tied to the tracks. *New York Times,* p. 17.

Quinton, E., Rutter, M., & Liddle, C. (1984). Institutional rearing, parenting difficulties and marital support. *Psychological Medicine, 14,* 107–124.

Randall, T. (1992). ACOG renews domestic violence campaign, calls for changes in medical school curricula. *JAMA, 267,* 3131.

Reid, J. B. (1986). Social-interactional patterns in families of abused and nonabused children. In C. Zahn-Waxler, E. M. Cummings, & R. Iannotti (Eds.), *Altruism and aggression: Biological and social origins* (pp. 238–255). Cambridge: Cambridge University Press.

Reid, J. B., Taplin, P. S., & Lorber, R. (1981). A social interactional approach to the treatment of abusive families. In R. Stuart (Ed.), *Violent behavior: Social learning approaches to prediction, management, and treatment* (pp. 83–101). New York: Brunner/Mazel.

Reiss, A. J., & Roth, J. A. (Eds.). (1993). *Understanding and preventing violence.* Washington, DC: National Academy Press.

Reiss, D., & Schulterbrandt, J. (1990). The Family Research Consortium: At the crest of a major wave? In G. R. Patterson (Ed.), *Depression and aggression in family interaction* (pp. 1–10). Hillsdale, NJ: L. Erlbaum.

Reppucci, N. D., & Haugaard, J. J. (1989). Prevention of child sexual abuse: Myth or reality. *American Psychologist, 44,* 1266–1275.

Rich, R. F., & Sampson, R. J. (1990). Public perceptions of criminal justice policy: Does victimization make a difference? *Violence and Victims, 5,* 109–118.

Richardson, D. C., & Campbell, J. L. (1980). Alcohol and wife abuse: The effects of alcohol on attributions of blame for wife abuse. *Personality and Social Psychology Bulletin, 6,* 51–56.

Riggs, D. S., Murphy, C. M., & O'Leary, K. D. (1989). Intentional falsification in reports of interpartner aggression. *Journal of Interpersonal Violence, 4,* 220–232.

Roscoe, B., Goodwin, M. P., & Kennedy, D. (1987). Sibling violence and agonistic interactions experienced by early adolescents. *Journal of Family Violence, 2,* 121–137.

Rose, R., Bernstein, I., & Gordon, T. (1974). Consequences of social conflict on plasma testosterone levels in rhesus monkeys. *Psychosomatic Medicine, 37,* 50–61.

Rossi, F., Waite, E., Bose, C. E., & Berk, R. (1974). The seriousness of crimes: Normative structure and individual differences. *American Sociological Review, 39,* 224–237.

Rowe, D. C. (1994). *The limits of family influence: Genes, experience, and behavior.* New York: Guilford Press.

Roy, M. (1977). A current survey of 150 cases. In M. Roy (Ed.), *Battered women: A psychosociological study of domestic violence* (pp. 25–44). New York: Van Nostrand Reinhold.

Ruble, D. N. (1977). Menstrual symptoms: A reinterpretation. *Science, 197,* 291–292.

Rushton, J. P., Fulker, D. W., Neale, M. C., Nias, D. K. B., & Eysenck, H. J. (1986). Altruism and aggression: The heritability of individual differences. *Journal of Personality and Social Psychology, 50,* 1192–1198.

Russell, D. E. (1975). *The politics of rape: The victim's perspective.* New York: Stein and Day.

Rutter, M. (1988). Functions and consequences of relationships: Some psychopathological considerations. In R. Hinde & J. Stevenson-Hinde (Eds.), *Relationships within families: Mutual influences* (pp. 332–353). Oxford: Clarendon.

Rutter, M. (1989). Intergenerational continuities and discontinuities in serious parenting difficulties. In D. Cicchetti & V. Carlson (Eds.), *Child maltreatment: Theory and research on the causes and consequences of child abuse and neglect* (pp. 317–348). Cambridge: Cambridge University Press.

Sagi, A., & Hoffman, M. L. (1976). Empathic distress in the newborn. *Developmental Psychology, 12,* 175–176.

Saunders, D. G., & Azar, S. T. (1989). Treatment programs for family violence. In L. Ohlin & M. Tonry (Eds.), *Family violence* (pp. 481–546). Chicago: University of Chicago Press.

Saunders, D. G., Lynch, A. B., Grayson, M., & Linz, D. (1987). The Inventory of Beliefs about Wife Beating: The construction and initial validation of a measure of beliefs and attitudes. *Violence and Victims, 2,* 39–57.

Saunders, D. G., & Size, P. B. (1986). Attitudes about woman abuse among police officers, victims, and victim advocates. *Journal of Interpersonal Violence, 1,* 25–42.

Saywitz, K. J., Geiselman, R. E., & Bornstein, G. K. (1992). Effects of cognitive interviewing and practice on children's recall performance. *Journal of Applied Psychology, 77,* 744–756.

Scarr, S., & McCartney, K. (1983). How people make their own environments: A theory of genotype → environment effects. *Child Development, 54,* 424–435.

Schmidt, J. D., & Sherman, L. W. (1993). Does arrest deter domestic violence? *American Behavioral Scientist, 36,* 601–609.

Schur, E. M. (1983). *Labeling women deviant: Gender, stigma, and social control.* Philadelphia: Temple University Press.

Sears, R., Maccoby, E., & Levin, H. (1957). *Patterns of child rearing.* Evanston, IL: Row, Peterson.

Sebastian, R. J. (1978). Immediate and delayed effects of victim suffering on the attacker's aggression. *Journal of Research in Personality, 12,* 312–328.

Seligman, M. E. P. (1975). *Helplessness: On depression, development, and death.* San Francisco: W. H. Freeman.

Shepard, M. (1992). Predicting batterer recidivism five years after community intervention. *Journal of Family Violence, 7,* 167–178.

Sherman, L. W. (1992). *Policing domestic violence: Experiments and dilemmas.* New York: Free Press.

Sherman, L. W., & Berk, R. A. (1984). The specific deterrent effects of arrest for domestic assault. *American Sociological Review, 49,* 261–272.

Sherman, L. W., Smith, D. A., Schmidt, J. D., & Rogan, D. P. (1992). Crime, punishment, and stake in conformity: Legal and informal control of domestic violence. *American Sociological Review, 57,* 680–690.

Shields, N. M., McCall, G. J., & Hanneke, C. R. (1988). Patterns of family and nonfamily violence: Violent husbands and violent men. *Violence and Victims, 3,* 83–97.

Shirk, S. R. (1988). The interpersonal legacy of physical abuse of children. In M. B. Straus (Ed.), *Abuse and victimization across the life span* (pp. 57–81). Baltimore: Johns Hopkins University Press.

Shotland, R. L., & Straw, M. K. (1976). Bystander response to an assault: When a man attacks a woman. *Journal of Personality and Social Psychology, 34,* 990–999.

Sigler, R. T. (1989). *Domestic violence in context.* Lexington, MA: Lexington.

Sigvardsson, S., Cloninger, C. R., Bohman, M., & von Knorring, A. L. (1982). Predisposition to petty criminality in Swedish adoptees. III. Sex differences and validation of the male typology. *Archives of General Psychiatry, 39,* 1248–1253.

Silverman, R. A., & Kennedy, L. W. (1988). Women who kill their children. *Violence and Victims, 3,* 113–127.

Simons, R. L., Whitbeck, L. B., Conger, R. D., & Chyi-In, W. (1991). Intergenerational transmission of harsh parenting. *Developmental Psychology, 27,* 159–171.

Singer, J. L., & Singer, D. G. (1986). Family experiences and television viewing as predictors of children's imagination, restlessness, and aggression. *Journal of Social Issues, 42,* 107–124.

Sirignano, S., & Lachman, M. (1985). Personality change during the transition to parenthood: The role of perceived temperament. *Developmental Psychology, 21,* 558–567.

Sivacek, J., & Crano, W. D. (1982). Vested interest as a moderator of attitude-behavior consistency. *Journal of Personality and Social Psychology, 43,* 210–221.

Skinner, B. F. (1969). *Contingencies of reinforcement: A theoretical analysis.* New York: Appleton-Century-Crofts.

Sonkin, D. J., Martin, D., & Walker, L. E. A. (1985). *The male batterer: A treatment approach.* New York: Springer.

Spencer-Molloy, F. (1992, July 19). Doctors missing signs of battering: Insensitivity, training blamed. *Hartford Courant,* pp. A1, A6.

Sprey, J. (1988). Sociobiology and the study of family conflict. In E. E. Filsinger (Ed.), *Biosocial perspectives on the family* (pp. 137–158). Newbury Park, CA: Sage.

Stark, R., & McEvoy, J. M. III (1970). Middle class violence. *Psychology Today, 4,* 56–65.

Starr, R. H., Jr. (1988). Physical abuse of children. In V. B. Van Hasselt, R. L. Morrison, A. S. Bellack, & M. Herson (Eds.), *Handbook of family violence* (pp. 119–155). New York: Plenum.

Statistical Abstract of the United States. (1992). Washington, DC: U.S. Department of Commerce.

Steele, C. M., & Southwick, L. (1985). Alcohol and social behavior I: The psychology of drunken excess. *Journal of Personality and Social Psychology, 48,* 18–34.

Straker, G., & Jacobson, R. S. (1981). Aggression, emotional maladjustment, and empathy in the abused child. *Developmental Psychology, 17,* 762–765.

Straus, M. A. (1979a). Family patterns and child abuse in a nationally representative American sample. *Child Abuse and Neglect, 3,* 213–225.

Straus, M. A. (1979b). Measuring intrafamily conflict and violence: The Conflict Tactics Scale. *Journal of Marriage and the Family, 41,* 75–88.

Straus, M. A., & Gelles, R. J. (1986). Societal change and change in family violence from 1975 to 1985 as revealed by two national surveys. *Journal of Marriage and the Family, 48,* 465–479.

Straus, M. A., Gelles, R. J., & Steinmetz, S. K. (1980). *Behind closed doors: Violence in the American family.* New York: Anchor/Doubleday.

Straus, M. A., & Kantor, G. K. (1987). Stress and child abuse. In R. E. Helfer & R. S. Kempe (Eds.), *The battered child* (4th ed., pp. 42–59). Chicago: University of Chicago Press.

Sudman, S., & Bradburn, N. M. (1982). *Asking questions: A practical guide to questionnaire design.* San Francisco: Jossey-Bass.

Sugarman, D. B., & Cohn, E. S. (1986). Origin and solution attributions of responsibility for wife abuse: Effects of outcome severity, prior history, and sex of subject. *Violence and Victims, 1,* 291–303.

Sugg, N. K., & Inui, T. (1992, June 17). Primary care physicians' response to domestic violence: Opening Pandora's box. *JAMA, 267,* 3157–3160.

Sutton-Smith, B., & Rosenberg, B. G. (1968). Sibling consensus on power tactics. *Journal of Genetic Psychology, 112,* 63–72.

Svare, B. B., & Mann, M. A. (1983). Hormonal influences on maternal aggression. In B. B. Svare (Ed.), *Hormones and aggressive behavior* (pp. 91–103). New York: Plenum.

Swann, W. B., Jr., & Ely, R. J. (1984). A battle of wills: Self-verification versus behavioral confirmation. *Journal of Personality and Social Psychology, 46,* 1287–1302.

Swann, W. B., Jr., Griffin, J. J., Predmore, S. C., & Gaines, B. (1987). The cognitive affective crossfire: When self-consistency confronts self-enhancement. *Journal of Personality and Social Psychology, 52,* 881–889.

Szinovacz, M. E. (1983). Using couple data as a methodological tool: The case of marital violence. *Journal of Marriage and the Family, 45,* 633–644.

Tannen, D. (1990). *You just don't understand: Women and men in conversation.* New York: William Morrow.

Taylor, S. E., & Brown, J. D. (1988). Illusion and well-being: A social psychological perspective on mental health. *Psychological Bulletin, 103,* 193–210.

Taylor, S. P., & Gammon, C. B. (1975). Effects of type and dose of alcohol on human physical aggression. *Journal of Personality and Social Psychology, 32,* 169–175.

Teichman, M., & Teichman, Y. (1989). Violence in the family: An analysis in terms of interpersonal resource-exchange. *Journal of Family Violence, 4,* 127–142.

Thomas, A., Chess, S., & Birch, H. G. (1968). *Temperament and behavior disorders in children.* New York: New York University Press.

Thomas, M. H., Horton, R. W., Lippincott, E. C., & Drabman, R. S. (1977). Desensitization to portrayals of real-life aggression as a function of exposure to television violence. *Journal of Personality and Social Psychology, 35,* 450–458.

Thorton, B. (1984). Defensive attribution of responsibility: Evidence for an arousal-based motivational bias. *Journal of Personality and Social Psychology, 46,* 721–734.

Toch, H. (1969). *Violent men.* Chicago: Aldine.

Tomita, S. K. (1990). The denial of elder mistreatment by victims and abusers: The application of neutralization theory. *Violence and Victims, 5,* 171–184.

Tooley, K. M. (1980). The young child as victim of sibling attack. In M. Elbow (Ed.), *Patterns in family violence* (pp. 26–29). New York: Family Service Association of America.

Tooley, V., Brigham, J. C., Maass, A., & Bothwell, R. K. (1987). Facial recognition: Weapon effect and attentional focus. *Journal of Applied Social Psychology, 17,* 845–859.

Trickett, P. K., & Kuczynski, L. (1986). Children's misbehaviors and parental discipline strategies in abusive and nonabusive families. *Developmental Psychology, 22,* 115–123.

Trickett, P. K., & Susman, E. J. (1989). Perceived similarities and disagreements about childrearing practices in abusive and nonabusive families: Intergenerational and concurrent family processes. In D. Cicchetti & V. Carlson (Eds.), *Child maltreatment: Theory and research on the causes and consequences of child abuse and neglect* (pp. 280–301). Cambridge: Cambridge University Press.

Trivers, R. L. (1972). Parental investment and sexual selection. In B. Campbell (Ed.), *Sexual selection and the descent of man 1871–1971* (pp. 136–179). Chicago: Aldine.

Troost, K. M. (1988). Sociobiology and the family: Promise versus product. In E. E. Filsinger (Ed.), *Biosocial perspectives on the family* (pp. 188–205). Newbury Park, CA: Sage.

Tutty, L. M., Bidgood, B. A., & Rothery, M. A. (1993). Support groups for battered women: Research on their efficacy. *Journal of Family Violence, 8,* 325–343.

Tversky, A., & Kahneman, D. (1986). Rational choice and the framing of decisions. *Journal of Business, 59,* S251–S278.

Virkkunen, M., DeJong, J., Bartko, J., Linnoila, M. (1989). Psychobiological concomitants of history of suicide attempts among violent offenders and impulsive fire setters. *Archives of General Psychiatry, 46,* 604–606.

Walker, L. E. (1978). Battered women and learned helplessness. *Victimology, 3,* 525–534.

Walker, L. E. (1979). *The battered woman.* New York: Harper & Row.

Walker, L. E. (1984). *The battered woman syndrome.* New York: Springer.

Walker, L. E. (1989). Psychology and violence against women. *American Psychologist, 44,* 695–702.

Wallach, M. A., & Wallach, L. (1983). *Psychology's sanction for selfishness: The error of egoism in theory and therapy.* San Francisco: W. H. Freeman.

Wallerstein, E. (1980). *Circumcision: An American health fallacy.* New York: Springer.

Webb, E. J., Campbell, D. T., Schwartz, R. D., & Sechrest, L. (1966). *Unobtrusive measures: Nonreactive research in the social sciences.* Chicago: Rand McNally.

Weis, J. G. (1989). Family violence research methodology and design. In L. Ohlin & M. Tonry (Eds.), *Family violence* (pp. 117–162). Chicago: University of Chicago Press.

Wells, S. (1988). On the decision to report suspected abuse or neglect. In A. Maney & S. Wells (Eds.), *Professional responsibilities in protecting children: A public health approach to child sexual abuse* (pp. 191–202). New York: Praeger.

Wells, G. L., & Murray, D. M. (1984). Eyewitness confidence. In G. L. Wells & E. F. Loftus (Eds.), *Eyewitness testimony: Psychological perspectives* (pp. 155–170). Cambridge: Cambridge University Press.

Widom, C. S. (1989a). Does violence beget violence? A critical examination of the literature. *Psychological Bulletin, 106,* 3–28.

Widom, C. S. (1989b). The cycle of violence. *Science, 244,* 160–166.

Widom, C. S., & Ames, A. M. (1988). Biology and female crime. In T. E. Moffitt & S. A. Mednick (Eds.), *Biological contributions to crime causation* (pp. 308–331). Dordrecht, The Netherlands: Martinus Nijhoff.

Wiehe, V. R. (1990). Religious influence on parental attitudes toward the use of corporal punishment. *Journal of Family Violence, 5,* 173–186.

Williams, L. B., & Pratt, W. F. (1990). Wanted and unwanted childbearing in the United States: 1973–88, Data from the National Survey of Family Growth. *Advance Data* (Whole #189). Washington, DC: U.S. Department of Health and Human Services.

Wilson, E. O. (1975). *Sociobiology: The new synthesis.* Cambridge, MA: Harvard University Press.

Wolf, R. S., & Pillemer, K. A. (1989). *Helping elderly victims: The reality of elder abuse.* New York: Columbia University Press.

Wolfe, D. A. (1987). *Child abuse: Implications for child development and psychopathology.* Beverly Hills: Sage.

Wolfe, D. A., Wekerle, C., & McGee, R. (1992). Developmental disparities of abused children: Directions for prevention. In R. DeV. Peters, R. J. McMahon, & V. L. Quinsey (Eds.), *Aggression and violence throughout the life span* (pp. 31–51). Newbury Park, CA: Sage.

Yllo, K. (1983). Sexual equality and violence against wives in American states. *Journal of Comparative Family Studies, 14,* 67–86.

Yussen, S. R., & Levy, V. M., Jr. (1975). Effects of warm and neutral models on the attention of observational learners. *Journal of Experimental Child Psychology, 20,* 66–72.

Zellman, G. L. (1990). Child abuse reporting and failure to report among mandated reporters: Prevalence, incidence, reasons. *Journal of Interpersonal Violence, 5,* 3–22.

Zigler, E., & Hall, N. W. (1989). Physical child abuse in America: Past, present, and future. In D. Cicchetti & V. Carlson (Eds.), *Child maltreatment: Theory and research on the causes and consequences of child abuse and neglect* (pp. 38–75). Cambridge: Cambridge University Press.

Zimbardo, P. G., & Leippe, M. R. (1991). *The psychology of attitude change and social influence.* Philadelphia: Temple University Press.

Zimring, F. E. (1989). Toward a jurisprudence of family violence. In L. Ohlin & M. Tonry (Eds.), *Family violence* (pp. 547–569). Chicago: University of Chicago Press.

Zuckerman, M., Buchsbaum, M. S., & Murphy, D. L. (1980). Sensation seeking and its biological correlates. *Psychological Bulletin, 88,* 187–214.

INDEX

Abbey, A., 31, 57
Abortion, 129
Abramson, L., 49, 54
Abuse, 6
   investigations of, 6
Abuse potential, 98, 140, 214
Abuse resistant youth, 115
Admitting guilt, 162
Adolescence, 9, 14, 63, 117, 120, 137
Adoption, 123, 132, 133–134
Adrenaline, 140
Aggression (see also violence, family
      violence), 2, 44, 137
   chronic, 137
   provoked, 137
   toward peers, 44
   verbal, 137
Ainsworth, M., 119
Ajzen, I., 44
Albee, G., 100
Alcohol, 41–42, 76, 115,
      148–152, 192
   as an excuse for violence, 150
   biochemical effects, 148–149
   education, 192
   and impaired judgment, 149
   individual differences, 151
   predictor or consequence of
      violence, 151
   use by victims of violence, 151–152
Alcohol and drug use, 147–152, 212
   and murder, 147

   and recidivism, 212
   and violence, 147–152
Alcoholics Anonymous, 206
Allegations about abuse,
      165–166, 172, 178
   children's lies, 165
   retracted, 172
Alloy, L:, 49
Allport, G., 21
Altruism, 123
Aman, C., 166, 167, 168
American Humane Association, 8, 25
Ames, A., 138, 140
Amphetamines, 149
Amundson, D., 196, 197
Androcentrism, 131
Anger, 70, 112, 139–140,
      203–204, 210
Antisocial behavior, 138
Approval of violence (see also tolerance
      of family violence), 28
Arias, I., 6, 39, 43, 58, 152
Armed conflict, 106
Arrest, 157–160, 162–163
   family vs. nonfamily offenses, 157
   general deterrence, 159
   long-term effects, 162
   mandatory, 158
   message to society, 159
   moderating effect of marriage and
      employment among
      perpetrators, 160

rates, 157
  specific deterrent, 160
  victim involvement, 163
Assertiveness, 76, 112, 119,
    193–194, 203
Assertiveness training, 207–208
Attachment to parents, 146
Attias, R., 180
Attitudes, 2, 27–46, 76
  behavior, 2, 44–45
  violence, 2
Attorney General's Task Force on
    Family Violence, 34, 157,
    163
Attractiveness, 70, 87
Attributions (see also blame,
    justification for violence,
    responsibility for abuse), 78
  relationship-enhancing vs. distress
    maintaining, 78
Austin, G., 159
Austin, T., 157, 163, 164
Axsom, D., 207
Azar, S., 198, 199, 206, 207, 209

Bail, 157
Ball-Rokeach, S., 45
Bandura, A., 33, 104, 105, 106, 107,
    109, 118
Bank, S., 83, 84
Barahal, R., 146
Barbieri, M., 183
Barnett, M., 39, 145, 146
Bartkno, J., 139
Bates, J., 113, 114
Battered women's syndrome, 175
Baumrind, D., 40, 70, 110
Beach, S., 6
Beachy, L., 42
Beating, 34
Bebber, C., 105, 106, 114
Becerra, R., 37, 40, 42, 43
Becker, H., 160
Becker, W., 45
Behavior change, 199–202
  framing benefits, 200
  smoking cessation programs, 199
  stages, 200–202
Belief in a just world, 31
Belsky, J., 48, 68, 69, 74, 88, 89, 188
Bem, D., 44, 139

Bem, S., 131
Bergeman, C., 132
Berk, R., 28, 29, 30, 34, 61, 158, 159,
    160, 161, 208
Berk, S., 163, 208
Berliner, L., 178, 183
Bernstein, I., 137
Bersani, C., 207
Besharov, D., 183
Biblical references to violence, 23
Bidgood, B., 209
Biglan, A., 75
Biological contributions to violence,
    121–142
  evolution, 122–131
  genetics, 131–136
  hormones, 136–139
  temperament and physiological
    reactivity, 139–140
Biology and violence, 107
Biosocial explanations for violence, 122
Birch, H., 72
Blackman, J., 49, 51, 52, 55
Blame, 31, 49, 51, 62, 78, 152, 198
  behavioral vs. characterological, 52
  perpetrator, 49, 51
  role of alcohol, 152
  self, 49, 175
  victim, 31, 32
Blaming the victim, 198
Blanchard, D., 104
Blanchard, R., 104
Blane, H., 150
Bleier, R., 131, 145
Bliss, E., 137
Blumental, M., 28, 35, 45
Blumstein, A., 159, 211
Bograd, M., 10, 207
Bohman, M., 132, 133, 134
Boldizar, J., 44, 85
Bond, C., 149, 150
Booth, A., 137
Borgia, G., 122, 123
Borgida, E., 175
Boriskin, J., 72
Bornstein, G., 168, 170
Bose, C., 28, 29, 30, 34
Bothwell, R., 55
Bottoms, B., 166, 167, 168, 172
Bowker, L., 63, 64, 65, 89, 200, 208
Bowlby, J., 88
Bradburn, N., 7, 171

Bradbury, T., 78
Brain damage, 140
Brehm, S., 207
Brice, P., 195
Briere, J., 169
Brigham, J., 55, 172, 174
Bromley, D., 50
Bross, M., 104–105
Brown, D., 159
Brown, J., 49, 52
Browne, A., 4, 5, 10, 12, 15, 18, 19, 49,
        53, 56, 57, 60, 61, 62, 63,
        147, 148, 151, 176, 177, 179,
        207, 209
Bruck, M., 165, 166
Bryant, B., 83
Buchsbaum, M., 140
Bugental, D., 72
Buhrmester, D., 83, 84
Bullock, L., 127
Bullying, 192
Burgdorf, K., 8, 9, 10
Burgess, A., 9
Burgess, R., 87, 123, 125, 126, 127,
        128, 129, 130, 150, 153, 198
Burt, M., 39
Buss, D., 122, 124, 131
Buzawa, E., 157, 163, 164

Cacioppo, J., 44
Caesar, P., 99, 114, 117
Cahn, T., 112, 203
Campbell, A., 160, 161
Campbell, D., 5
Campbell, J., 152
Campbell, S., 138
Carli, L., 32
Carlson, B., 60, 63
Carmody, D., 162
Caspi, A., 74, 87, 118, 139
Catharsis, 111
Causal thinking, 49–54
Causes of abuse, 77, 86–89
    environmental influences,
        86–88
    role of social support, 88–89
    spouse abuse, 77
Causes of violence, 2, 93–101
    biological, 2, 121–142
    learning, 2, 103–120
    memory, 94

multiple causation, 94
probabilistic thinking, 94
salient cues, 94
thinking about, 93–101
Ceci, S., 165, 166
Celano, M., 50
Chadiha, L., 28, 35, 45
Chang, A., 180
Channels, N., 157
Chapin, M., 104–105
Chen, H., 207
Chess, S., 72
Child abuse, 4, 8, 9–10, 23–25, 41, 43,
        48, 60, 98, 114, 116–117,
        119, 128–129, 140, 144, 148,
        199, 209–210, 213–215
    age differences, 8, 128
    coin-rubbing, 41
    consequences, 43, 48, 60,
        116–117, 144, 210
    by age of onset, 119–120
    definition, 4
    economic benefits of prevention,
        213–215
    effect of age of victim, 210
    historical perspective, 23–25
    incidence, 7, 8, 25, 98, 129
    intervention with victims, 209–210
    neglect due to alcohol use, 148
    perpetrators, 8
    physiological reactivity in
        perpetrator, 140
    prevention efforts, 189–191
    sex of perpetrator, 10, 129
    sex of victim, 9
    treatment, 203
    treatment for families, 199
Child abuse potential, 117
Children of battered women, 117
Child-to-parent aggression, 118
Chyi-In, W., 99, 108, 109, 113, 118,
        119, 131
Cialdini, R., 31
Circumcision, 41
Clark, J., 184
Clarke, A., 138
Clarke, C., 208
Clarke-Stewart, K., 70
Clasen, M., 178
Classical conditioning, 104
Cloninger, C., 132, 133, 134, 135, 136,
        203

Coates, D., 31, 57
Cognitive/behavioral treatment with
    perpetrators,
    202–204
Cognitive restructuring, 203
Cohen, J., 159
Cohn, E., 39
Cole, G., 28, 35, 45
Coleman, D., 80
Coller, S., 39
Collins, M., 182
Colombotos, J., 195
Compas, B., 70
Competition, 146
Conaway, L., 112
Concordance, 132
Conflict management, 190
    during marriage, 190
Conflict resolution, 110
Conflict Tactics Scale, 6, 8
Conger, R., 70, 99, 108, 109, 113, 118,
    119, 131
Conte, J., 169, 182
Coombs, R., 118
Cooper, J., 207
Coopersmith, S., 70
Coping, 115
Copycat effect, 105
Cornell, C., 3, 12, 15, 85, 88
Corporal punishment (see discipline of
    children)
Cosgrove, J., 3, 41
"Cost" of battering, 200
Cousins, C., 172, 174
Crano, W., 44
Criminality, 133–135, 139, 190
    and adoption, 133–134
    against persons vs. property, 135
    sex differences in propensity for,
    133
Criminals, 117, 137
Criminogenic, 133
    circumstances, 133
Critical period, 189
Crittenden, P., 54
Cross-cultural studies of alcohol use
    and violence, 151
Cross-cultural studies of family
    violence, 19, 21–23,
    80–82, 90, 127

Cross-generational violence (see also
    cycle of violence), 108, 116
Cross-sectional designs, 80, 82
Crowne, D., 6
Crying, 140, 145
Crying and abuse, 128
Crying/distress, 168
    and memory for events, 168
Cultural support for violence,
    89–90, 106
Curley, A., 208
Cycle of violence, 86, 114, 117
Cyclical hypothesis of abuse,
    95–101, 107

Dabbs, J., 137, 138
Darley, J., 100
Daro, D., 190, 193, 210, 213, 214
Dating, 2
Davidson, E., 105, 117, 195, 197
Davies, G., 165
Davis, M., 144, 145
Dawkins, R., 145
Decision-making, 126, 172
    in households, 126
    by jurors, 172
Deffenbacher, J., 202
DeFries, J., 130, 132, 136, 146
DeJong, J., 139
Denno, D., 140
Dent, D., 152
Denton, R., 207
Dependence upon abuser, 60
Depression, 49
Desensitization to violence, 42, 57–60,
    105
Desistence, 208, 212
    and shelter stays, 208
    stages of, 212
Desisters vs. persisters vs. innocents,
    211
Deterrent to violence, 159–163
DiClemente, C., 200, 201, 202, 205,
    209
Differences between victims/
    nonvictims, 56
DiLalla, D., 54
DiLalla, L., 131, 132, 136
Dillon, M., 50, 51, 55
Disabilities, 128

Discipline of children, 35, 37, 40, 45,
    60, 70, 73–74, 97–98,
    110–111, 145, 189, 194
  authoritative vs. authoritarian
    rearing, 40
Dishion, T., 19, 75
Disinhibition, 105, 149
Divorce/separation, 162
Dix, T., 70, 107
Dobash, R. E., 31, 32, 33, 89, 90
Dobash, R. P., 31, 32, 33, 89, 90
Dodge, K., 113, 114, 147, 210
Donnerstein, E., 104–105, 196
Donovan, W., 72
Dopamine, 149
Downey, G., 74
Drabman, R., 33
Draper, P., 123, 125, 126, 127, 128,
    129, 130, 150, 153
Drugs, 115
Drug use, 192
  education, 192
Dunn, J., 84
Dunsavage, I., 53
Dweck, C., 52

Easterbrooks, M., 83
Edelson, J., 78
Edgerton, R., 150
Education, 40, 76, 188–194, 214
  to prevent violence, 188–194, 214
EEG, 140
Egalitarian parenting, 119
Egeland, B., 98, 115, 119
Ehrenkranz, J., 137
Einbender, A., 49
Eisikovits, Z., 78
Elder, G., 74, 87, 118, 139
Elder Abuse, 15, 16
Elderly, 85
  strain on caretaker, 85
Elderly abuse, 13–16, 85, 88, 192,
    210–211
  economic stress, 85, 88
  intervention with victims, 210–211
  perpetrator characteristics, 86
  prevention efforts, 192
  sex differences, 15, 85
  socioeconomic status, 85
Elliott, D., 157, 159, 162, 163
Ely, R., 100

Emde, R., 83
Emotional abuse, 43
Emotional support, 115
Empathy, 30, 144–147
  of abuse perpetrators, 144
  altruism, 145
  biological determinants,
    144–147
  genetic contribution, 145
  interaction between social and
    biological determinants,
    146–147
  social determinants, 145–147
  sociobiology and evolution, 145
  of victims, 144
Empathy and violence, 144–147
Employment, 126
  of mothers, 126
Empowerment of victims,
    193–194
England, P., 173, 183
Erickson, M., 119, 140
Eron, L., 195
Ervin-Tripp, S., 83
Escalation of violence, 38–39
Eth, S., 173, 182–183
Evolution and family violence, 122–131
Expectations, 70, 85
  about child development, 70
Expert testimony, 169, 174–178
Eysenck, H., 144, 145, 146, 147, 192

Fagan, J., 21, 60, 89, 211–212
Family, 3, 68
  definition, 3
  subsystems, 68
Family and nonfamily violence, 212
Family life, 33, 67–91, 125
  difficulties of, 33
  roles, 125
Family violence (see also child abuse,
    elderly abuse, sibling abuse,
    spouse abuse), 3–5,
    18–21, 25, 107–120,
    122–136, 139, 141, 148, 156,
    160, 163–176, 188, 198
  across cultures, 19, 21–23,
    80–82, 90, 127
  alcohol and drug use, 148
  biosocial explanations,
    130–131

cause of, 141
consequences, 3
    by sex of perpetrator,
       118–119
    by sex of victim, 118–119
definition, 3, 25
differing perspectives, 3, 4
and evolution, 122–131
and genetics, 131–136
hormonal contributions, 136
ill-temperament, 139
incidence, 5
    relative to nonfamily violence,
       18–21
intention, 3, 4
and learning, 107–120
penalty to perpetrator, 160
perspectives on causation, 188
prosecution, 163–178
severity, 5
tolerance of, 156–158
treatment programs, 198–213
Farrington, D., 211
Fazio, R., 45
Fear, 60, 140, 175, 193
Feierstein, M., 39
Feingold, A., 122, 124, 131
Felson, R., 84
Ferguson, T., 38
Feshbach, N., 144, 145
Fetus, 41
Fincham, F., 75, 78
Finkelhor, D., 3, 9, 10, 43
Fischer, P., 195
Fishbein, M., 44
Fisher, B., 42
Fishman, H., 68, 75
Fiske, S., 94, 180
Flanzraich, M., 53
Flewelling, R., 18, 19
Flitcraft, A., 181
Floody, O., 123, 138
Fogarty, L., 182
Foley, M., 165
Foot-in-the-door, 37–38
Franz, C., 146
Freud, S., 111
Friedman, D., 198, 199
Friedrich, W., 49, 72
Frieze, I., 4, 5, 10, 12, 15, 32, 48, 49,
      50, 60, 61, 62, 80, 147, 148,
      151, 207

Frodi, A., 72, 128, 140
Fulker, D., 144, 145, 146, 147, 192
Furman, W., 83, 84

Gabrielli, W., Jr., 133, 134, 135
Gammon, C., 148
Gandelman, R., 136–137
Garbarino, J., 3, 4, 5, 8, 9, 39, 87, 120,
      125, 130
Garbarino, M., 24
Gardner, W., 95, 96
Gavelek, J., 144
Gediman, D., 194
Geen, R., 111
Geiselman, R., 168, 170
Gelles, R., 3, 8, 9, 10, 12, 13, 15, 24,
      25, 32, 35, 60, 75, 80, 81, 85,
      88, 97, 98, 101, 111, 118,
      119, 126, 127, 156, 157, 184,
      194, 198
Gene pool, 123
Generalization, 109
Genes, 99, 107, 123, 131,
      135–136
    and antisocial behaviors, 135
    and family violence, 99, 131
    and juvenile crime, 136
    and marital instability, 135
    and mate selection, 123
Genetic basis of behavior, 131
George, C., 144
Gerbner, G., 195, 197
Gil, D., 7, 37
Giovannoni, J., 37, 40, 42, 43
Golding, J., 172
Goldsmith, H., 139
Goldsmith, T., 122, 123, 124, 127, 129
Goldstein, H., 180
Gombossy, G., 156
Gondolf, E., 206
Goodman, G., 166, 167, 168, 172, 173,
      183
Goodman, J., 171
Goodwin, J., 180
Goodwin, M., 13, 14, 84, 85
Goolkasian, G., 34, 56, 141, 157, 159,
      160
Gordon, T., 137
Gottesman, I., 131, 132, 135, 136, 139
Gottman, J., 75
Gray, E., 3, 34, 41

Grayson, M., 44
Green, A., 109
Greenblat, C., 34, 35, 36, 39, 40, 82
Greene, E., 175
Gresham, A., 175
Griffin, J., 49
Groth-Marnat, G., 6
Grusec, J., 70, 107
Grych, J., 75
Guttmann, E., 3, 78

Habituation (see also desensitization to
        violence), 33
Hackett, G., 11
Haith, M., 172
Hall, D., 165
Hall, J., 33, 85
Hall, N., 23, 128, 148
Hamilton, E., 160, 161
Hampton, R., 25, 43, 180
Hanneke, C., 21, 212
Hanneken, J., 206
Hansen, D., 109, 112
Hardy, J., 31
Hartman, C., 9
Hartup, W., 83
Hastings, J., 23
Haugaard, J., 193
Heart rate, 140
Heath, L., 117
Help-seeking, 207
    sex differences in, 207
Henderson, C., Jr., 130, 189, 190, 191
Hensley, J., 105
Heritability, 132, 136
Herrenkohl, E., 115, 128
Herrenkohl, R., 115, 128
Herscovici, B., 172
Herzberger, S., 5, 31, 33, 43, 50, 51,
        55, 58, 59, 60, 85, 97, 99,
        100, 101, 144, 157, 180
Hexter, A., 180
Hilberman, E., 61
Hill, J., 42
Hilton, J., 100
Hinchey, F., 144
Hoerig, J., 31
Hoffman, J., 34, 204
Hoffman, M., 70, 145
Holden, G., 72, 75, 120
Holland, A., 100, 101
Holtzworth-Munroe, A., 78, 212

Homemakers, 81
Hopkins, J., 138
Hops, H., 75
Hormones and aggression,
        136–138
    cause and effect, 138
    among females, 138–139
    among males, 136–138
Horney, J., 138
Hornung, C., 78
Horton, R., 33
Hostile personality, 113
Hostility, 112, 114
Hotaling, G., 4, 13, 15, 17, 19, 20, 56,
        76, 78, 85, 88, 99, 109, 110,
        117, 118, 128, 147, 151, 212
Household decision-making,
        80–81
Howe, A., 58
Huesmann, L., 195
Hull, J., 149, 150
Hunter, R., 114
Hutchings, B., 133, 134, 135

Imitation, 105, 118
Immanent justice, 50
Impulsivity, 70, 149
Inciardi, J., 148
Incompatibility, 78
Inequality, 4, 78, 125–126
    and spouse abuse, 78–82
Infancy, 119, 123, 127–128
Infanticide, 136
Infidelity, 35, 124, 126–127
Injury, 113, 116, 129, 157, 213
Insecurity, 146
Interplay between biology and
        environment, 141
Intervention, 61–63, 115, 192
    help-seeking, 62
    police, 61–62
    in schools, 192
    services for victims, 61
    at a young age, 192
Interviewing children, 168,
        170–171
Inui, T., 179
Investigation of family violence,
        180–181
    biased processing of evidence,
        180–181

Irritability, 138–139
Isolation, 60, 86, 89

Jacklin, C., 39, 72, 118, 119
Jacob, M., 31
Jacobson, N., 78
Jacobson, R., 144
Jacobvitz, D., 98, 115
Jaet, B., 39
Jaffe, P., 118, 159
Janoff-Bulman, R., 32, 48, 52, 207
Jary, M., 136
Jayaratne, T., 28, 35, 45
Jealousy, 124, 126–127
Jennings, J., 45, 88, 199, 204–205
Jensen, B., 54, 112, 194, 207
Johnson, C., 178
Johnson, M., 165
Johnson, P., 39, 43, 58
Jones, D., 173, 183
Jung, J., 148, 149, 151
Justification for violence, 31–34, 44,
    150
Juvenile delinquency/criminality,
    132–133, 139, 149, 190

Kahn, M., 83, 84
Kahneman, D., 200
Kalmuss, D., 99, 110, 117, 119, 131
Kantor, G., 87, 88, 89
Kantrowitz, B., 42
Katz, A., 88
Kaufman, J., 70, 71, 97, 98, 99, 188
Kelder, L., 60, 63
Kennedy, D., 13, 14
Kennedy, L., 128
Kennell, J., 189
Kenrick, R., 31
Kihlstrom, N., 114
Klap, R., 160, 161
Klaus, M., 189
Klein, R., 195
Knudsen, D., 25
Koestner, R., 146
Korbin, J., 41
Koski, P., 19, 39, 43
Kovera, M., 175
Kropp, J., 70
Krug, R., 45
Kruttschnitt, C., 115, 117
Kuczynski, L., 110, 210

Labeling abuser, 200
Labeling perpetrator as deviant, 160
Lachman, M., 72
Lahey, B., 70
Lamb, M., 72, 119, 140
Landsverk, J., 118
LaPiere, R., 44
Larrance, D., 50
Larzelere, R., 111
Lau, R., 49
Launius, M., 54, 112, 194, 207
Laursen, B., 83
Lavoie, F., 31
Laws and acceptance of violence,
    194–195
Lawson, A., 126
Learned helplessness, 53
Learning to be aggressive, 99, 103–120
    indirect path, 108, 113
    susceptibility to learning, 116–120
Leavitt, L., 72
Left-hemisphere dysfunction, 140
Leippe, M., 172, 174, 199, 200
Leonard, K., 150
Lerner, M., 31
Levenson, R., 144, 145
Levin, H., 74
Levinson, D., 19, 21, 22, 23, 80, 81, 82,
    89, 90, 125, 126
Levy, V., 105
Lewin, L., 75
Lewis, B., 56
Lewis, J., 72
Lewis, M., 72
Lichter, S., 196, 197
Liddle, C., 115, 116
Lidz, C., 95, 96
Liebert, R., 105, 117, 195, 197
Lindblad, J., 175
Lindquist, C., 54
Linnoila, M., 139
Linz, D., 44, 104–105, 196
Lippincott, E., 33
Livesley, W., 50
Lloyd, S., 75, 76
Loaded questions, 171
Lockwood, D., 148
Loeber, R., 19, 75, 84, 211
Loehlin, J., 146
Loftus, E., 164, 165, 168, 169, 171
Longitudinal studies, 110, 139

Lorber, R., 73, 210
Lore, R., 125
Loseke, D., 163
Loss of control, 112
Love, 115
Lutzker, J., 203
Lying, 6–7, 165
Lynch, A., 44
Lynn, S., 60, 63

Maass, A., 55
MacAndrew, C., 150
Maccoby, E., 39, 72, 74, 118, 119
Machismo, 45
MacMillan, V., 112
Macrae, C., 39
Magnusson, D., 140, 141
Main, M., 144
Maiuro, R., 112, 203
Malamuth, N., 196
Male victims (see also spouse abuse), 6, 10, 80
Malinosky-Rummell, R., 109
Maney, A., 158, 178
Mangold, W., 19, 39, 43
Mann, C., 10, 207
Mann, M., 131, 138
Mantyla, S., 72
Marcus, M., 138
Margolin, G., 78
Marijuana, 149
Marital relations (see also partner relations), 75–83
Marital satisfaction, 78
Marlatt, G., 150
Marlowe, D., 6
Martin, D., 206
Martin, G., 31
Martin, H., 146
Masbad, I., 39, 145
Masochism, 56–57
Maternal investment (see also parental investment), 129
Mate selection, 123–125
Mazur, A., 137, 138
McCall, G., 21, 212
McCartney, K., 146
McCarty, J., 70
McClearn, G., 130, 132, 136
McCullough, B., 78
McEvoy, J., 34, 35, 40

McFarlane, J., 127
McGee, R., 210
McHugh, M., 80
McIntire, R., 29
McKillop, P., 11
McNamara, J., 60, 63
McNeely, R., 10, 207
Media, 105, 157, 195–197
    influence on public policy, 157
    portrayal of violence, 195–197
    providing a script for violence, 105
Mednick, S., 133, 134, 135
Memory, 166–168
    for abuse incidents, 166–168
Mendonca, P., 207
Menstruation and aggression, 138–139
Metalsky, G., 49
Meyer, C., 52, 53
Milgram, S., 38
Miller, D., 51, 62
Milner, J., 98, 99, 100, 115, 117, 140
Minimization of violence, 61
Minnett, A., 84
Minuchin, S., 68, 75
Moitra, S., 211
Monogamy, 124
Morgan, M., 195, 197
Morris, J., 178
Moyer, K., 140
Multiple forms of violence, 15, 17, 19, 85, 110, 131
Mulvey, E., 95, 96
Munson, K., 61
Murder, 18, 128–129, 209
    by battered women, 176–177
    lack of social support for battered victim, 209
    sex differences, 18
Murphy, C., 6, 7
Murphy, D., 140
Murray, D., 172
Mydans, S., 38
Myers, J., 41
Myers, S., 207

Nachson, I., 140
Nagi, S., 178
Nagin, D., 159
Nalepka, C., 180
National Center on Child Abuse and Neglect, 9, 129, 178, 182

National Institute of Justice Research in
Brief, 170
National Study of the Incidence and
Severity of Child Abuse and
Neglect, 8
Native Americans, 24
Natural selection, 122, 125
and child abuse, 127
and wife beating, 125
Neale, M., 144, 145, 146, 147, 192
Neff, C., 72
Neglect of elderly, 86
Neidig, P., 198, 199
Nesselroade, J., 132
Newberger, C., 144
Newberger, E., 43, 180, 184
Newhill, C., 63
Newton, P., 208
Nguyen, T., 9, 87
Nias, D., 144, 145, 146, 147, 192
Nonfamily violence, 17–21, 109, 148
Norcross, J., 200, 201, 202, 205, 209
''Normal'' violence, 12, 15, 33, 55, 114
Novaco, R., 202, 203
Nurse visitors, 189
Nurturance, 115, 146

Ogbu, J., 46, 69
Oglesby, A., 180
Olds, D., 130, 189, 190, 191
O'Leary, K., 6, 7, 70, 76, 77, 89, 99,
198, 208
Oliver, J., 131
Olweus, D., 137, 140, 192
Operant conditioning, 104
Opiates, 149
Oppenheim, D., 119
O'Toole, R., 180

Pachella, R., 178
Pagelow, M., 10, 12, 14, 15, 23, 33, 55,
56, 60, 61, 62, 85, 129, 148,
194
Pallotta, G., 112
Palmer, J., 164, 165, 168
Papatola, K., 98, 115
Parental certainty, 123, 126
Parental investment, 123–124, 126, 129
Parent-child relations, 69–75, 83, 115,
146, 189–191
child effects, 72

effect of marital relations, 74, 83
effect of support services, 189–191
interaction between child and parent
factors, 72–74
parent effects, 69–71
Parent education, 189
Parent-infant bonding, 189
Parenting, 68, 120
model of, 68
Parents Anonymous, 206
Parke, R., 110
Parker, B., 127
Parlee, M., 138
Partner abuse (see also spouse abuse),
205–209
intervention with victims, 207–209
self-help groups for perpetrators,
205–206
Partner relations, 2, 75–83
effect of child rearing, 78
marital, 2
satisfaction, 75
Pate, A., 160, 161
Patriarchy, 33–34, 39, 78–82
Patterson, G., 33, 72, 84, 211
Paulson, M., 118
Pavlov, I., 104, 109
Pedersen, N., 132
Penrod, S., 105, 196
Perception of consequences, 85
Perceptions of abuse, 55
as unusual, 55
Perpetrator characteristics,
56–57, 63, 75, 77, 202–204
behavior of perpetrator, 56–57, 77
cognitive/behavioral treatment,
202–204
control, 57
partner abuse, 75
promises to stop, 63
repentance, 57
Perry, D., 30, 38, 44, 57, 85, 118
Perry, L., 30, 38, 44, 57, 85, 118
Personality, 70
of perpetrators, 70, 75–76
victims of spouse abuse, 76
Pettit, G., 113, 114
Petty, R., 44
Phares, V., 70
Philips, D., 105
Physiological arousal/reactivity, 105,
139

Piaget, J., 50
Pianta, R., 119
Pierce, R., 86, 181
Pillemer, K., 15, 85, 86, 88, 192, 211
Pleck, E., 23, 24
Plomin, R., 130, 132, 136, 146
Police discretion, 158–159
Policing vs. Privacy, 42
Pollock, C., 70
Pornography, 195–197
Port, L., 173, 183
Porter, C., 51, 62
Postpartum depression, 138
Pottieger, A., 148
Potts, D., 50, 51, 55, 100, 101
Power differences, 79–82, 84, 125–126
    partners, 79–82
    siblings, 84
Prado, L., 173, 183
Pratt, W., 129
Predicting violence, 95–97, 100
Predictors of child abuse, 71
Prevention of abuse, 32, 53,
        61–62, 188–189, 193, 198,
        213–215
    economic benefits, 213–215
    illusions about ability to, 32
    multifaceted efforts needed, 198
    secondary, 198
    sexual abuse programs, 193
    victims' sense of control, 53, 61–62
    vs. treatment, 213
Privacy, 34, 158
Problem-solving ability, 54,
        112–113, 119, 203
Prochaska, J., 200, 201, 202, 205, 209
Professional reactions, 41, 58
Project 12-Ways, 203
Prosecution, 163–171, 182–184
    accuracy of testimony,
        164–171
    confidence in testimony,
        171–172
    effect on victim and witnesses,
        182–183
    effects of interview style, 168,
        170–171
    truthfulness of child witness, 165
    use of expert witnesses,
        174–178
    vs. treatment, 184
Provocation, 31–32

Provoking violence, 175
Pruitt, D., 140
Psychopathology, 70, 76, 115
    of abusers, 70, 72
    and parenting, 115
Punishment, 104, 105
Puritans, 24
Pynoos, R., 173, 182–183

Quackenbush, S., 39
Quade, V., 42
Quanty, M., 111
Quindlen, A., 38
Quinton, E., 115, 116

Race/ethnicity, 40
Raitz, A., 175
Randall, T., 179
Rape, 31, 32, 39–40, 62
Reasoning, 110–111
    inductive, 145
Rebound effect of alcohol, 149
Recidivism (see also desistance), 133,
        211–212
Regan, P., 175
Reid, J., 73, 74, 112, 210
Reinforcement, 111
Reiss, A., 18, 128, 139, 147, 149, 150,
        151, 192, 198, 214, 215
Reiss, D., 208
Relaxation training, 203
Religion, 78
Reporting of abuse, 5, 25, 158, 178–184
    ambiguous evidence, 178
    belief that reporting is wrong,
        181–183
    benefits, 183–184
    bias in, 5, 180
    differences between adult vs. child
        victims, 181
    effect on disclosure, 181
    failure to report, 178–183
    following victim denial,
        179–180
    mandatory for professionals, 158
    underreporting, 6, 8
Reppucci, N., 193
Repressed memory for abuse, 168–169
Repudiation of violence, 115
Resick, P., 39
Responsibility, 44

Responsibility for abuse, 49–53, 58–59,
    73, 198
  perceptions of adult victims, 49–53
  perceptions of child victims, 50–52,
    58–59
Retaliation, 33, 35, 37, 38, 63, 80, 162,
    175
  battered women's syndrome, 175
Retribution (see also retaliation), 37,
    163
Retrospective designs, 7
Rewards, 75, 104–105
Rice, J., 203
Rich, R., 40
Richardson, D., 152
Riggs, D., 6, 7
Ritchie, K., 75
Robertson, K., 98, 99, 100, 115, 117
Rogan, D., 159, 161, 184
Rogers, D., 98, 99, 100, 115, 117
Rohsenow, D., 150
Role models, 115, 119, 146
Role-reversal behavior, 54
Role taking, 146
Romanczyk, A., 172, 174
Roscoe, B., 13, 14, 84, 85
Rose, R., 137
Rosenbaum, A., 208
Rosenberg, B., 84
Rosenblum, L., 72
Rossi, F., 28, 29, 30, 34
Roth, J., 18, 128, 139, 147, 149, 150,
    151, 192, 198, 214, 215
Rothery, M., 209
Rowe, D., 99, 104, 131, 132, 136
Roy, M., 151
Ruble, D., 138
Rudy, L., 166, 167, 168, 173, 183
Ruef, A., 144, 145
Rule, B., 38
Rushton, J., 144, 145, 146, 147, 192
Russell, D., 49, 56
Rutter, M., 70, 88, 115, 116

Sagi, A., 145
Sampson, R., 40
Santrock, J., 84
Saunders, D., 43, 44, 61, 198, 199, 206,
    207, 209
Saunders, L., 39
Saywitz, K., 168, 170

Scarr, S., 146
Schmidt, J., 159, 161, 162, 184
Schmitt, D., 122, 124, 131
Schulterbrandt, J., 208
Schultz, L., 125
Schur, E., 31, 32
Schwartz, R., 5
Screening for family violence, 179
Sears, R., 74
Sebastian, R., 104
Sechrest, L., 5
Seeley, J., 3
Sela-Amit, M., 78
Selective mating, 131
Self-blame (see blame)
Self-defense plea, 177
Self-destruction, 109, 139
Self-directedness, 106
Self-esteem, 49, 70, 76, 209
Self-fulfilling prophecy, 100
Self-help groups, 204–207
Self-perception of victims, 48–65
  belief that treatment is unusual, 55
  causal thinking, 48–53
  unrealistic expectations, 53
Self-reinforcing behavior, 104
Self-sacrifice, 123
Seligman, M., 53, 54
Serotonin, 139, 148
Services for victims (see also
    intervention), 12, 15
Sexism (see also inequality, patriarchy),
    131
Sex segregation, 125–126
Sexual abuse, 2, 43, 180, 193
Shaver, P., 172
Sheard, M., 137
Sheble, M., 115
Shelters, 56, 208
Shepard, M., 212
Shepherd, J., 39
Sherman, L., 61, 158, 159, 160, 161,
    162, 184
Sherry, D., 72
Shields, N., 21, 212
Shirk, S., 210
Shotland, R., 30, 45
Sibling abuse, 12, 13, 15, 33, 55
  incidence, 19
  intervention, 211
  sex differences, 13, 14

Sibling conflict, 83–85
  age differences, 83
  parental influence, 84–85
  positive consequences, 83
  sex differences, 84–85
Sigler, R., 10, 12, 24, 28, 35, 45
Signorielli, N., 195, 197
Sigvardsson, S., 132, 133, 134
Silverman, R., 128
Simons, R., 99, 108, 109, 113, 118,
    119, 131
Singer, D., 195
Singer, J., 195
Sinisi, C., 39
Sirignano, S., 72
Sivacek, J., 44
Size, P., 43, 61
Size of family, 128
Skinner, B., 104
Slaby, R., 110
Slapping, 35–36
Smith, D., 159, 161, 184
Smoking, 41
Snow, M., 72
Social construction of violence, 26
Social desirability, 6
Social learning, 104
Social perception, 114
Social support, 115, 126
Society for the Prevention of Cruelty to
    Children, 24
Sociobiology, 126
Socioeconomic status, 40, 76, 78, 150
Soeken, K., 127
Sonkin, D., 206
Southwick, L., 149
Spanking (see discipline of children)
Spencer-Molloy, F., 179
Spouse abuse, 4, 7, 10, 12, 18–19,
    23–25, 99, 114, 117, 126,
    202–203
  affection for perpetrator, 61
  consequences, 4, 117
  definition, 10
  historical perspective, 23–25
  and household decision-making,
    80–81
  incidence, 7, 10, 19, 25, 99, 126
  and inequality, 78–82,
    125–126

sex differences, 18
sex of perpetrator, 10, 12
treatment, 202–203
victim characteristics, 76
Sprafkin, J., 105, 117, 195, 197
Sprey, J., 125, 130
Squabbling, 76
Sroufe, L., 115
Stark, R., 34, 35, 40
Starr, R., 70
Statistical Abstract of the United States,
    126, 129
Steele, B., 70
Steele, C., 149
Steinberg, Joel, 11
Steinmetz, S., 10, 13, 60, 80, 81, 97,
    98, 111, 118, 119
Stepchildren, 123
Stewart, M., 136
Straker, G., 144
Straus, M., 4, 6, 8, 10, 13, 15, 17, 19,
    20, 23, 25, 35, 60, 80, 81, 85,
    87, 88, 89, 97, 98, 101, 109,
    110, 111, 117, 118, 119, 128,
    156, 157, 184, 194, 198, 212
Straw, M., 30, 45
Stress, 73, 86–88, 129, 140–141, 150,
    189, 209
  and alcohol/drug use, 150
  home environment, 73
  of new baby, 189
  social and economic, 86–88
Stuart, G., 212
Substantiation of abuse cases, 5, 182
Sudman, S., 7, 171
Sugarman, D., 39, 56, 76, 78, 88, 99,
    109, 147, 151
Sugg, N., 179
Suggestibility, 164–168
  of children, 165–168
Sugimoto, T., 78
Support groups
  for perpetrators, 204–207
  for victims, 209
Survival of the fittest, 122
Susman, E., 114
Sutton-Smith, B., 84
Svare, B., 131, 138
Swann, W., 49, 100
Szinovacz, M., 6

Tannen, D., 172
Taplin, P., 73, 210
Taub, E., 173, 183
Taylor, S., 49, 52, 53, 94, 148, 180
Teasdale, J., 54
Teichman, M., 75
Teichman, Y., 75
Televised violence, 195–197
Television, 104, 117
Telford, A., 159
Temperament, 139
Tengs, T., 84, 211
Tennen, H., 31, 43, 58, 59, 60, 144
Testimony, 171–172
    of children, 173
    relationship between confidence and
        accuracy, 171–172
    retracted allegations, 172
Testosterone, 136
    cause and effect of changes in level,
        137
    and dominance, 137
    and family relations, 137
Tetreault, P., 39, 145
Theory of reasoned action, 44
Thomas, A., 72
Thomas, M., 33
Thorton, B., 39
Thrill-seeking, 140
Thurman, Tracy, 156–157
Time out, 211
Timko, C., 32
Tishelman, A., 112
Toch, H., 104
Toedter, L., 115
Tolerance of family violence,
        28–46, 58, 118,
        156–158, 194
    characteristics of the victim and
        perpetrator, 43–44
    context effects, 34–39
    education and socioeconomic status,
        40
    ethnic/racial/cultural differences,
        40–41
    explanations, 30
    gender roles, 39–40, 43
    guilt, 118
    professional orientation, 41, 58
Tomita, S., 86
Tooley, K., 13

Tooley, V., 55
Tousignant, J., 165
Treatment, 45, 157, 198–214
    cost of, 213–214
    evaluation, 206–207
    of family violence, 198–213
    of family vs. nonfamily violence,
        157
    for perpetrators, 45
    pharmacological, 203–204
    self-help, 204–207
    stages of behavior change, 200–202
    varied by type of offender, 211–213
Trickett, P., 110, 114, 210
Trivers, R., 123, 124, 129
Troost, K., 125
Trotta, R., 86, 181
Turbett, P., 180
Tutty, L., 209
Tversky, A., 200
Twentyman, C., 50
Twins, 131–132

Vandell, D., 84
Verbal aggression, 76
Vicarious learning, 105
Victimization, 48
Violence (see also family violence), 2,
        45, 117, 124, 127–128, 130,
        144–150, 213–215
    biochemical effects of alcohol/drug
        use, 148–149
    costs to society, 213–215
    definition, 2
    family vs. nonfamily, 124
    multiple forms of, 117
    personality characteristics of
        alcohol/drug users, 150
    and pregnancy, 127
    role of empathy, 144–147
    sex differences in reaction to
        alcohol, 148, 150
    social consequences of alcohol/drug
        use, 148–152
    and socioeconomic class, 128, 130
    unplanned, 45
Virkkunen, M., 139
Vitaliano, P., 112, 203
Vondra, J., 48, 74, 88, 89, 188
Von Knorring, A., 132, 133, 134

Waite, E., 28, 29, 34
Walker, L., 12, 49, 53, 61, 62, 89, 127,
    146, 148, 152, 206, 207
Wallace, H., 180
Wallach, L., 144
Wallach, M., 144
Wallerstein, E., 41
Wang, D., 11
Ward, D., 115, 117
Waterman, J., 146
Weaning, 127–128
Weapon use, 157
Webb, E., 5
Weinberger, J., 146
Weis, J., 3, 5, 6, 7, 10
Weiss, R., 38, 78, 85, 118
Wekerle, C., 210
Wells, G., 172
Wells, S., 181, 182
Western, B., 160, 161
Wexler, S., 60
Whitbeck, L., 99, 108, 109, 113, 118,
    119, 131
White, K., 144
Widom, C., 97, 109, 117, 138, 140, 190
Wiehe, V., 23
Williams, K., 12, 18, 162, 207, 209

Williams, L., 129
Williard, J., 30, 57
Wilson, E., 123, 145
Wilson, S., 118
Witnessing crime, 172
    credibility of eyewitness, 172
Witnessing violence, 163–164
    effects of, 76, 99, 107, 110, 144
    special arrangements for children in
        court, 173
Wolf, R., 15, 85, 86, 88, 192, 211
Wolfe, D., 70, 118, 159, 210
Wortman, C., 31, 57

Yang, R., 70
Yllo, K., 78, 79, 80, 82
Yussen, S., 105

Zambarano, R., 120
Zellman, G., 181, 182
Zigler, E., 23, 70, 71, 97, 98, 99, 128,
    148, 188
Zimbardo, P., 199, 200
Zimring, F., 156, 158
Zuckerman, M., 140